The Middleboro Casebook

THIRD EDITION

The Middleboro Casebook

HEALTHCARE STRATEGY AND OPERATIONS

Lee F. Seidel | James B. Lewis

AUPHA

Health Administration Press, Chicago, Illinois

Association of University Programs in Health Administration, Washington, DC

Library of Congress Cataloging-in-Publication Data is on file at the Library of Congress, Washington, DC.

ISBN: 978-1-64055-352-1

The paper used in this publication meets the minimum requirements of American National Standard for Information Sciences—Permanence of Paper for Printed Library Materials, ANSI Z39.48-1984. ♾ ™

Acquisitions editor: Jennette McClain; Manuscript editor: Sharon Sofinski; Cover designer: James Slate; Layout: To Come

Found an error or a typo? We want to know! Please e-mail it to hapbooks@ache.org, mentioning the book's title and putting "Book Error" in the subject line.

For photocopying and copyright information, please contact Copyright Clearance Center at www.copyright.com or at (978) 750-8400.

Health Administration Press
A division of the Foundation of the American
  College of Healthcare Executives
300 S. Riverside Plaza, Suite 1900
Chicago, IL 60606-6698
(312) 424-2800

Association of University Programs
  in Health Administration
1730 Rhode Island Ave, NW
Suite 810
Washington, DC 20036
(202) 763-7283

Dedicated to Errol L. Biggs, PhD, FACHE.

Errol devoted his professional career to health and hospital administration. He served as director of graduate programs in health administration at the School of Business, University of Colorado, Denver, until his recent retirement. In 1994 he welcomed this book into the capstone course for the Executive MBA in Health Administration program. Prior to his academic career, he served as CEO and president of a number of hospitals. Over many years, he contributed advice and examples to assist students in using this book. We acknowledge and thank him for his many contributions.

BRIEF CONTENTS

DETAILED CONTENTS

ACKNOWLEDGMENTS

To ensure that all cases are realistic, we asked senior healthcare executives to review and comment on each case. Cathy, Dan, Dennis, Ellen, Eugene, Fritz, Jay, Mike, Steve, Tim, Tom, and Yousef have read these cases and given us their perspectives as successful managers in different sectors of our industry. Many others have volunteered advice as we continue to strive to provide our students with an effective foundation. Over the years, the cases also have benefited from the insights and suggestions of faculty members, senior healthcare executives, and students—especially the students and faculty in the Executive MBA program at the University of Colorado, Denver. Errors in the many tables of data, however, are solely our responsibility.

Map Legend

 Mountains

 County and State Roads

Interstate Highway

Interstate Highway
(Under Construction)

❶ Hillsboro Health (HH)–Middleboro and Jasper
❷ Physician Care Services (PCS)–Mifflenville and Jasper
❸ Middleboro Medical Center (MIDCARE)–Middleboro
❹ Webster Hospital (WH)–Middleboro
❺ Medical Associates (MA)–Middleboro and Jasper
❻ Jasper Gardens (JG)–Jasper
❼ Hillsboro County Health Department (HCHD)–Middleboro
❽ Middleboro Community Mental Health Center (MCMHC)–
Middleboro
❾ Jasper Emergency Services (JES)–Jasper
❿ Jasper Ambulatory Surgery Center (JASC)–Jasper
⓫ The Oaks (OAKS)–Jasper
⓬ Capitol City General Hospital (CCGH)–Capitol City
⓭ Valley Medical Center (VMC)–Capitol City

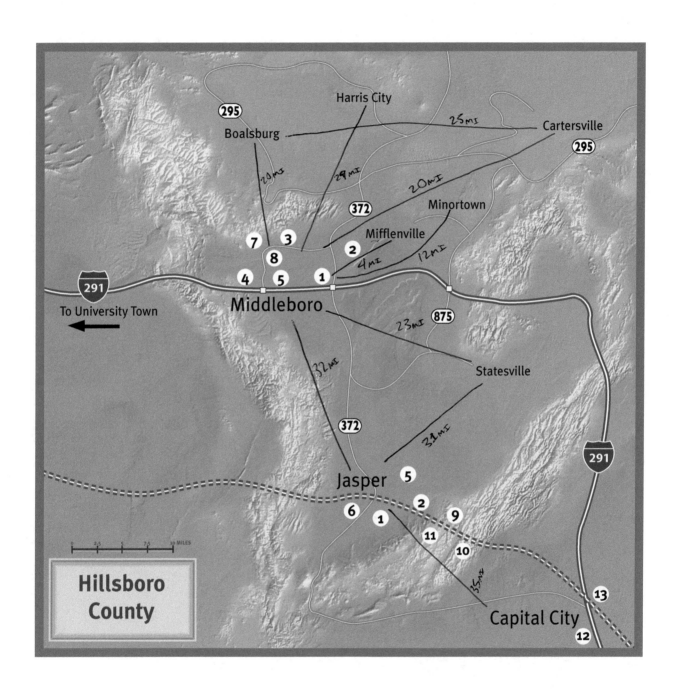

Harris City

295

Boalsburg

25mi

Cartersville

295

29mi

29mi

20mi

372

Minortown

7   3

Mifflenville

2

12mi

8

4mi

1

4   5

291

To University Town

Middleboro

23mi

875

32mi

Statesville

372

31mi

Jasper   5

2

6   9

1

11

10

13

35mi

Capital City

12

0   2.5   5   7.5   10 MILES

Hillsboro
County

LIST OF TABLES

Case 11

Case 12

Case 13

Case 14

Case 15

Appendixes

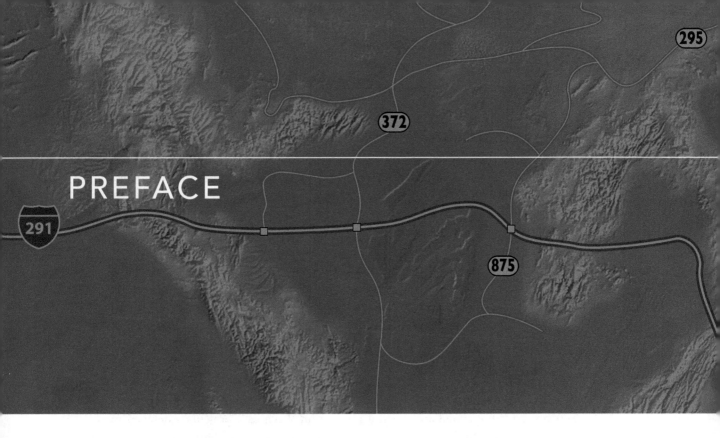

PREFACE

The Middleboro Casebook is a flexible and integrated case study that focuses on the strategy and operations of a regional healthcare system located in and around the communities of Middleboro and nearby Jasper in Hillsboro County, USA. The opening case introduces students to the communities as well as their demographic, socioeconomic, political, economic, epidemiological, and environmental characteristics. Data presented in the tables enable students to analyze the communities in detail, focusing on those factors that drive the need for and use of healthcare services as well as framing the strategic decisions made by healthcare organizations. The cases provide information about the primary healthcare organizations in Middleboro and the surrounding area. Each case includes the organization's history, governance, organizational structure, programs and services, finances, and particular issues and challenges.

CONCEPT OF THE BOOK

We developed The Middleboro Casebook to bring authentic management and policy issues into the classroom and to assist students and faculty with integrating an academic curriculum in health administration. As well as describing a "typical" regional healthcare system, it also provides the basis for identifying many types of problems and issues and for formulating management plans and strategies. Since its inception, the casebook has assisted faculty with providing a robust integrating seminar between traditional academic study and professional practice.

All the cases and the setting are totally fictitious, removing "what really happened" scenarios from any management plans and strategies provided by students. Each healthcare organization is described in detail in the context of its common setting. The cases blend the impact of national forces and issues that influence the management of healthcare organizations today with the local forces and issues that make managing healthcare organizations unique. Sensitivity to local events, circumstances, and issues is essential, just as in professional practice.

Middleboro provides the opportunity and flexibility to achieve many different types of learning outcomes. For example, students can be asked to define a comprehensive strategy for a specific business unit or to complete a focused analysis on a specific aspect of an organization (e.g., financial, marketing, population health). Students can assess multiple organizational arrangements, including mergers and acquisitions, as well as the opportunity for horizontal and vertical integration. Each case presents a detailed picture of the structure, function, and operation of a different type of healthcare organization. To engender flexibility, no specific student assignments have been included in the book. This allows the instructor—with the help of the Instructor Resources provided—to define how the book is used and to select assignments, as well to determine if additional information might be needed.

THE THIRD EDITION

The Middleboro Casebook reflects contemporary, plausible realities—realities influenced by many events and forces. This edition acknowledges the impact of a pandemic as well the emergence of telehealth and other healthcare systematic adaptations. The third edition also includes new presentations describing a freestanding emergency room (FES), a freestanding ambulatory surgical center (ASC), a continuing care retirement center (CCRC), an accountable care organization (ACO), and the primary referral medical centers—Capital City General and Valley Medical—located in Capital City. *Note that the data in the third edition have no relationship with the data in the first two editions. Each edition is independent.*

As was true of earlier editions, this edition can be used in many ways. First, it can be the primary text for a course and/or used as resource for topical management courses in such areas as strategic planning, marketing, population health, and financial management. Second, as some faculty members have done, the casebook can be used in a course that introduces students to the US healthcare system, its organizations, and its issues. In this context, *The Middleboro Casebook* is used as a microcosm of the real world to familiarize students with the structure and function of a typical regional healthcare system. Third, it can be used in multiple foundation courses in which students develop strategic analyses and business plans based on specific course objectives and then in a program's capstone course as a culminating integrating experience. This model approach, which we call "Middleboro Across the Curriculum," provides depth, breadth, and integration for many courses. When used in a capstone course, *The Middleboro Casebook* also provides a unique opportunity to assess student attainment of intended curricula competencies.

THE INSTRUCTOR'S MANUAL

The Instructor's Manual is a critical component of this text and will allow instructors to make the most of each case for students. It includes suggestions related to problem-based learning and case-method teaching, short essays with guidance on using the cases effectively, and recommended assignments. Additional information regarding the full Instructor Resources follows.

CONCLUSION

Middleboro, Jasper, Hillsboro County, Capital City, and all the organizations and people described in the book are, again, totally fictitious. Any similarity to real people, places, or events is merely an unintended consequence. (For the record, Middleboro, Jasper, and Hillsboro County are not in New Hampshire.) The data and the issues in the cases are realistic and derived from many sources and advice from many healthcare executives. Recognizing that management is both an art and a science, we hope students use both to define and address problems and challenges, improve access and quality, and lower costs.

Remember that every case is layered, so students—and other users of the book—should peel it like an onion. Read it over, numerous times. Look for connections. Explore it. Think about it. Understand that the cases are related and integrated. Even though an assignment may focus on one organization, relevant information can be gathered from the other cases.

Health services management requires both educational and experiential preparation. We hope this book provides some of each. Welcome to Middleboro and Hillsboro County. It is exactly midnight on December 31, 2024. The year 2024 has just ended and 2025 has just begun.

Lee F. Seidel, PhD
James B. Lewis, ScD

INSTRUCTOR RESOURCES

This book's Instructor Resources include the following:

Instructor's Manual

- *Using Middleboro* presents many issues and suggestions related to problem-based learning and case-method teaching applied to each case. This section includes using Assignment Letters and Case Assignments to create the "problems" for student attention.

- *Teaching Notes* provides short essays that describe what the instructor needs to know to use these cases effectively.

- *Suggested Assignments* recommends assignments in three categories: (1) assignments for each individual case (e.g., Webster Hospital); (2) assignments by subject (e.g., marketing); and (3) assignments for specific companion texts, including the following:

  Dunn, R. T. 2021. *Dunn and Haimann's Healthcare Management,* 11th edition. Chicago: Health Administration Press.

  Harris, J. M. 2017. *Healthcare Strategic Management,* 4th edition. Chicago: Health Administration Press.

  Olden, P. C. 2019. *Management of Healthcare Organizations: An Introduction*, 3rd edition. Chicago: Health Administration Press.

  Reiter, K. L., and P. Song. 2018. *Gapenski's Fundamentals of Healthcare Finance,* 3rd edition. Chicago: Health Administration Press.

  Reiter, K. L., and P. Song. 2021. *Gapenski's Healthcare Finance: An Introduction to Accounting and Financial Management*, 7th edition. Chicago: Health Administration Press.

  Thomas, R. K. 2020. *Marketing Health Services*, 4th edition. Chicago: Health Administration Press.

  White, K. R., and J. R. Griffith. 2019. *The Well-Managed Healthcare Organization,* 9th edition. Chicago: Health Administration Press.

Middleboro as Internship

- This is a modified guide to using *The Middleboro Casebook* in an internship format.

  For the most up-to-date information about this book and its instructor resources, go to ache.org/HAP and search for the book's order code (2459I). This book's instructor resources are available to instructors who adopt this book for use in their course. For access information, please email hapbooks@ache.org.

STUDENT RESOURCES

Excel versions of all tables are available online at ache.org/books/Middleboro3.

CASE 1

THE COMMUNITY

Many people regard Hillsboro County as a comfortable place to raise a family. It is an area known for its social and economic stability. While the residents are generally aware of national and world events, the local media coverage is dominated by news about the area's youth teams, social and fraternal organizations, church outings, and high school sports. Multiple generations of families live in Middleboro and the surrounding towns that make up Hillsboro County.

DEMOGRAPHIC CHARACTERISTICS

Middleboro and Hillsboro County are classified as non-metropolitan areas. Middleboro has been the economic, political, and social hub for Hillsboro County. The average family size is 2.57 people. Basic demographic data are given at the end of this case. (Note that the entire casebook is set at the start of 2025, so all tables are dated for the preceding years.)

The other major town in Hillsboro County is Jasper, located 32 miles southeast of Middleboro. Jasper is a growing community that benefits from being close to Capital City, the state capital, and is continuing to develop an economy that is independent from Middleboro.

GEOGRAPHIC CHARACTERISTICS

Surrounded on two sides by relatively high mountains, Middleboro is 60 miles northwest of Capital City and 68 miles east of University Town, the location of State University. Access to Middleboro is limited to rail (freight), bus, automobile, and truck. The majority of private and commercial travel is done on the four-lane, east–west interstate highway, which is typically closed an average of three days per year because of weather conditions. Commercial air travel is available in Capital City. The mountains on the east and west make winter travel outside Middleboro difficult. The fertile valleys on the north and south are known for agricultural activities.

Outside of Middleboro and Jasper, the population lives in small, scattered villages. The only transportation linkages to Middleboro from these scattered communities are the rural county and state highways. Limited bus service is available throughout Hillsboro County. Middleboro serves as the regional transportation hub, and the bus station in Middleboro offers connections to major population centers in the state. Jasper is also served by this bus system. Recently, a commuter bus system began linking Jasper with Capital City. A commuter rail system between Jasper and Capital City is expected to open in 18–24 months. It eventually will be extended to University Town and points west.

Hillsboro County stretches 65 miles to the north, 25 miles to the west, 28 miles to the east, and 47 miles to the south of Middleboro. The Lonely Pines Mountains run between Jasper and Capital City. Seventy-one percent of the total area is developed, and the remainder is taken up by forest, the state park, and rivers. This area experiences four distinct seasons, but tourists find it especially attractive during the fall and spring. Sports of all types play an important role in the life of its communities. Table 1.1 indicates the distance between the communities located in Hillsboro County.

Middleboro is located along Swift River, which was instrumental in the commercial development of the city in the early 1800s. Before the turn of the twentieth century, Swift River and the commercial barges that traversed it were the city's primary linkage with the rest of the state. Now the river is used for recreational purposes, and some limited redevelopment of the riverside property has begun.

Swift River divides Middleboro into two almost equal parts. The north side of the river is the site of the central business district, large manufacturing plants, the railroad station, older residential neighborhoods, and the county government. During the 1970s, federal funds were used to develop low-income housing on the north side. The south side of the river, which is closer to the interstate highway, is the site of newer residential neighborhoods, the new Middleboro High School, and small shopping centers. To date, the City of Middleboro has not approved any significant development—residential or commercial—in the vacant 150-acre land adjacent to the interstate highway.

SOCIAL AND EDUCATIONAL CHARACTERISTICS

The population of Hillsboro County is predominantly of German, Irish, and English extraction. Most of the African Americans arrived in the 1960s. Most of the other minority groups arrived in the late 1970s. The minority population is primarily located in Middleboro, although recent immigrants, particularly from Asia, Africa, and Latin America, are moving to Jasper in larger numbers.

In Middleboro, 16.6 percent of households are headed by a woman. The median education level of the population older than 25 years is 10.7 years. Approximately 13.5 percent of the population has completed college, and 89.3 percent has completed high school. The current dropout rate from area high schools is 3 percent, an improvement over the 17 percent rate experienced 20 years ago.

Middleboro is the site of numerous elementary schools (K–6), a regional middle school (7–8), and a high school (9–12) that serve students from all over the city. Other communities in the county can send their children to Middleboro schools, using tuition arrangements on a space-available basis. Although all the schools are owned and operated by the City of Middleboro, a separately elected Middleboro School Board makes educational policy. One-third of the nine-member school board is elected each year in a special school-district election held in Middleboro. Each year, the school board submits a recommended budget for consideration by the Middleboro City Council. The city council approves the school budget before it is submitted, as part of the town's total budget, for voter approval. All employees of the Middleboro School Department—except the school superintendent, Dr. Sam Drucker—are unionized. Abby O'Hara is currently the chair of the school board, a position she has held for the past ten years. The new $32.5 million high school located in Middleboro opened last year after being considered by the city council for about eight years. The town is heavily involved in high school sports. Middleboro Memorial Stadium is a landmark in regional high school football.

Jasper is the site of numerous elementary schools, a regional middle school (5–8), and a high school (9–12). A state-supported junior college is scheduled to open in September 2026. A five-member elected school board that is independent of the town governs the Jasper Regional Educational Cooperative. Each year, this school board submits a recommended budget directly to the voters. Once approved, the funds are collected by the Town of Jasper from local taxes. The Jasper Regional Educational Cooperative has expressed interest in working with the state to develop a regional vocational high school to complement the new Hillsboro County Junior College.

State University (SU) in University Town is the land-grant university within the state. It has a nursing, public health, and allied health school connected to its relatively large liberal arts and agricultural schools. Its 20,000 students make SU the largest public university in the state. A private liberal arts college of 1,000 students is also located in Capital City. SU maintains a small branch campus in Capital City as well.

Church membership remains strong in Hillsboro County. Aside from their religious influence, churches sponsor many of the youth sports leagues and are the site of many social gatherings.

Local chapters of Rotary International meet monthly in Middleboro and Jasper. AARP—formerly called the American Association of Retired Persons—maintains a chapter in Middleboro. The local chapter of the American Red Cross, located in Middleboro, sponsors monthly blood drives throughout the county.

When statistics are adjusted for demographic characteristics, crime rates in the county are 10 percent below the national averages for non-metropolitan areas.

POLITICAL CHARACTERISTICS

Middleboro and its surrounding communities are politically conservative. Unlike other areas in the state, the same political party has dominated Middleboro for the past 45 years, except in presidential elections. Its politicians have gained statewide political power by consistently being reelected to office. The city is especially proud that the area's representative to the US Congress, James Giles, is a Middleboro native who retains his law practice in town.

Middleboro is governed by a six-member city council whose members are elected every two years. By tradition, the council member who receives the largest number of popular votes is appointed by the council to serve as mayor. Although the office's powers are mostly ceremonial, the mayor has the ability to influence decisions by presiding over council meetings and by making appointments to boards and commissions. Keith Edwards, a local retailer, has held the position of mayor for 17 years. Other members of the Middleboro City Council are Frederick Washburn, Diana Story, David Alley, Patricia Hood, and Michael York. The city's largest department is the school department, and the second largest is public works. York is the council member who has lead responsibilities for all healthcare-related issues and programs.

The City of Middleboro has recently begun legal action to block the licensing of three group homes for the developmentally disabled population. Group Homes Inc., a national corporation, has a contract with the state to own and operate these homes. Middleboro Community Mental Health Center currently owns and operates Justin Place, a four-bed group home in Middleboro. Group Homes Inc., a national corporation, has a contract with the state to own and operate these homes. According to Mayor Edwards, the Hillsboro County Health Department has failed to take into consideration the serious implications these homes will have on Middleboro. Mayor Edwards recommends that the application for licensure be turned down on grounds related to negative community impact. Stephanie Jervis-Washburn, the executive director of Middleboro Community Mental Health Center, has also questioned the need for additional group homes, although at the same time indicating that her organization would be willing to assess the need for such services and possibly develop them should a need be identified.

Middleboro is the county seat for Hillsboro County. Three county commissioners elected by the population at large govern Hillsboro County. While the county level of government is not a powerful political subdivision in this region, it does control the court system, the penal system, and the registry of motor vehicles; it also provides some human service programs. Hillsboro County owns and operates Manorhaven, a nursing home located in Middleboro. It is a major county employer in Middleboro. The current Hillsboro County Commissioners are Janet Ruseski, Bill Nelligan, and Mary Harrison.

Jasper is governed by a 12-member town council and a mayor. All are elected for four-year terms. William Hines is the mayor, a position he has held for the past nine years. The town council employs a professional city manager, Susan Giles-Harrison. The Jasper Industrial Development Authority (JIDA)—authorized by the voters 25 years ago—is a subunit of the town council and has the authority to issue bonds to support industrial development in Jasper. State law allows a municipal government to use tax-increment financing for purposes of economic development. Giles-Harrison also serves as the executive director of JIDA. Two years ago, JIDA formed a special committee to consider the feasibility of a hospital located on its property that was to be owned and operated by the town. This committee is chaired by Sharon Lee, who is the spouse of a Jasper physician, a member of the town council, and a former consultant for a national consulting firm that specializes in healthcare. Other members of this committee include Mayor Hines and town councilor Ed Hicks. Giles-Harrison provides staff support for the committee.

THE PANDEMIC

In March 2021, a previously unknown virus appeared in the United States. Although the roots of the virus are not certain, the virus first appeared almost simultaneously in April 2021 in locations outside the United States, including Asia and Europe, and spread rapidly. Scientists quickly ascertained that the new disease had a natural origin rather than resulting from manufacture, laboratory accident, or terrorism. Coronaviruses are the cause of many diseases, ranging from the common cold to Middle East respiratory syndrome (MERS). The new virus is a coronavirus that is transmitted via an aerosol route between humans. Due to international travel and trade, the disease rapidly evolved into a global pandemic affecting virtually every country in the world by June 2021. It was not COVID-19.

Although the pandemic affected people of all ages, its incidence and mortality rates both increased with patient age. Children under age ten rarely contracted the virus, and their symptoms were typically minor. In addition, a substantial segment (estimated to be about one-fourth) of those contracting the virus, particularly among younger age groups, were asymptomatic. Symptoms of the disease varied considerably, although among more serious cases the virus most frequently compromised the respiratory system.

When the virus appeared, several laboratories and researchers developed suitable tests to identify the virus in individuals. The levels of specificity and sensitivity of the tests were not ideal but were nonetheless acceptable. In Hillsboro County, and the entire country, there was no system in place for distribution of the tests, and there was substantial resistance to use of the tests among segments of the population. Devising a plan to coordinate testing was left to individual states and counties, a task for which Hillsboro and many other counties were ill-prepared. During the pandemic, several communities, including Middleboro, Harris City, and Carterville, were considered hotspots based on the number of cases per 1,000 population. Others had higher-than-average rates of incidence.

As is true for many viruses, the incidence of this new virus increased and decreased in waves. An effective treatment or cure has eluded scientists, although various treatments have achieved some success in reducing the severity of the illness caused by the virus, particularly among the most severe cases.

Vaccines became available to high-risk populations in Hillsboro County in January 2023. The Hillsboro County Health Department estimated that by November 2024 approximately 60 percent of the county's population over age 16 had received the recommended vaccination. As with most viruses, this one produced mutations or variants from the original strain. Effectiveness of the vaccine against these variants was not ascertained with certainty, although it was felt to be at least of some utility in lessening the seriousness of the disease. Due to the relatively high percentage (approximately 40 percent) of area residents not receiving the vaccine and the ongoing evolution of the virus, herd immunity was determined to be an unlikely outcome. Ultimately, public health experts came to believe that individuals would need to receive booster immunizations, probably annually, to maintain the highest possible levels of immunity.

By March 2022, it was apparent that public health measures such as social distancing and wearing face masks were at least somewhat effective in reducing transmission of the virus. At the same time, these strategies met with resistance among large segments of the population who viewed them as contrary to individual freedom and choice. This resistance was greater in rural communities, such as Northern Hillsboro County, where it was difficult to effect either social distancing or mask wearing. Neither the state nor the county imposed mask mandates, even at the height of the pandemic. Further, implementation of public health measures ran counter to the beliefs of state and county business and industry leaders, who felt such strategies had an excessively negative impact on economic performance. Resistance to economic shutdowns was particularly strong in Jasper. It was true that many businesses that closed during the pandemic or shifted to remote working experienced a negative impact on their financial performance. Several employers were forced to reduce or even eliminate health insurance coverage for their workforce. Tension between the business and public health communities was exacerbated by battles among various political factions, both local and beyond.

To date, the impact of the pandemic on the community and healthcare providers has also been extensive. An increased number of people infected by the virus showed up in emergency departments and local hospitals, which were intermittently short of the resources (intensive care and general beds, ventilators, personal protective equipment, etc.) needed to handle the workload. In addition, many patients refrained from using healthcare resources altogether, fearing exposure to the virus. This impact was felt in many areas, such as elective surgery, preventive care, and dental care. One area that experienced dramatic growth, however, was telehealth.

MacWilliams and Co., a national consulting firm hired by the state to assess the effect of the pandemic on healthcare, described the impact in Hillsboro County as extensive. It called attention to the significant financial losses sustained by most health sector organizations as well as the significant increase in early retirements of critical clinicians including physicians and nurses. The number of physician practices located in rural communities that closed or relocated out of the county was also cited as a "significant concern." Every hospital and all long-term care providers (including home health) also experienced utilization changes, as well as changes in operating costs. As noted earlier, the report indicated that the pandemic led to several closings among large and small employers throughout the county, as well as statewide delays on almost all public works projects. The report also called attention to the estimated 20 percent of the county's population who chose not to be vaccinated (anti-vaxxers).

Based on 2023 state legislation, the Hillsboro County Health Department has been designated as the local agency to continue to monitor all reported cases in the county and to implement appropriate public health measures, including increasing the percentage of the population maintaining their immunity using vaccinations. Data regarding the pandemic and its impact appear in the several tables in this chapter. Table 1.2 displays the incidence of the virus by town and year.

In terms of utilization of hospital resources, Hillsboro County fared relatively well, although it had to transfer a small number of patients to Capital City General Hospital for 19 days when pandemic volume was particularly high. The peak number of hospital beds in use for pandemic patients at any one time was 78, which occurred in October 2022. The peak number of intensive care unit (ICU) beds in use by pandemic patients at any one time was 14, which also occurred in October 2022. At that time, enough non-pandemic patients were able to be temporarily transferred out of the ICU to accommodate the increased demand for beds. The peak number of ventilators in use by pandemic patients was 11. This peak occurred twice, in October 2022 and February 2023. During these peaks, MIDCARE and Webster Hospital borrowed ventilators from other area facilities to accommodate increased need.

Under a program supported by the federal Department of Homeland Security approximately six years ago, prior to the onset of the pandemic, the mayors of all the communities located in Hillsboro County and their fire and police officials created a task force to estimate surge capacity in an emergency or mass casualty situation. Officials from the two Middleboro hospitals—MIDCARE and Webster—have attended task force meetings. The task force continues to update its estimate of potential evacuation or triage locations and beds that could be used. The Office of the Governor supports this project by funding a countywide assessment of surge capacity conducted by State University.

Initial findings and results from the study, published in December 2020, indicate the following:

◆ At least 285 hotel or motel rooms are available in Hillsboro County.

◆ Public schools can hold 4,500 citizens, although none has provisions for emergencies.

◆ The disaster plans for both hospitals have not been coordinated. Each has its own plan and has estimated that it can accommodate at least 150 percent to 180 percent of its inpatient capacity for one week.

◆ No countywide, centralized communication system or command-and-control system exists that can direct resources and responses in the face of a significant disaster.

The experience of the pandemic has caused the task force to revisit the issue of surge capacity, and a more comprehensive assessment and plan is expected within six months.

Since 2009, Hillsboro County has sponsored a Community Emergency Response Team program to educate residents about disaster preparedness for hazards that may arise such as fires, floods, and weather-related disasters. Classes are held three times a year; to date, approximately 120 residents have completed training. Program instructors have been drawn from local police and fire departments, both local hospitals, and the Hillsboro County Health Department. It is anticipated that community interest in this program will increase following the pandemic.

For the past five years, the state legislature has attempted to make the state a right-to-work state. Although the bill was not passed, it did secure 52 percent approval in the state senate last year. The current governor has indicated that if the legislation passes in both houses, he will veto it. His political opponents have indicated their support for the right-to-work legislation.

ECONOMIC CHARACTERISTICS

Middleboro's tax profile reflects the conservative nature of the community. Increases in property taxes have just barely kept pace with inflation. The state has both a graduated income tax and a sales tax. By state law, any incorporated city is allowed to add a 0.5 percent local sales tax to the state sales tax. The Middleboro City Council has repeatedly rejected all proposals to do this.

Middleboro is the site of important wholesale and retail trade in Hillsboro County. Its major industries include manufacturing, finance, and service. Jasper is also establishing itself as a manufacturing center. Agriculture, which once dominated, now accounts for 20 percent of income and 16 percent of all employment in the county. Manufacturing accounts for 32 percent of income and 30 percent of employment. Per capita income is 5 percent below the national average. Fourteen percent of the county's population falls below the federal poverty standard. In Capital City, 18 percent of the population is under the federal poverty level.

Local banks estimate that approximately 3 percent of the single homes in the county have outstanding mortgages greater than the homes' current market value. The regional foreclosure rate is 1 percent greater than the national rate.

Until recently, three of Middleboro's manufacturing companies employed approximately 15 percent of the community's workforce, down 7 percent from five years ago:

1. Carlstead Rayon, a privately controlled textile corporation, employed 4.1 percent of the workforce. Sold to an overseas corporation, it ceased operation in Middleboro on December 31, 2024. Under a state and union supervised plan, all workers are provided six months' wages and benefits and immediate access to their vested retirement benefits.

2. River Industries, a division of National Auto Technology, manufactures rubber products for automobiles. For the past three years, it has reduced its workforce by 9 percent but still accounts for 4.5 percent of the workforce.

3. Master Tractor, formerly a division of United Agricultural Supply, was recently sold to a Japanese firm, which indicated that some parts for tractors will be imported from offshore and South American suppliers. A leader in the market for small tractors, Master Tractor employs 4.6 percent of the workforce.

Western Arms, Inc., manufactures and distributes shotguns, rifles, pistols, and ammunition. The company has purchased some of Carlstead Rayon's property and begun needed modifications. Western Arms plans to be fully operational in five months. It has not released any specific employment estimates.

Following are the larger employers in Jasper:

◆ Blue Bear Ale is a popular, locally owned, statewide microbrewery. Its sites are located in Middleboro, Mifflenville, and Jasper.

◆ U.S. Parts, a division of a national corporation that manufactures components for large air-conditioning units, relocated to Jasper three years ago. Today, it employs 2.9 percent of Jasper's workforce.

◆ National Yearbooks, a corporation headquartered in a major western city, established a modern printing and manufacturing plant in Jasper last year, using resources provided by JIDA. The company specializes in manufacturing yearbooks for colleges and high schools. Although currently it employs only 81 workers, it estimates that employment will increase 10 percent for each of the next ten years as it reduces its existing regional manufacturing sites and concentrates its entire North American manufacturing at the Jasper plant. National Yearbooks is not unionized and offers a full range of health insurance options to its full-time workers.

◆ Office Pro, a retail and wholesale provider of office supplies and office furniture, operates its regional warehouse in the Jasper Industrial Park, located on the western boundary of Jasper.

◆ University Research Park is located on Route 491A halfway between Jasper and University Town. In 2021, it opened with its first research and development (R&D) and manufacturing facility for solar technologies, Sunenco. It has recently announced that an international corporation has also purchased space to build its R&D laboratory in collaboration with State University for advanced robotics technologies.

Agriculture and construction companies in the rest of Hillsboro County are primarily small, family-owned businesses. Chicken Farms, Inc., located in Harris City, is a national corporation that specializes in raising chickens for fast-food restaurants. It recently began to acquire family farms in the area and has announced plans to locate a processing plant somewhere in the county.

Countywide, housing construction permits have declined over the past seven years, and the decline was particularly large during the pandemic. The housing stock is considered old—except in Jasper—by both national and state standards. Real estate development has been relatively robust in the area between Jasper and Capital City.

Hillsboro County has one state-chartered commercial bank—Middleboro Trust Company—that has offices in Middleboro, Mifflenville, Statesville, Harris City, and Jasper. The county also has seven savings-and-loan (S&L) institutions. Major capital financing is available through Middleboro Trust Company, a correspondent bank of a major national financial institution, or through a commercial bank located in Capital City. Bankers' Cooperative, a multistate commercial bank headquartered in another state, has recently announced plans to expand into Jasper.

MEDIA RESOURCES

The major newspaper in the county is the *Middleboro Sentinel*. It has a daily as well as a Sunday edition, and it maintains a comprehensive website. Its circulation is 32,000 for the daily edition and 18,200 for the Sunday edition. Three years ago, National News Stands, Inc., a national owner and operator of local newspapers, acquired the *Middleboro Sentinel*. Jack Donnelly has been its editor for 16 years. In Jasper, *The Capital City News* reaches approximately 25 percent of all households in Hillsboro County. Its advertising rates are similar to those of the *Middleboro Sentinel*.

Middleboro has three local radio stations—AM-75, AM-1220, and FM-89.7— that cover local news and current events. TV Channel 32 is a FOX-affiliated station located in Middleboro. It provides network and some independent programs. Other affiliates of national television networks (ABC, CBS, NBC, and FOX News) are located in Capital City, and their broadcasts reach most residents in the county. Cable TV and high-speed Internet from national and local providers are available throughout most of the county as well.

MEDICAL RESOURCES

HILLSBORO HEALTH (CASE 2)

This tax-exempt, Medicare-certified home health agency provides a broad range of home-based services throughout the county. Six years ago, the agency was formed after a merger and expanded its mission and focus. It established a Medicare-certified hospice service and curtailed a number of community health programs. It uses funds provided by the towns and cities in the area, Hillsboro County, and United Way to support indigent care associated with its services. It transferred maternal and child health programs, funded by a grant from the state's Department of Health and Human Services, to voluntary health agencies. Martha Washington is Hillsboro Health's CEO, and Janet Myer is president of its board of directors.

PHYSICIAN CARE SERVICES, INC. (CASE 3)

Physician Care Services (PCS), Inc., is a private, tax-paying corporation that owns and operates two urgent care/occupational health centers—one located in Mifflenville and the other in Jasper. PCS employs physicians and other professionals to provide walk-in ambulatory care, a full range of diagnostic services, and an occupational health program. Currently, PCS is considering opening a third center in the Jasper Industrial Park. Dr. Stephen Tobias is the president/CEO and medical director of PCS.

MIDDLEBORO COMMUNITY MENTAL HEALTH CENTER (CASE 4)

In 1964, Middleboro Community Mental Health Center (MCMHC) was established as a tax-exempt 501(c)(3) corporation. MCMHC provides a range of services and programs, including adult, child and family, emergency, and education. In addition, it owns and operates a central office called Gardner Place as well as a four-bed group home called Justin Place; both facilities are located in northwest Middleboro. Stephanie Jervis-Washburn serves as MCMHC's executive director.

WEBSTER HOSPITAL (CASE 5)

Webster Hospital, a 501(c)(3) corporation, is a fully accredited, tax-exempt, 70-bed hospital located in Middleboro adjacent to the interstate highway. Named after its founder Dr. Edward W. Webster, this hospital was founded in 1930 to practice osteopathic medicine. Until 30 months ago, it was an affiliate member of the Osteopathic Hospitals of America (OHA) network. This network ceased operations with the bankruptcy and sale of Osteopathic Medical Center's assets in Capital City to a national proprietary hospital chain. Webster Hospital is in the process of redefining its mission, structure, and place in the regional market.

MIDCARE, INC. (CASE 6)

Middleboro Medical Center, or MIDCARE, is a health system established on January 1, 2015, to "meet the needs of Hillsboro County." The system grew out of Middleboro Community Hospital, a fully licensed, tax-exempt acute care hospital founded in 1890 on the north side of Middleboro. Most of MIDCARE's current beds are located in wings originally constructed in 1962 and 1966 with the assistance of federal Hill-Burton funds; these wings have now been modernized. In 2014, this modernization involved converting a significant number of semiprivate rooms into private rooms and updating the birthing facilities. MIDCARE provides a full range of diagnostic, outpatient, therapeutic, and emergency medical services, including a cancer center. Adjacent to the hospital is the Middleboro Medical Office Building; ample parking is available for both facilities. Although licensed for 272 beds, the hospital had to reduce its inpatient capacity to lower costs and adjust to new hospital utilization patterns.

In 2015, the system signed a renewable ten-year agreement to become an affiliate member of Treeline Health Systems, Inc. Under this affiliation, MIDCARE pays dues to be part of Treeline; in return, Treeline provides medical oversight and direction for MIDCARE's cancer center, access to its national supply chain management system, and technical assistance and support for MIDCARE's clinical data systems. In addition, both parties agreed to develop a clinical residency program for primary care practitioners. James Higgens is the president of MIDCARE.

MEDICAL ASSOCIATES (CASE 7)

Medical Associates is a multispecialty physician group with offices in downtown Middleboro and in Jasper. Founded in 1951, it is a tax-paying private corporation organized as a professional partnership. Physicians in the group provide specialty and subspecialty care on an ambulatory basis, and in the Jasper location, they also offer ambulatory surgical services. All of its physicians are board certified and maintain active medical staff privileges at area hospitals. Over the past three years, to facilitate the expansion of its primary services, the group has added more physicians in its Jasper office as well as advanced registered nurse practitioners in both locations. In 2019, it introduced Medical Associates Express, a 24/7 walk-in clinic, to its Jasper office. The group contracts with Wythe Laboratories in Capital City for all medical tests and with Radiology Partners for all diagnostic images. Cynthia Worley is the executive manager at Medical Associates.

JASPER GARDENS (CASE 8)

Jasper Gardens Nursing Home is a private, tax-paying, 125-bed long-term care facility located in Jasper on a 100-acre campus. It qualifies for Medicare, Medicaid, all private insurance plans, and self-pay. Its owners—Jefferson Partners, LLC, of Capital City—recently announced plans to expand its inpatient and outpatient rehabilitation services. Jayne Winters is the licensed administrator of Jasper Gardens.

HILLSBORO COUNTY HEALTH DEPARTMENT (CASE 9)

Located in Middleboro, this department is responsible for the distribution of state health agency funds to local health agencies, immunizations, environmental health, the long-term care facility Manorhaven, and the implementation of county health priorities using county tax revenues. Using a statewide data system, the department gathers vital and mortality statistics and provides the data to the state as part of its annual report to the Hillsboro County Commissioners. John Snow is the director of the health department. The current chair of the Hillsboro County Board of Health oversees this municipal department. The board comprises 12 members, each of whom is appointed for an overlapping five-year term by the Hillsboro County Commissioners. Other professionals the department employs include registered nurses, public health assistants, and experts in public health.

OTHER HEALTH SERVICES

Aside from Medical Associates, many small, single-specialty and solo medical practices operate out of Hillsboro County. Other services include:

The Carter Home—located north of Middleboro and Jasper near Mifflenville—is a tax-paying, 110-bed long-term care facility that qualifies for both Medicare (as a skilled nursing facility) and Medicaid (as an intermediate care facility). Jack H. Carter has been president of the Carter Home Corporation, Inc., for the past 20 years and is currently the administrator of the Carter Home. Recently, the corporation opened Carter Village, an assisted living facility comprising 50 two-bedroom apartments with a congregate meal facility, 24-hour access to nursing services, access to physical and occupational therapists, and van service to shopping areas in Middleboro.

Jasper Emergency Services (case 10), an affiliate of Capital City General Hospital, is located in Jasper. The facility is open 24/7 and is fully accredited by The Joint Commission.

Jasper Ambulatory Surgical Center (case 11), an affiliate of Capital City General Hospital, co-owned by the hospital and the Capital City Medical Group, is located in Jasper. Services are provided six days a week in the facility's three operating rooms and two procedure rooms. The center is accredited by the Accreditation Association for Ambulatory Health Care.

Manorhaven, located in Middleboro, is a 110-bed long-term care facility that is owned and operated by Hillsboro County. It also operates a limited adult day care program for residents of Middleboro. It cooperates with Hillsboro Health to provide inpatient hospice services. Services at the facility qualify for both Medicare and Medicaid reimbursement. Jennifer Jones has been Manorhaven's administrator for the past eight years.

The Oaks (case 12) is a continuing care retirement community located near Jasper Gardens between Jasper and Capital City. It has 100 residential units.

Rock Creek—located north of Mifflenville near Harris City—is a private, 126-bed nursing home and 84-bed assisted living facility. It qualifies for Medicaid insurance, but it serves no Medicare patients. Five years ago, a statewide proprietary chain purchased Rock Creek. Its current administrator is John Lipman.

Senior Living of Mifflenville, located between Middleboro and Mifflenville, is an assisted living facility that offers two types of living arrangements. In the 45-unit assisted living facility, residents rent a private, one- or two-bedroom apartment with a small kitchen. Amenities include congregate meals, transportation services, and a full recreational program. In the adult home, 125 residents are provided either private or semiprivate room accommodation. A 24-hour nursing staff provides supervision. Senior Living of Mifflenville opened four years ago and is owned and operated by a national corporation. Its adult home is not a licensed nursing home.

Sockalexis Center, located in Jasper, has the contract to provide behavioral health and counseling services to the Jasper schools and is moving aggressively into the corporate substance abuse and employee assistance program market. The center is staffed by four doctorally trained clinical psychologists, three master's-level social workers, and three substance abuse counselors.

Greenwood Group, located just east of Jasper, is a provider of substance abuse therapy known for its "upscale" setting. It is staffed by psychiatrists, clinical psychologists, a social worker, substance abuse counselors, and health and wellness personnel. The organization has targeted commercially insured clients.

Royman Oaks, LLC, offers employment counseling and job placement for clients with a history of behavioral disorders.

Grosvenor Arms, located in Jasper, is a seven-bed adult group home. Its staff includes residential counselors, a clinical psychologist, a social worker, and a marriage-and-family therapist.

Churches throughout Hillsboro County coordinate and provide Meals on Wheels, a program that delivers hot lunches to homebound elderly and disabled populations.

In Middleboro, the Fire Department provides emergency services staffed with emergency medical technicians (EMTs). In Jasper, the Fire Department uses paramedics to provide emergency services. Other communities rely on volunteer firefighters and emergency responders, some of whom require basic EMT certification. This year, the county launched a countywide 911 emergency dispatch system.

Statewide Blue Cross and Blue Shield is headquartered in Capital City, along with the state chapters of the following organizations:

◆ AARP

◆ Alzheimer's Association

◆ American Cancer Society

◆ American Diabetes Association

◆ American Heart Association

◆ American Lung Association

◆ Brain Injury Association of America

◆ Epilepsy Foundation

◆ Mental Health America (formerly National Mental Health Association)

◆ Muscular Dystrophy Association

◆ Planned Parenthood Federation of America

◆ United Cerebral Palsy

The statewide Alzheimer's Association has publicly expressed its priority to establish a membership office in Middleboro and throughout Hillsboro County.

The state has two medical schools. One is public and located on the state's eastern boundary, and the other one is private with an osteopathic focus and located on the state's northern boundary. Both are located in major cities and are more than 250 miles away from Capital City. Over the past 30 years, the hospitals in Capital City have become major referral centers for the community hospitals located within a 100- to 150-mile geographic circle. Capital City General Hospital (case 13) and Valley Medical Center (case 14)—the two largest hospitals in the city—maintain teaching affiliations with the two medical schools in the state. Osteopathic Medical Center's facilities were sold to Valley Medical Center, Inc.,—a national chain of proprietary hospitals and related services—as part of the Osteopathic Medical Center's Chapter 7 bankruptcy. Also located in Capital City is the Swift Water Accountable Care Organization (case 15). A state-supported, 154-bed inpatient psychiatric institution is located nearly 150 miles northeast of Middleboro. Six licensed mortuaries work in the county—four in Middleboro and two in Jasper.

STATE REGULATIONS: CERTIFICATE OF NEED

The state continues to maintain a certificate-of-need (CON) law for all acute and specialty hospitals and long-term care facilities that receive Medicaid and/or Medicare. Home health agencies were exempted from the law 12 years ago. Also specifically excluded from the law are private physician offices, clinics, and dispensaries for employees and health maintenance organizations. The thresholds for application of CON are $6 million for major medical equipment, $15 million for new construction, any transfer of ownership, and any increase in the number of licensed bed size equal to or greater than 10 beds or 20 percent of the facility (whichever is less). CON proposals are evaluated on the basis of the proposal's ability to better address the needs of the service area, immediate and long-term financial viability, cost control, and quality-of-care implications. The first step in securing a CON is a letter of intent that addresses a specific question. Once the CON board rules that a CON is needed, the applicant is granted permission to submit a detailed application. Currently, there is one active letter of intent to seek a CON: Horizon Health Care, Inc., has filed a letter of intent to open a 65-bed hospital in Statesville to treat drug and alcohol addiction.

CON applications are forwarded to the State Commissioner of Health and Welfare and then analyzed by the State Bureau of Healthcare Services. The state's CON Board renders the final decision. The governor, following the recommendation of the state legislature, appoints the seven-member board. Jack Carter, the only local representative on this board, owns a nursing home in Hillsboro County. Working with a committee in the state legislature, within eighteen months, the governor will be issuing recommendations on whether CON should be reauthorized, changed, or allowed to lapse as a state statute.

COMMUNITY CONCERNS AND ISSUES

Local political leaders have long recognized that Middleboro is economically stagnant. They have discussed the need to build a major industrial park adjacent to the interstate highway. Local business leaders, however, have resisted this venture, arguing that the funds designated for an industrial park be invested instead in improving the central business district to bolster the city's existing retail trade business. As a result of these competing views, Middleboro has not invested in either development.

The entire city has been affected by the national downturn in the traditional industrial and manufacturing sector. The current unemployment rate in Hillsboro County is 3.4 percentage points higher than the state's overall rate. Most of this unemployment is in the Middleboro area. The recent demise of Carlstead Rayon and uncertainty concerning Western Arms has created unemployment concerns in the greater Middleboro area.

In 2019, the *Middleboro Sentinel* ran a series of stories on the environmental hazards caused by Carlstead Rayon's questionable handling of waste materials through the years. Subsequently, the Hillsboro County Health Department requested a Health Consultation of the Carlstead site by the Agency for Toxic Substances and Disease Registry of the US Department of Health and Human Services, Public Health Service. The 2022 consultation report indicated that portions of the Carlstead Rayon site are hazardous waste sites and thus subject to remediation requirements. This is considered one of the reasons for the sale and closing of Carlstead Rayon and the sale of some of its real estate not considered to be a hazardous site to Western Arms. Active litigation between the owners of Carlstead Rayon, Hillsboro County, and the state is underway to hold Carlstead Rayon financially accountable to remediate the site. If these efforts fail, responsibility for remediation falls upon the municipal government.

The Middleboro City Council has repeatedly asked all tax-exempt healthcare providers to make a payment in lieu of taxes to cover municipal services costs. Last year, Steven Local ran for city council with one campaign promise: He would convince nonprofit hospitals and other healthcare "free riders" to "pay their fair share" or face consequences from the city, including court action. He lost the election by 21 votes but vowed to return next year with an even stronger campaign. For the past five years, Hillsboro County has received an annual payment of $28,000 under the federal Payment in Lieu of Taxes program (Public Law 113-79).

For the past five years, Middleboro politics has been dominated by three issues: (1) the increases in property taxes, (2) the cost of schools, and (3) the use of funds included in Medicaid to pay for abortions. Planned Parenthood continues to attract demonstrations and protests. Except for unemployment concerns, economic development issues typically do not characterize the local political campaigns.

Major economic development has occurred in Jasper. U.S. Parts arrived in town, and today the company occupies almost 60 percent of the Jasper Industrial Park.

National Yearbooks is expected to fill the remaining capacity in the Jasper Industrial Park within two years. Plans are also underway to construct another industrial park adjacent to the new interstate highway between Jasper and Capital City. City officials in Middleboro are still being criticized for letting Jasper "beat out" Middleboro in attracting these major employers.

In 18 months, the state will open a moderate-security prison as part of the plan to develop regional prison facilities. The prison will have a capacity of 600 inmates and will be outside Hillsboro County, approximately 40 miles southwest of Jasper.

Issues involving growth continue to dominate the politics in Jasper. While the entire community seems very satisfied with the success of JIDA, many are dissatisfied with the impact the developments have had on municipal services and the local education system. Responsible Growth, a four-year-old group comprising 100 Jasper residents who voice community concerns, succeeded in electing two of its members—Jennifer Kip and Kevin Khalil—to the Jasper Town Council. Both expressed concern that Jasper was too quickly becoming a bedroom community to Capital City.

National Development Corp. has recently presented to the Jasper Planning Board a proposal to construct an 800-unit subdivision of moderately priced housing on land adjacent to the new interstate highway west of Jasper. The proposal holds the developer responsible for all infrastructures.

New Interstate Highway

Seven years ago, Representative Giles announced with the governor that a new four-lane interstate highway would be built from Jasper to Capital City and University Town. This road would shorten the travel distance from downtown Jasper to downtown Capital City (currently, 35 miles) to 16 miles and from Jasper to University Town (currently, 45 miles) to 40 miles.

Currently, the new road is finished from University Town to approximately 20 miles West of Jasper and from Capital City to approximately 20 miles east of Jasper. Given the mountainous terrain, the road to University Town is scheduled to be completed in approximately 22 months, while the remaining section between Jasper and Capital City should completed in 18 months.

Construction has already begun on a high-speed commuter rail link between Jasper and Capital City. The Capital City Transportation Authority has purchased land in both Capital City and Jasper and secured the right-of-way adjacent to the new highway. It is expected that this rail system will be operational within 48 months.

Over the past three years, the south of Jasper and land between Jasper and Capital City have experienced significant attention and a number of development proposals. For example, the Jasper Town Council, based on recommendations from the town and county planning boards, has approved the zoning application for a major shopping mall complex, which will be located adjacent to the new highway and at the edge of Jasper—approximately six miles from downtown Jasper. Given the impact of the recent pandemic on retail trade, it is possible this approval will be revisited.

COUNTYWIDE GRIEVANCES

In 2021, Middleboro had a significant Black Lives Matter rally followed by many meetings between the community's Black and political leaders to identify and resolve issues involving policing practices, employment opportunities, and *de facto* educational segregation based on the catchment areas of specific elementary schools. Recent demonstrations and events have attracted local and statewide media coverage.

Citizens Against Abortions is a small but vocal political force in Jasper. On three occasions, the group has picketed in front of the offices of physicians known to have performed abortions at hospitals in either Middleboro or Capital City and a Planned Parenthood clinic. TV Action 12, the largest TV station in Capital City, broadcasted on the evening news two of these demonstrations in Jasper. This group has announced plans to picket area hospitals. The *Middleboro Sentinel* has estimated that this organization has 75 to 130 members.

Leaders from other communities in Hillsboro County—Harris City, Boalsburg, Minortown, and Carterville—have begun to meet monthly to discuss common concerns. The group recently issued a statement directed at the Hillsboro County Commissioners. The statement indicated that too many county resources are being devoted to develop the southern part at the expense of the northern, smaller communities.

Philanthropy has continued to decline in the county, a situation exacerbated by the pandemic. The rate of giving throughout the county has declined 30 percent, and the amount disbursed by United Way has also shrunk by 16 percent. Even though all large industries and many small employers in the county cooperate with United Way, measures suggest that philanthropy from corporate donors has significantly decreased over the past ten years.

All employers in the state are required to obtain workers' compensation insurance. Currently, employees injured on the job are free to choose which healthcare provider would treat them. A new workers' comp law has been recently enacted, however. In six months, the responsibility for choosing the medical provider to care for an injured worker will be, by law, the employer's—not the employee's. This legislation also changes the workers' comp appeal process. Appeals will continue to flow through the circuit court and the State Supreme Court, and employees will still have 30 days from the time of the injury to initiate an appeal. However, questions reviewed under the new appeals process will pertain to law only and will not permit a jury trial. The old process permitted reviews of law and fact as well as a jury trial. In addition, the new law will increase competition for workers' comp business among healthcare providers. Most residents and observers feel that the changes amount to a tightening up of the workers' comp system, at the expense of employees. By all indications, the new law and its yet-to-be-seen impacts will be watched carefully. For example, a recent article in *The Capital City News* reported that a study by the Teamsters and Service Workers Unions found that, under the current system, the state's rejection rate of workers' comp claims was extremely high and had been rising for at least the past four years. According to the study, rejected claims are not paid by the state but by the employees' regular health insurance plans, which often include deductibles and copayments. The unions identified the shift of insurance coverage from the state workers' comp system to the employees and employers as a major way of increasing health insurance expenses.

Table 1.1
Distance (Miles) Between Hillsboro County Communities

City/Town	Boalsburg	Carterville	Harris City	Jasper	Middleboro	Mifflenville	Minortown	Statesville
Boalsburg	0	25	9	62	20	16	8	39
Carterville		0	18	44	20	16	15	15
Harris City			0	61	29	25	26	57
Jasper				0	32	36	46	31
Middleboro					0	4	12	23
Mifflenville						0	7	30
Minortown							0	37
Statesville								0
Outside Hillsboro County								
Capital City	55	80	55	35	60	64	45	32
University Town	88	89	96	45	68	72	80	76

Table 1.2
Pandemic Cases
in Hillsboro
County, Capital
City, and
University Town
by City/Town
and Year

City/Town	2024	2023	2022	2021	Total
Middleboro	820	1,493	1,579	753	4,645
Jasper	1,069	1,474	1,389	358	4,290
Statesville	405	753	268	143	1,569
Harris City	326	384	236	104	1,050
Mifflinville	183	454	192	79	908
Carterville	78	81	99	108	366
Minortown	32	38	59	23	152
Boalsburg	30	47	55	9	141
Hillsboro County Total	**2,943**	**4,724**	**3,877**	**1,577**	**13,121**
Capital City	2,628	5,442	6,078	1,987	16,135
University Town	2,304	2,383	2,744	1,673	9,104

Table 1.3
Hillsboro
County
Population

City/Town	1999	2004	2009	2014	2019	2024
Jasper	39,871	42,657	46,902	49,247	51,230	54,293
Middleboro	45,861	46,995	47,364	47,590	48,502	49,003
Statesville	11,750	11,790	12,750	14,350	14,780	14,903
Harris City	12,203	12,953	12,951	12,904	12,835	11,895
Mifflenville	10,623	10,945	10,952	11,240	11,253	11,134
Carterville	2,367	2,145	2,378	2,066	2,198	2,078
Minortown	2,163	2,190	2,056	2,103	2,005	2,109
Boalsburg	1,885	1,893	1,891	1,935	1,965	1,985
Total	**126,723**	**131,568**	**137,244**	**141,435**	**144,768**	**147,400**
Outside Hillsboro County						
Capital City	120,450	155,340	160,230	163,440	177,560	188,102
University Town	61,044	61,370	63,560	64,500	65,840	67,802

City/Town	Total	Ages						
		Under 5	5–14	15–24	25–44	45–64	65–74	75+
Jasper	54,293	4,831	9,229	9,061	15,902	10,684	2,806	1,780
Male	27,443	2,478	4,821	4,545	8,020	5,687	1,102	790
Female	26,850	2,353	4,408	4,516	7,882	4,997	1,704	990
Middleboro	49,003	4,214	8,330	8,181	14,354	9,684	2,583	1,657
Male	24,378	2,178	4,170	4,097	7,190	4,912	1,091	740
Female	24,625	2,036	4,160	4,084	7,164	4,772	1,492	917
Statesville	14,903	1,282	2,534	2,487	4,371	2,945	795	489
Male	7,331	644	1,275	1,290	2,245	1,350	323	204
Female	7,572	638	1,259	1,197	2,126	1,595	472	285
Harris City	11,895	902	2,001	1,853	3,484	2,440	625	590
Male	5,795	423	980	913	1,777	1,202	297	203
Female	6,100	479	1,021	940	1,707	1,238	328	387
Mifflenville	11,134	957	1,893	1,858	3,268	2,198	585	375
Male	5,407	463	950	908	1,560	1,156	202	168
Female	5,727	494	943	950	1,708	1,042	383	207
Carterville	2,078	168	369	350	601	412	110	68
Male	1,031	85	180	179	312	209	42	24
Female	1,047	83	189	171	289	203	68	44
Minortown	2,109	182	359	352	618	415	110	73
Male	1,042	96	183	178	312	204	40	29
Female	1,067	86	176	174	306	211	70	44
Boalsburg	1,985	171	338	334	582	391	103	66
Male	987	89	160	171	298	202	44	23
Female	998	82	178	163	284	189	59	43
Total	147,400	12,707	25,053	24,476	43,180	29,169	7,717	5,098
Male	73,414	6,456	12,719	12,281	21,714	14,922	3,141	2,181
Female	73,986	6,251	12,334	12,195	21,466	14,247	4,576	2,917

Table 1.4
Hillsboro County Age Profile by Sex, 2024

Table 1.5
Hillsboro
County
Population by
Race

City/Town	Population	White	Black	Other
Jasper				
2024	54,293	50,101	1,544	2,648
2019	51,230	47,162	1,534	2,534
Middleboro				
2024	49,003	29,912	17,278	1,813
2019	48,502	30,191	16,344	1,967
Statesville				
2024	14,903	14,641	28	234
2019	14,780	14,371	42	367
Harris City				
2024	11,895	11,267	38	590
2019	12,835	12,230	45	560
Mifflenville				
2024	11,134	10,971	102	61
2019	11,253	11,079	114	60
Carterville				
2024	2,078	2,012	6	60
2019	2,198	2,104	16	78
Minortown				
2024	2,109	2,106	3	0
2019	2,005	1,989	9	7
Boalsburg				
2024	1,985	1,978	0	7
2019	1,965	1,956	0	9
Total				
2024	**147,400**	**122,988**	**18,999**	**5,413**
2019	**144,768**	**125,997**	**11,169**	**7,602**

	Percentage of Coverage					
	Not Covered Any Time During the Year	Covered by Employment-Based Insurance	Covered by Self-Employment Insurance	Covered by Medicaid	Covered by Medicare	Covered by Medicare and Medicaid
All Residents	19.5	51.5	3.5	19.5	18.2	1.8
Employer Size, Workers Aged 18–64						
Fewer than 25 Employees	28.5	32.8	17.6	20.3	1.8	0.6
25–99 Employees	24.3	64.3	7.4	5.3	0.1	0
100–499 Employees	16.9	75.3	5.3	3.5	0.2	0.3
500–999 Employees	18.4	78.8	0	3.6	0.2	0.3
Household Income						
Less than $25,000	28.3	13.9	8.2	43.5	8.1	0.5
$25,000–$49,999	22.8	35.4	23.6	9.2	12.5	0
$50,000–$74,999	13.2	61.4	30.5	0	7.5	0
$75,000 or more	9.3	72.4	39.4	0	5.7	0

Table 1.6
Hillsboro County Health Insurance Profile, 2024

Note: Percentages may exceed 100%, depending on changes during the year of study and multiple coverage.

Table 1.7
Health
Insurance
Benefits
of Major
Employers
in Hillsboro
County, 2024

Employer	Fee-for-Service		Managed Care		
	Deductible ($)	Coinsurance (%)	Deductible ($)	Coinsurance per MD Visit (%)	Other Features
River Industries					Behavioral
LD	3,600	70/30			Vision
HD	7,200	60/40			
Master Tractor					Behavioral
PPO			4,500	60/40	HSA
HMO			500	80/20	
HD	7,200	60/40			
U.S. Parts					
PPO			7,200	60/40	HSA
HMO			7,200	70/30	Vision
National Yearbooks					
PPO			1,000	70/30	Behavioral
HMO			800	80/20	HSA
HD	7,200	80/20			
POS	1,400	60/40			
Office Pro	2,500	60/40			
Chicken Farms, Inc.	7,200	50/50	300	85/15	Behavioral
Middleboro Trust Company					
PPO			2,000	70/30	Behavioral
HMO			1,500	80/20	Dental
HD	7,200	60/40			Vision

Notes: (1) Deductibles shown are for family coverage. (2) State law mandates mental health coverage in any insurance plan with more than 25 participants. The plan must include 30 hours coverage for outpatient visits and 20 days for inpatient. (3) HD: high deductible; HMO: health maintenance organization; LD: low deductible; POS: point of service; PPO: preferred provider organization.

Coverage	2024	2023	2022	2019	2014
No Insurance	19.5	17.5	15.3	13.5	12.9
Medicaid	19.3	19.2	16.3	15.2	14.8
Any Private Plan	51.5	50.5	56.3	58.4	59.6
Medicare	18.2	15	14.9	14.1	13.7
Military Healthcare	1.9	2.4	2.4	2.8	2.5

Table 1.8 Hillsboro County Estimated Health Insurance Coverage

Note: Numbers are a percentage of total. Total insured and totals may exceed 100% due to multiple coverages.

City/Town	Population	Discharges	Hospital Patient Days			
			Total	Webster	MIDCARE	Other*
Jasper						
2024	54,293	5,366	25,977	1,503	12,804	11,670
2019	51,230	4,771	25,859	4,668	12,000	9,191
2014	49,247	5,352	24,088	3,013	17,100	3,975
2009	46,902	4,878	22,926	3,078	17,664	2,184
Middleboro						
2024	49,003	6,076	26,950	4,890	21,563	497
2019	48,502	6,023	32,343	5,037	27,002	304
2014	47,590	6,201	35,346	7,076	27,830	440
2009	47,364	6,394	33,889	4,850	28,185	854
Statesville						
2024	14,903	1,623	6,928	2,256	4,482	190
2019	14,780	1,528	8,918	2,490	6,356	72
2014	14,350	1,530	7,191	3,020	4,056	115
2009	12,750	1,469	7,938	3,175	4,673	90
Harris City						
2024	11,895	1,272	6,756	4,980	1,607	169
2019	12,835	1,581	8,468	6,590	1,720	158
2014	12,904	1,730	8,996	6,743	2,020	233
2009	12,951	1,756	12,117	9,866	2,006	245

Table 1.9 Hillsboro County Hospital Discharges and Patient Days

continued

Table 1.9
Hillsboro
County Hospital
Discharges and
Patient Days
(continued)

City/Town	Population	Discharges	Hospital Patient Days			
			Total	Webster	MIDCARE	Other*
Mifflenville						
2024	11,134	1,132	6,094	2,022	3,921	151
2019	11,253	1,324	7,378	2,291	4,938	149
2014	11,240	1,456	7,280	2,839	4,288	153
2009	10,952	1,687	8,939	3,320	5,475	144
Carterville						
2024	2,078	212	1,174	366	748	60
2019	2,198	275	1,442	390	1,000	52
2014	2,066	194	1,716	596	1,077	43
2009	2,378	338	1,891	702	1,177	12
Minortown						
2024	2,109	177	1,126	98	1,020	8
2019	2,005	194	1,127	94	1,001	32
2014	2,103	420	2,408	601	1,796	11
2009	2,056	317	1,963	508	1,448	7
Boalsburg						
2024	1,985	241	1,074	488	580	6
2019	1,965	229	1,326	528	798	0
2014	1,935	220	1,217	681	513	23
2009	1,891	236	1,395	747	608	40
Hillsboro County Resident Totals						
2024	147,400	16,099	76,079	16,603	46,725	12,751
2019	144,768	15,925	86,861	22,088	54,815	9,958
2014	141,435	17,103	88,242	24,569	58,680	4,993
2009	137,244	17,075	91,058	26,246	61,236	3,576
Noncounty						
2024		21	133	99	34	
2019		26	126	71	55	
2018		32	176	86	90	
2009		24	126	44	82	
Overall Total						
2024		16,120	76,212	16,702	46,759	12,651
2019		15,951	86,987	22,159	54,870	9,958
2014		17,135	88,418	24,655	58,770	4,993
2009		17,099	91,184	26,290	61,318	3,576

*Hospitals outside Hillsboro County

2024 Hospital Discharges by Town and Hospital				
City/Town	Total	Webster	MIDCARE	Other
Jasper				
Discharges	5,366	437	2,785	2,144
Patient Days	25,977	1,503	12,804	11,670
Middleboro				
Discharges	6,076	856	5,139	81
Patient Days	26,950	4,890	21,563	497
Statesville				
Discharges	1,623	570	1,017	36
Patient Days	6,928	2,256	4,482	190
Harris City				
Discharges	1,272	902	340	30
Patient Days	6,756	4,980	1,607	169
Mifflenville				
Discharges	1,132	429	674	29
Patient Days	6,094	2,022	3,921	151
Carterville				
Discharges	212	71	132	9
Patient Days	1,174	366	748	60
Minortown				
Discharges	177	28	148	1
Patient Days	1,126	98	1020	8
Boalsburg				
Discharges	241	112	127	2
Patient Days	1,074	488	580	6
Hillsboro County Resident Totals				
Discharges	16,099	3,405	10,362	2,332
Patient Days	76,079	16,603	46,725	12,751
Noncounty Residents				
Discharges	21	16	5	
Patient Days	133	99	34	
Total				
Discharges	16,120	3,421	10,367	2,332
Patient Days	76,212	16,702	46,759	12,751

Table 1.9
Hillsboro
County Hospital
Discharges and
Patient Days
(continued)

Table 1.10
Hillsboro
County
Physicians
by Specialty,
City/Town,
and Hospital
Affiliation

Specialty	Total	MIDCARE	WH
Family Practice	25	5	20
Middleboro	7	0	7
Jasper	2	0	2
Harris City	2	0	2
Statesville	2	1	1
Mifflenville	6	1	5
Carterville	2	1	1
Minortown	2	1	1
Boalsburg	2	1	1
Internal Medicine General	33	31	2
Middleboro	13	11	2
Jasper	9	9	0
Harris City	2	2	0
Statesville	2	2	0
Mifflenville	2	2	0
Carterville	2	2	0
Minortown	2	2	0
Boalsburg	1	1	0
Pediatrics	16	14	2
Middleboro	14	12	2
Jasper	2	2	0
Allergy Immunology	3	3	0
Middleboro	2	2	0
Jasper	1	1	0
Cardiology	5	5	0
Middleboro	5	5	0
Gastroenterology	6	6	0
Middleboro	4	4	0
Jasper	2	2	0
Psychiatry	8	8	0
Middleboro	6	6	0
Jasper	2	2	0
Other Medical*	16	14	2
Middleboro	14	12	2
Jasper	2	2	0

continued

Specialty	Total	MIDCARE	WH
Orthopedic Surgery	**9**	**6**	**3**
Middleboro	**9**	6	3
General Surgery	**12**	**8**	4
Middleboro	**10**	6	4
Jasper	**2**	2	0
OB/GYN	**13**	**7**	**6**
Middleboro	**10**	4	6
Jasper	**3**	3	0
Other Surgical**	**17**	**15**	**1**
Middleboro	**16**	15	1
Jasper	**0**	0	0
Subtotal	**163**	**122**	**40**
Hospital-Based			
Anesthesiology	**15**	11	4
Emergency	**21**	12	9
Hospitalists	**10**	10	0
Radiology	**18**	14	4
Pathology	**12**	9	3
Subtotal	**76**	**56**	**20**
Total Active Staff	**239**	**178**	**60**
Total Consulting Staff	**58**	**35**	**23**
Overall Total	**297**	213	83

Table 1.10
Hillsboro
County
Physicians
by Specialty,
City/Town,
and Hospital
Affiliation
(continued)

Notes: (1) Detailed table includes only physicians who have active medical staff privileges or are employed by an accredited hospital in Hillsboro County. City/Town means office location. (2) WH: Webster Hospital; * includes dermatology, pulmonology, endocrinology, otolaryngology, pulmonary medicine, ear/nose/throat, oncology, and hematology; ** includes vascular surgery, bariatric surgery, ophthalmology, plastic surgery, thoracic surgery, urology, and neurosurgery.

Vital Statistics	2024	2019	2014	2009	2004
Live Births	1,942	2,254	2,935	2,678	2,205
Deaths (Except Fetal)	1,240	1,193	1,236	1,210	1,085
Infant Deaths	16	15	17	14	14
Neonatal Deaths*	9	7	6	8	10
Postneonatal Deaths**	7	8	11	6	4
Maternal Deaths	1	3	2	1	2
Out-of-Wedlock Births	287	256	355	299	216
Marriages	921	995	981	1,051	901

Notes: * fewer than 28 days after birth; ** within 28–365 days of birth.

Cause of Death	2024	2019	2014	2009
Diseases of the Heart	408	399	401	418
Malignant Neoplams	254	262	256	245
Cerebrovascular Diseases	84	78	93	86
Chronic Lower Respiratory	74	60	40	36
All Accidents	71	62	64	70
Influenza and Pneumonia	54	37	30	34
Alzheimer's Disease	42	38	34	34
Pandemic	41	0	0	0
Diabetes Mellitus	40	32	33	33
Nephritis, Nephrotic Syndrome, and Nephrosis	23	20	22	21
Intentional Self-Harm	22	17	24	26
Total Deaths from Leading Causes	**1,113**	**1,005**	**997**	**1,003**
All Deaths	**1,240**	**1,193**	**1,236**	**1,210**

Cause of Death	Total	Under 1	1–4	5–14	15–24	25–44	45–64	65–75	75+
Disease of the Heart									
2024	408	0	1	0	0	19	68	135	185
2019	399	1	0	0	3	18	72	128	177
2014	401	2	0	0	2	14	58	124	201
2009	418	0	0	0	0	11	50	139	218
Malignant Neoplasms									
2024	254	1	0	0	4	12	30	68	139
2019	262	2	0	2	3	20	34	67	134
2014	256	1	0	1	1	24	38	79	112
2009	245	0	0	2	4	19	24	75	121
Cerebrovascular Diseases									
2024	84	0	0	0	0	3	9	29	43
2019	78	0	0	0	0	2	12	28	36
2014	93	0	0	0	1	3	10	26	53
2009	86	0	0	0	0	2	14	23	47
Chronic Lower Respiratory Disease									
2024	74	0	0	0	0	0	10	16	48
2019	60	0	0	0	0	0	15	20	25
2014	40	0	0	0	0	0	13	13	14
2009	36	0	0	0	0	0	11	9	16
All Accidents									
2024	71	4	6	10	10	7	6	8	20
2019	62	3	5	10	10	5	7	9	13
2014	64	5	2	9	8	6	7	8	19
2009	70	3	4	4	18	15	12	5	9
Influenza and Pneumonia									
2024	54	2	2	3	0	0	6	16	25
2019	37	1	1	0	0	0	2	14	19
2014	30	1	0	0	0	0	1	12	16
2009	34	1	2	0	0	0	2	8	21

Table 1.13
Hillsboro County Causes of Resident Death by Age Group, 2024

continued

Table 1.13
Hillsboro County Causes of Resident Death by Age Group, 2024 *(continued)*

Cause of Death	Total	Under 1	1–4	5–14	15–24	25–44	45–64	65–75	75+
Alzheimer's Disease									
2024	42	0	0	0	0	0	1	14	27
2019	38	0	0	0	0	0	0	12	26
2014	34	0	0	0	0	0	2	3	29
2009	34	0	0	0	0	0	1	8	25
Pandemic									
2024	41	0	0	0	4	6	5	10	16
2019	0	0	0	0	0	0	0	0	0
2014	0	0	0	0	0	0	0	0	0
2008	0	0	0	0	0	0	0	0	0
Diabetes Mellitus									
2024	40	0	0	0	0	0	2	18	20
2019	32	0	0	0	0	0	3	14	15
2014	33	0	0	0	0	0	5	12	16
2009	33	0	0	0	0	2	10	12	9
Nephritis, Nephrotic Syndrome, and Nephrosis									
2024	23	1	1	0	0	1	7	5	8
2019	20	0	1	0	1	3	3	4	8
2014	22	0	1	0	1	2	4	5	9
2009	21	0	0	1	2	4	6	2	6
Intentional Self-Harm									
2024	22	0	0	0	8	1	5	5	3
2019	17	0	0	1	6	2	3	2	3
2014	24	0	0	0	2	2	9	5	6
2009	26	0	0	4	6	6	4	2	4
Total from Listed Causes									
2024	1,113	8	10	13	26	49	149	324	534
2019	1,005	7	7	13	23	50	151	298	456
2014	997	9	3	10	15	51	147	287	475
2009	1,003	4	6	11	30	59	134	283	476

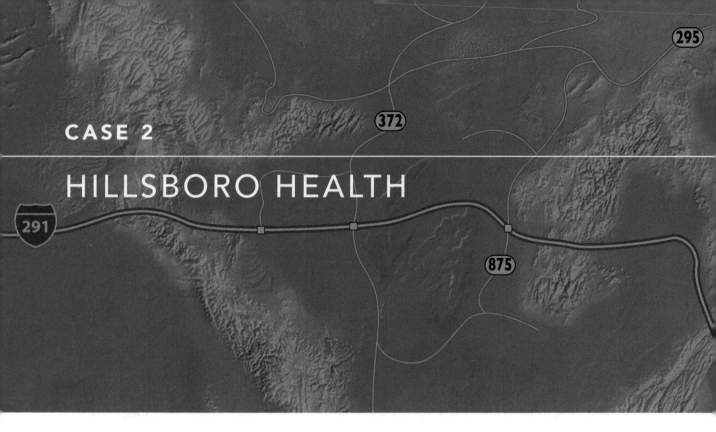

HILLSBORO HEALTH

Hillsboro Health is a 501(c)(3) corporation created in 2019 by the merger of Hillsboro County Home Health Agency (HCHHA) and Valley Hospice. HCHHA—originally named Middleboro Visiting Nurses Association—was founded in 1946 as a nonprofit home health agency to provide healthcare services to the county's population. Valley Hospice began serving residents in the county in 1980, providing palliative care and support for the terminally ill and their families. Volunteers provided most of the hospice services. Until the merger, Valley Hospice had been unable to qualify for Medicare certification. In 2015, it realized that it lacked the needed capital and expertise to become Medicare certified, so it sought a merger partner. Today, Hillsboro Health is an integrated healthcare organization providing home care, private duty services, hospice and palliative care, and community health services.

MISSION AND VISION

The following mission and vision of Hillsboro Health were approved by the board of directors in 2017.

Our Mission

We strive to provide comprehensive quality home health care and support services, for the purpose of restoring, advancing, and maximizing the level of independence to individuals and families in their place of residence. We believe that all clients will thrive in the comfort of their own home and attain the highest quality of life while respecting their need for dignity and compassionate care. We provide continuity in care for the terminally ill and their families. We strive to maintain the comfort and dignity of the client through palliative care, with relief of physical symptoms and provision of emotional and spiritual support. We value the quality of life to the end of life while recognizing the ongoing needs of the client, family, and staff with emotional and bereavement support.

Our Vision

Hillsboro Health strives to set the standard of excellence in home care and hospice by demonstrating cutting-edge results in client outcomes; performance improvement; and client, family, physician, and employee satisfaction.

GOVERNANCE

Overall responsibility for Hillsboro Health rests with its board of directors. The 15-person corporate board meets quarterly to review the status of the corporation. All directors serve for a five-year term and may be reelected by the board. The executive committee nominates individuals for membership on the board, and the new board then elects its officers. The election of directors is done by the full board at its June meeting. New directors and officers take their positions beginning July 1st.

The executive committee—composed of the president, vice president, secretary, and treasurer—meets monthly and as needed with the chief executive officer (CEO) to resolve special issues and plan board meetings. Every April, the executive committee prepares a slate of nominees for new board members. The finance and audit committee meets monthly with the executive director to review the financial status of the agency. It also reviews the annual budget and recommends it to the full board for approval. The professional advisory committee meets monthly to review issues related to clinical care and quality standards. The current leadership of the Hillsboro Health Board of Directors is as follows:

- ◆ Janet Myer, president. She lives in Middleboro and is a senior vice president at Middleboro Trust Company. This year marks her 12th consecutive year as board president, and she has one year remaining on her current five-year term.

◆ Dylan Matthew, vice president. He lives in Mifflenville and is the owner of Luxury Auto Sales in Middleboro and Jasper. He has been a member of the board for 18 years.

◆ Mary Steel, JD, the secretary. She lives in Middleboro and maintains a solo law practice in Mifflenville. She has been on the board for 16 years.

◆ James Philip, the Treasurer. He lives in Statesville and is the senior partner in the accounting firm of Philip and Associates in Middleboro. He has served on the board for 17 years. As treasurer, he is an ex-officio member of the finance and audit committee.

The 11 other members of the board are as follows; the (number)* indicates the number of years served on the HCHHA and/or Valley Hospice board and the number of years remaining on the current board term:

Ruth Berrie, RN (12, 3)*

   Board position: Professional Advisory Committee

   Occupation: Retired, former director, Faith-Based Nursing Program

   Residence: Statesville

Nancy Blau (7, 2)

   Board position: Fund Raising Committee

   Occupation: Retired, former Hillsboro County Commissioner, and member, Middleboro School Board

   Residence: Middleboro

William Bond (19, 5)

   Board position: Finance and Audit Committee, Chair

   Occupation: Vice president, Master Tractor, Inc.

   Residence: Mifflenville

Marquis Cushing, MD (16, 1)

   Board position: Professional Advisory Committee, chair

   Occupation: Retired, former internist

   Residence: Jasper

Jack Donnelly (16, 5)

  Board position: Finance and Audit Committee

  Occupation: Editor, *Middleboro Sentinel*

  Residence: Mifflenville

Leroy Paige (17, 1)

  Board position: Fundraising Committee, chair

  Occupation: Farmer, Major General, US Army Retired

  Residence: Boalsburg

Melissa Giles, JD (7, 3)

  Board position: Publicity Committee

  Occupation: Legislative aide to US Representative James Giles

  Residence: Jasper

Marsh Logic, JD (14, 4)

  Board position: Professional Advisory Committee

  Occupation: Attorney, Jasper Legal Assistance Clinic

  Residence: Jasper

Reverend Philip Martin (21, 4)

  Board position: Publicity Committee, chair

  Occupation: Minister, former vice president, Valley Hospice

  Residence: Middleboro

Owen Richard, CPA (11, 2)

  Board position: Fundraising Committee

  Occupation: Principal, Financial Planning Services of Capital City

  Residence: Jasper

Alicia Tierry (5, 5)

  Board position: Publicity Committee

  Occupation: Art historian and curator, Middleboro Art Association

  Residence: Middleboro

Every month, the members of the board of directors are provided with operational and financial data on Hillsboro Health's "dashboard." As a condition of board service, each member must agree to protect individual confidentiality and guarantee no conflicts of interest. All board members are expected to support Hillsboro Health's fundraising and community activities and to participate in board development activities. Other than Dr. Marquis Cushing, no other physician serves on Hillsboro Health's corporate board because physician interest in doing so has been minimal.

COMMUNITY ADVISORY BOARDS

Community advisory boards were created to ensure that the community had direct input into operations of all programs. Hillsboro Health managers in charge of these programs meet with the advisory boards and are responsible for maintaining effective and open communications with these members, giving them updates on program accomplishments and plans. Most members of the advisory boards are former board members of HCHHA or Valley Hospice. They meet semiannually and participate in the annual strategic planning work session of the corporate board. Members serve three-year terms and are then reappointed by the Hillsboro Health CEO with the approval of the board of directors. Vacancies are filled as needed based on the recommendation of the CEO. Following are the current membership lists of the two advisory boards; the (number)* indicates the number of years remaining on current advisory board term:

Home Care Services Community Advisory Board

Janet Doe, RN (2)*

 Retired, Former director of school nursing, Middleboro School Department. Resident of Middleboro.

Joan McCory, RN (2)

 Community health consultant. Resident of Middleboro.

Thomas Patrick, MD (3)

 Principal, Omega Point Medical Consultants. Resident of Mifflenville.

Matty O'Brien, OTR (2)

 Professor emerita of Occupational Therapy, State University. Resident of Jasper.

Prudence Regan, RN (1)

 Director of Nursing, Manorhaven LTC Center. Resident of Jasper.

Hospice and Palliative Care Advisory Board

Cindy Donnelly (3)

Retired, former newspaper reporter for the *Middleboro Sentinel*. Resident of Mifflenville.

Alice Meadows (3)

Vice president, Middleboro Golf Course. Resident of Middleboro.

Lois Metz, LISW (2)

Independent social worker. Resident of Middleboro.

Grace Niebauer (2)

Homemaker. Former trustee of Capital City Medical Center.

Victoria Seed (1)

Vice president, Mid State Oil Company.

Emilia Perez-Ramos LCSW (1)

Retired, former director, Social Services, at Capital City General Hospital. Resident of Statesville.

MANAGEMENT TEAM

CHIEF EXECUTIVE OFFICER

Martha Washington, RN, was hired in 2010. She has a four-year renewable contract, which the corporate board recently extended (after a formal review) for another four years and with an increase in salary. Prior to being CEO, she served as regional director for a large for-profit chain of home health agencies, managing the affairs of 13 separate agencies. In the past, she was the director of marketing for a large medical products firm head-quartered in Capital City and was a visiting nurse for ten years with a large visiting nurse association (VNA) in a major midwestern city. Today, she is the vice president of the State Home Health Association board and maintains an active presence in the state legislature to lobby for home care issues. Her management style emphasizes the delegation of clearly expressed responsibilities.

Since her arrival, Washington has reorganized the organization in accordance with its mission. To date, her accomplishments include the expansion and development of the Private Duty Services program; the HCHHA merger with Valley Hospice; and the increased use of technology and information systems to support home care services, including the installation of an agencywide medical record system and medical information system. Her direct reports include the chief operating officer, chief financial officer, chief quality improvement officer, and project assistant.

CHIEF OPERATING OFFICER (COO)

Catherine Newfields, RN, was hired by HCHHA in 2011 to manage the Home Care Services Division. She was promoted to her current position at the time of the merger. Before that, she was an assistant professor of community health nursing at State University and worked for 17 years in all aspects of home care, including briefly as executive director of a small VNA. As COO, her direct reports include the program directors of Home Care Services, Private Duty Services, Community Health Services, and Hospice and Palliative Care as well as the directors of Administration, Information Systems Management, and Marketing.

CHIEF FINANCIAL OFFICER (CFO)

John Gochnaur, CPA, manages the fiscal resources of Hillsboro Health. He joined Hillsboro Health in 2016 and became the first employee it recruited using an executive search firm. Prior to that, he was chief financial officer of a VNA in a large midwestern city. He has more than 20 years of experience with home health and hospice and has been a speaker at regional meetings of home care financing. Since joining Hillsboro Health as CFO, he has been elected to the fiscal affairs committee of the State Home Health Association. A native of Middleboro, he has a daughter who teaches in the Middleboro School Department.

MEDICAL DIRECTOR

Dr. Jane Campbell has served as Hillsboro Health's medical director since 2017, working closely with the Home Care and Hospice divisions. She is trained in internal medicine and is board certified in geriatric medicine, with a subspecialty certification in hospice and palliative care. Born and raised in Statesville, she completed her training at an East Coast medical school and her residencies in both the United States and England. Prior to this position, she was the deputy medical director of a large VNA in an adjacent state.

CHIEF QUALITY IMPROVEMENT OFFICER (CQIO)

As CQIO, Judith Herman, RN, is responsible for all aspects of quality improvement and utilization review at Hillsboro Health. She is a graduate of State University and holds a master's degree in nursing quality improvement from a private university. She has approximately 15 years of experience in quality improvement in home health care and worked with the CEO in another organization before coming to HCHHA. Along with Selma Kessler, she cochairs Hillsboro Health's information systems development committee.

PROGRAM DIRECTOR OF HOME CARE SERVICES

Roberta (Bobbie) Allen, RN, worked for HCHHA for ten years before she was promoted to her current position. Previously, she worked in home care and with the VNAs in Capital City; Washington, DC; and the rural Midwest. She is active in the State Nurses Association and sponsors an intern from the nursing graduate program at State University.

PROGRAM DIRECTOR OF PRIVATE DUTY SERVICES

Michael Carlstead, LPN, was a home health aide and licensed practical nurse for more than 30 years, and 24 of those years were with HCHHA. At Hillsboro Health, he oversees the Private Duty Services Division and program development and growth. Aside from providing essential nursing services to the community, the division has consistently contributed to Hillsboro Health's other programs and services. He completed his nursing training 18 years ago but just recently earned a bachelor's in business administration from a small college that offers distance education for active professionals. He plans to retire in six months.

PROGRAM DIRECTOR OF COMMUNITY HEALTH SERVICES

Angela Lopez, RN, serves in this capacity only part-time, having been appointed to the position right after the merger and the retirement of the former program director. She has worked for the agency (before and after the merger) for five years. Previously, she was an intern and program assistant for the Hillsboro County Health Department and for the state's Office of Health Promotion. She has a bachelor's degree in community health nursing from State University and a master's in public health from a major midwestern university.

PROGRAM DIRECTOR OF HOSPICE AND PALLIATIVE CARE

Prior to the merger, Middleboro native Mary Care, RN, CHPN, was the part-time executive director of Valley Hospice for three years. She brings to her full-time role at Hillsboro Health more than 24 years of experience working in hospice and palliative care programs, certifications in all aspects of hospice and palliative care nursing, and professional knowledge of community-based and inpatient hospice services. At Valley Hospice, she was the leading force behind the merger and the development of a Medicare-certified program.

Under her leadership, Valley Hospice created an effective and extensive network of trained community volunteers who provided palliative and bereavement care as well as assisted with fundraising.

DIRECTOR OF ADMINISTRATION

Steve Graham is responsible for all aspects of administration, including inventory management, human resources management, telecommunication systems management, facilities management, and all vendor contracts. Prior to joining HCHHA 18 years ago, he was employed in a similar position with the local cable company.

DIRECTOR OF INFORMATION SYSTEMS MANAGEMENT

Selma Kessler, the chief information officer, was recruited through a regional executive search firm at the time of the merger. Her knowledge of and experience with healthcare hardware and software systems are vast, including overseeing the development and implementation of information systems at a VNA in the eastern part of the state. She holds a graduate degree in medical information systems and business processing from a private university on the West Coast. She and her husband are originally from Mifflenville.

DIRECTOR OF MARKETING

Eliska Pile was promoted into this position right after the merger. Before the merger, she was the part-time marketing and public relations assistant for Valley Hospice. Also, she was the regional marketing manager for a retail pharmaceutical chain in Capital City and a market representative for a national pharmaceutical corporation. She holds a master's in marketing from State University.

ORGANIZATIONAL STRUCTURE

Hillsboro Health is organized into four divisions on the basis of mission, clientele, and reimbursement. Each division is a unique service line. Two—Home Care Services and Hospice and Palliative Care—primarily rely on Medicare financing. Two others—Private Duty Services and Community Health Services—do not rely on Medicare funding. Each division has a program director who reports to the COO, and each division has a budget. The functional units of the organization are finance, quality improvement, information systems management, administration, and marketing. These units support the operations of the four divisions.

HOME CARE SERVICES DIVISION

This division provides nursing and other services—occupational therapy, physical therapy, and speech therapy—to clients in their homes. Medicare, Medicaid, self-pay, and private insurance fund the division. This division continually pursues contracts with local managed care organizations. As a result of these efforts, contracts are in place with Central States Good Health Network and with a commercial health maintenance organization.

Medicare requires the beneficiary to be "confined to the home under the care of a physician. Services are based on an approved care plan established, certified, and periodically reviewed by a physician." Medicare pays Hillsboro Health a predetermined base payment. The rate is established for each 60-day episode of needed care. In addition, Medicare covers the need for skilled nursing on "an intermittent basis" as well as the needs for physical therapy, speech-language pathology, and occupational therapy. As such, Medicare covers part-time or intermittent skilled nursing services, part-time or intermittent home health aide services, physical therapy, speech-language pathology, occupational therapy, medical social services, medical supplies, and durable medical equipment.

Registered nurses (RNs) assess and monitor all clients. They are responsible for treatment planning, administration of medications, and other nursing services. Home health aides work as team members in implementing treatment plans and assisting with self-care activities within the context of Medicare and Medicaid regulations. Therapists and other contract professionals—such as physical therapists, occupational therapists, speech therapists, social workers, and nutritionists—are available to consult and to implement treatment plans. Staff members have reported that clients served by this program immediately following a hospital discharge have required more intensive services than in the past.

The division also provides pediatric care to children who are born prematurely, who are recovering from surgery, or who are experiencing a chronic disease. Special therapy is also available. Typically, these services are covered by health insurance plans, Medicare, and Medicaid. Use of Home Care Division services declined during the pandemic as both providers and clients were reluctant to open homes to outside visitors. As a result, several clients saw their healthcare status deteriorate and their needs for augmented services increase. This will be a challenge as the community emerges from the pandemic.

When interviewed, Bobbie Allen, the program director, indicated that "Even before the pandemic, staff turnover was a real, and sometimes very critical, issue. I believe our staff—especially our RNs—work harder and are paid less than those in a hospital, and the pandemic only made the staffing dilemma even more challenging." She said that matching staff talents with client needs creates staffing issues. Currently, all RNs are certified to administer intravenous (IV) therapies, and some have special training and certification in palliative care and gerontology. Allen is concerned that hospitals in Capital City are referring their clients who live in Jasper to the Capital City VNA and Hospice and not to Hillsboro Health. She admitted to feeling annoyed when she hears a radio commercial extolling the services of the Capital City VNA and Hospice as she drives into Jasper. She shared that a frequent challenge for her division is getting the required physician recertification every 60 days for clients with Medicare.

When asked about her assessment of the agency, Allen commented on the impact of the four-division model, stating that "health promotion and education should not be isolated in a specific division—such as Community Health Services—but instead woven into all services provided by Hillsboro Health." She added, "sometimes our silos get in our way." She points out that the division needs the opportunity to expand its emergency preparedness and that Medicare's rule that requires a person to be "homebound" to be eligible continues to prevent the division from meeting the needs of a number of individuals. "Too often we have to explain to senior citizens that they do not qualify for Medicare Home Care because they are not homebound as defined by Medicare," she reported.

HCHHA equipped all clinical staff with a computer tablet for data entry and report generation. The tablets directly interface with the agency's master information system, which includes the client's medical record. The goal of this electronic point-of-care documentation system is to eventually eliminate all paper records, especially charts that need to be done during the home visit. Going beyond this practice, Hillsboro Health provided all clients served by the Home Care Services Division with a free tablet to enable them to maintain contact with staff, to facilitate client education, and to be the basis of expanded telemedicine applications.

Allen said, "My most significant management issue is cost control. Our financial margins are very small. We need to track and manage everything. Fortunately, I have access to a number of qualified colleagues who are responsible for quality reporting, billing, cost reporting, and information systems. Another difficulty we face is getting physicians to recertify a client's condition by face-to-face examination, and it can be a source of payment delay."

When asked about productivity, she volunteered that the "clinical staff is highly skilled and productive, but over the past two years, a number of our senior staff members have retired. The division uses the following productivity guidelines: Nurses are expected to generate, on average, 30 points/standard hours per week. For a routine visit, the time standard is 1.25 hours. This breaks down to 45 minutes for the actual visit, 15 minutes for documentation, and 15 minutes for travel time. "We expect around 30 points per week," she said. "This leaves sufficient time for case conferences, meetings, and in-service education." Allen indicated that points need to be constantly monitored as clients are increasingly needing more time, especially for education.

PRIVATE DUTY SERVICES DIVISION

Begun in 2012 at HCHHA, the Private Duty Services program provides assistance with activities of daily living (ADLs) and other in-home services as needed. Medicare does not pay for these services; all funding comes from Medicaid, self-pay, or private insurance. The division and its programs were developed for both service and financial reasons. A formal marketing study completed in 2011 indicated a strong demand for these types of services in Middleboro and surrounding communities. Initially, demand for these services has surpassed expectations. All services are purchased hourly, daily, or weekly. Medicaid sets its own hourly rates by service.

Program offerings include the following:

◆ Basic nursing care or assistance, such as medication administration and blood pressure screening, provided by licensed practical nurses and home health aides

◆ Physical, occupational, and speech therapy provided by professional therapists

◆ Social work services provided by licensed social workers

◆ 24/7 companion services provided by personal care attendants or others

◆ Light housekeeping, grocery shopping, meal preparation, laundry, and other in-home duties provided by homemaker/housekeeper aides

◆ Assistance with ADLs and respite care provided by personal care attendants

Clients can select from a menu of services—and prices—that meet their needs. No medical authorization is required.

When interviewed, Michael Carlstead, the program director, stated, "As with most of our services, the pandemic negatively affected our private duty activities. Normally, we never seem to have enough staff to meet our clients' needs. Not everyone is suited to do this type of work, and I expect these staffing issues will return now that the pandemic is over." He attributed the high staff turnover to low pay and modest benefits. Reflecting on his own experience, he said, "The paperwork really gets me down. In the past 20 years, the paperwork has just increased and never seems to end. But I love my loyal and great staff and I really enjoy working with them. I will miss them all when I retire. Over the last few years, we have been facing growing local competition that frequently charge less than we do. Competition in our market is getting to be fierce."

Clients contract for a specific number of hours per week and are billed at the end of the week. Most clients pay with a credit card, but some pay with cash or check. Clients with an outstanding balance for more than two weeks are reviewed and potentially dropped from the program. For Medicaid to pay, the client must be Medicaid eligible and the service plan must be approved by Medicaid before services are provided.

Carlstead expressed concerns about the human resources dimension of the agency: "It is essential that we have current information on the professional status of all of our employees; sometimes we don't. Sometimes, we need more staff who have had the required background checks and who have undergone a formal review of their credentials. Credentialing and background checks are an issue that could get us into trouble. Another issue we face is the poor and potentially unhealthy condition of a client's home because of that person's inability to care for the home or because of too many family pets."

COMMUNITY HEALTH SERVICES DIVISION

The range of services offered by the Community Health Services Division depends on the funding it receives directly from state, county, town, and other grants. Following are the current programs it runs:

◆ *Maternal and child health program.* It provides education, direct services, and health screening to expectant and new mothers with children under one year old as well as child home care visits to qualifying infants under one year old. Bilirubin photo light therapy is also available as needed. Funding for this program is provided by state Medicaid and an annual grant. All recipients of state public assistance are eligible to receive the service without charge, while others may pay with a modest contribution. Classes and clinics are held in Middleboro and Jasper if a grant is received from the state, county, or town. The Prenatal Program—which has been well received in the community—includes a home visit from a maternity nurse to evaluate the health of both mother and child and to provide counseling on breast-feeding, diet, and infant care.

◆ *High blood pressure screening program.* It provides not only screening but also referrals to physicians as appropriate. Screenings are done in public locations, such as shopping centers, churches, and schools. Funding for this program is obtained from United Way through an annual application. Recently, United Way has requested a comprehensive assessment of the cost-effectiveness of the program as a condition of continued funding.

◆ *Community health activities program.* It provides physicals; immunizations; drug and alcohol testing; and, by appointment, smoking cessation and health education to high-risk individuals. CPR and first-aid classes are available per a grant from the county's chapter of the American Red Cross. All services take place at Hillsboro Health's offices in Middleboro and Jasper. Physicals and immunizations required for students of public elementary and secondary schools are free of charge to residents. Special classes are held in topics such as nutrition, foot care, and post-stroke care and recovery. Financial support for this program comes primarily from annual, voter-approved town appropriations.

◆ *Senior health clinics program.* It provides services such as foot care, blood pressure monitoring, earwax removal, injections, medication management support, immunizations, and preventive care. Funded by the State Office on Aging, this program is free to seniors older than age 65; a modest fee is charged for seniors younger than age 65. Clinics are held in Middleboro and occasionally in other towns in Hillsboro County.

◆ *Head lice program.* It provides lice education, prevention, and treatment to schoolchildren and their family. The program relies on referrals from school nurses. Services are available in Hillsboro Health's offices and by appointment. The program is completely financed by an annual grant from the Retail Pharmacy Association of Hillsboro County.

As with many healthcare services, utilization was suppressed during the pandemic. Normally, the Community Health Services Division is expected to cover all its direct costs and an appropriate share of its indirect costs. Unique to the division is the need to write grant applications for private, state, and local funds and to attend town meetings to secure funding for its programs. When interviewed, Angela Lopez, program director, indicated that she is concerned that many community needs are left unfulfilled because of a lack of funds. She also noted that even if state and town funding were adequate today, Hillsboro Health may have a problem making ends meet in the future. United Way has already expressed concern that Hillsboro Health had been "so active and successful in its own fundraising that future allocation decisions—or money coming from United Way—would be weighed carefully against the more substantial needs of other worthy organizations." A recent letter to the editor printed in the *Middleboro Sentinel* highlights Hillsboro Health's need to raise funds. The letter was written by an angry family member of a low-income program participant who had to pay for services; it noted, "The agency is supposed to be there for the community, and it turns a large profit every year! And we support them through United Way."

The division's relationship with the Hillsboro County Health Department is tenuous. "We probably need to meet more often," Lopez admitted. "They typically want us to take on contracts for less than our costs. We have issues with them." Neither of the two hospitals in Middleboro financially contribute to the division's programming as part of their community benefit responsibility, and program coordination with the hospitals is also a problem.

HOSPICE AND PALLIATIVE CARE DIVISION

Hospice care is supported by a number of private health insurance plans as well as Medicare. To be eligible for Medicare funding, the individual must be certified as having a terminal illness with a medical prognosis of six months or less. Electing hospice care precludes the individual from receiving Medicare support for curing the terminal illness. Physician services, nursing care, medical equipment and supplies, drugs for pain and symptom management, hospice aide and homemaker services, physical therapy, occupational therapy, speech-language pathology services, social worker services, dietary counseling, spiritual counseling, grief and loss counseling, and short-term inpatient care for pain control and symptom management and for respite care are all covered by Medicare.

Medicare-supported hospice is available for two periods of 90 days and an unlimited number of subsequent 60-day periods. Medicare pays a daily rate for each day a client is enrolled in the hospice benefit period. Daily payments are made regardless of the number of services furnished on a given day. The client pays for all eligible costs associated with the plan of care. Four payment levels are used: routine home care, continuous home care, inpatient respite care, and general inpatient care. Adjustments to these rates include a service-intensity add-on, to acknowledge the extra costs associated with the last seven days of life. As a Medicare-certified hospice, the division is required to report to Medicare a number of quality measures related to opioid use in treatment, pain screening and assessments, and dyspnea screening and treatment as well as related quality indicators.

Medicare and Medicaid do not pay for palliative care. At the time of the merger, Hillsboro Health made the decision to provide palliative care regardless of the person's ability to pay as long as the need for such care is endorsed by the agency's hospice care team (including its physician, nurse, and social worker). Because a significant number of palliative care clients eventually become eligible for hospice, this decision was deemed appropriate.

Palliative care, in contrast to hospice care, is intended to make the client feel better. People who receive curative care (e.g., radiation therapy, chemotherapy, surgery) frequently need the benefits of palliative care to address the discomfort, symptoms, and stress of serious illness and curative treatments. People with cancer, congestive heart failure, chronic obstructive pulmonary disease, kidney failure, and AIDS frequently need palliative care. The palliative care team comprises nurses and social workers and, sometimes, registered dietitians, music therapists, and counselors. Volunteers are used as appropriate.

When interviewed, Mary Care, the program director, sounded pleased with the division's success: "Our Medicare-certified services have surpassed our original expectations.

Since beginning, we have grown in scope and sophistication. Today, we offer a full range of services and are able to manage the complex financial systems and quality reporting. We were fortunate to hire Dr. Cecily Saunders as the hospice's medical director. Dr. Saunders has more than 20 years' experience in hospice and palliative care. Identifying and hiring the staff we needed to provide Medicare services was a challenge. The management team has been very supportive. In just two years, we have grown into our mission." When asked about the competition, she indicated that Jasper is a concern, saying, "There are multiple Medicare-certified hospices in Capital City, and all of them advertise that they serve all of Hillsboro County, especially Jasper residents."

At the time of the merger, Hillsboro Health decided not to begin a freestanding inpatient service. Instead, it signed a multiyear collaborative agreement with Manorhaven, the owned and operated nursing home, to reserve and renovate two private rooms for Hillsboro Health's hospice clients. Under this agreement, when the rooms are used, Hillsboro Health pays Manorhaven for service and can augment the hospice client's care team as needed. In the past two years, 68 percent of Hillsboro Health's hospice clients died in their place of residence (including their nursing home), 20 percent died in a dedicated private room at Manorhaven, and another 10 percent died as a hospital inpatient.

SUCCESSES AND CHALLENGES

The merger that formed Hillsboro Health required a significant upgrade to many management systems, but issues still remain. Martha Washington, the CEO, explained, "The coordination between our clinical personnel and business office and administrative services office still needs to be improved. For example, last year, in more than 20 cases, we failed to adhere to the 60-day physician review requirements. Also, too often, we begin providing home care services even before we have the signed physician's certificate. This jeopardizes and delays our qualification under Medicare."

She added, "Our financial margins are small, and we are very dependent on community fundraising, something that Valley Hospice excelled at and helped us build upon their bases. I am very grateful that almost all of the former volunteers with Valley Hospice are now working with our hospice program. They have embraced Hillsboro Health's expanded mission and vision and help us significantly access community philanthropy and provide superior service."

Although all employees are assigned to a specific division or functional area, the agency uses a flexible staffing model. A number of workers are cross-trained so that some can work effectively in more than one division. The management systems are sufficiently robust to appropriately charge the division that benefits from an employee's work. For example, if a home health aide assigned to the Hospice and Palliative Care Division works in the Private Duty Services Division, the latter is charged for the associated staff expenses. This staffing flexibility and a collaborative team of program directors have been essential in Hillsboro Health's growth in some areas and in its contracts with other organizations. Every two weeks, the senior management team meets formally to review operations and to problem-solve. For the full board meetings, only Washington, the CFO, the medical director, and the COO usually attend.

The continued application of technology and expansion of telemedicine are essential to the agency's mission and vision. "Government funding will never pay us what it should, so we need to find ways to provide the best-quality service with what funding is available to us," she explained. "Our primary challenge in the future will be to hold on to our markets as more and more competition develops. How either or both of the community hospitals in our service area will position themselves in this changing market is an open question." Hillsboro Health's current marketing program has not established a strong relationship with primary care physicians in Middleboro and beyond. Washington is aware of this shortcoming, noting, "In home health, marketing is more than advertising. We need to better secure our clients at the source—namely, their primary care physician. As the local hospitals have acquired more primary care practices, the physicians and nurse practitioners have looked first to the hospital for services; we are, at best, second."

She foresees steadily declining revenue and funding for the Community Health Services Division. "The general public just did not seem to realize that the 'grey tsunami' is upon us. Patients are being discharged from hospitals quicker and sicker, and this situation—coupled with the Affordable Care Act—has created a complex situation for home health," she noted. "I am optimistic that hospitals, primary care providers, nursing homes, and home health agencies working together will improve health and lower costs. Our goal is to be the home care provider of choice."

On a recent Sunday morning public affairs show broadcast on Middleboro's TV Channel 32, Washington was a guest panelist. She was asked how NGOs (nongovernmental organizations) could make people's lives better. She framed her answer around Hillsboro Health's specific core competencies. "As healthcare providers, we need to reduce hospital admissions and readmissions and the need for emergent care. We also need to accurately diagnose patients' needs and treat and care for them with the highest level of professionalism," she began. "It is also essential that we accurately code cases for reimbursement and provide payers with all the needed documentation to ensure timely payment. We have to meet realistic productivity benchmarks and become even smarter in providing clinical care using comprehensive information about our patients." This TV appearance garnered her an invitation to be a keynote speaker at the upcoming State Conference of Home Health Leaders in Capital City.

Although some members of the corporate board still want Hillsboro Health to remain the sole provider of home health, private duty, and hospice and palliative care services in Middleboro, Washington has told the board the goal is unrealistic. Instead, she is focused on continuing the agency's highly positive reputation. "We are known for our prudent administration of funds, high quality of care, and can-do attitude. Healthcare professionals throughout the county view us as a highly professional place to work," she said. "Our Medicare-certified hospice has identified us as a key and essential player in the state's healthcare system and a champion for the needs of our citizens. That's what I hope we can retain—this positive public image. It has multiple advantages." Washington explained that competition is growing in home care, private duty, and hospice services. Private for-profit agencies have started to enter the markets in Capital City and its suburbs as well as in Jasper.

Table 2.1
Hillsboro Health
Operational
Statistics

Division	2024	2023	2022	2021
Home Care				
Unduplicated Client Census	1,884	1,838	1,748	1,801
RN Visits	38,170	37,659	36,053	36,421
LPN Visits	750	698	703	703
HH Aide Visits	16,208	15,087	15,018	14,330
PT Visits	4,495	4,692	4,741	4,957
OT Visits	1,012	954	1,044	960
ST Visits	190	160	196	190
SW Visits	511	510	555	503
Total Visits	**61,336**	**59,760**	**58,310**	**58,064**
Private Duty				
Unduplicated Client Census	478	462	476	415
RN In-Home Hours	1,057	1,100	1,115	1,003
LPN In-Home Hours	13,620	13,263	13,888	13,475
PCA In-Home Hours	24,771	22,510	23,106	23,339
HH Aide In-Home Hours	24,958	25,308	26,270	24,997
Other In-Home Hours	657	390	500	500
Total Hours	**65,063**	**62,571**	**64,879**	**63,314**
Community Health				
Ante/Postpartum Visits	349	341	336	301
Child Health Visits	345	362	383	316
Prenatal Class Enrollees	113	103	128	118
Children Seen	716	797	840	784
High Blood Pressure Screening				
People Screened	7,103	7,804	8,138	7,439
MD Referrals	384	421	469	412
Senior Health Clinic Clients	1,091	1,041	1,199	1,201
Hospice and Palliative Care				
Palliative Care Unduplicated Client Census	111	123	120	88
Number of Veterans Served	19	16	12	11
3-Year Average, % Palliative Care Patients Who Died, Died at Home	69.2%	69.8%	61.4%	67.5%
Hospice Care Unduplicated Client Census	267	271	280	265
Hospice Median Length of Service (Days)	21.3	21.6	19.8	21.3
Hospice Mean Length of Service (Days)	70.1	59.3	63.1	65.1
% Patients in Hospice Over 180 Days	14.4	12.3	11.9	11.5

continued

Table 2.1
Hillsboro Health
Operational
Statistics
(continued)

Division	2024	2023	2022	2021
Bereavement Service (Hours) Provided to Families and Friends	770	789	799	799
Total Volunteer Hours	1,856	2,014	2,054	2,144
Mean Hours per Volunteer	51	47	45	43
Home Nursing and Aide Visits	4,258	4,145	4,356	4,230
Home SW and Chaplain Visits	671	640	648	612
% Families Who Reported Their Bereavement Needs Were Met	89.0%	89.4%	93.6%	92.6%
% Discharged Hospice Patients with 3+ Types of Advanced Planning Instruments	79.0%	75.3%	74.5%	71.4%

Note: HH: home health; LPN: licensed practical nurse; MD: physician; OT: occupational therapist; PCA: personal care attendant; PT: physical therapist; RN: registered nurse; ST: speech therapist; SW: social worker.

Table 2.2A Hillsboro Home Health Utilization by Town: Home Care

Home Care	Client Census	RN Visits	LPN Visits	HH Aide Visits	PT Visits	OT Visits	ST Visits	SW Visits	Total Visits
Boalsburg									
2024	28	512	16	301	86	9	0	7	931
2023	33	564	16	312	120	9	0	7	1,028
2022	38	654	18	356	131	18	3	10	1,190
Carterville									
2024	49	890	21	312	123	28	6	10	1,390
2023	48	834	19	302	134	27	4	13	1,333
2022	46	881	17	362	152	28	3	11	1,454
Harris City									
2024	73	1,534	40	712	151	115	25	25	2,602
2023	92	2,198	62	801	267	112	22	30	3,492
2022	107	2,258	60	911	337	101	23	34	3,724
Jasper									
2024	314	6,443	112	1,601	503	105	49	62	8,845
2023	312	6,398	103	1,534	615	87	40	59	8,836
2022	301	6,332	118	1,545	603	102	35	56	8,791
Middleboro									
2024	970	19,439	412	9,541	2,734	552	78	298	33,054
2023	945	18,834	360	8,649	2,695	541	67	304	31,450
2022	895	17,946	354	8,589	2,645	588	82	331	30,535
Mifflenville									
2024	257	4,869	98	2,537	612	118	19	63	8,316
2023	234	4,438	90	2,251	593	102	12	45	7,531
2022	205	4,167	89	2,056	590	125	28	56	7,111
Minortown									
2024	45	801	12	448	103	28	5	12	1,409
2023	42	749	12	456	101	22	3	20	1,363
2022	40	770	14	434	105	30	6	28	1,387
Statesville									
2024	148	3,712	39	756	183	57	8	34	4,789
2023	132	3,644	36	782	167	54	12	32	4,727
2022	116	3,045	33	765	178	52	16	29	4,118
Total									
2024	1,884	38,170	750	16,208	4,495	1,012	190	511	61,336
2023	1,838	37,659	698	15,087	4,692	954	160	510	59,760
2022	1,748	36,053	703	15,018	4,741	1,044	196	555	58,310

Note: HH: home health; LPN: licensed practical nurse; OT: occupational therapist; PT: physical therapist; RN: registered nurse; ST: speech therapist; SW: social worker.

Table 2.2B
Hillsboro
Home Health
Utilization by
Town: Private
Duty

Private Duty	Client Census	RN in Home Hours	LPN In-Home Hours	PCA In-Home Hours	HH Aide In-Home Hours	Other In-Home Hours	Total Hours
Boalsburg							
2024	8	12	125	132	63	0	332
2023	9	17	131	145	60	4	357
2022	9	19	130	156	58	2	365
Carterville							
2024	8	9	208	83	37	7	344
2023	7	12	184	71	39	3	309
2022	10	13	192	64	46	0	315
Harris City							
2024	24	20	392	402	85	7	906
2023	22	25	403	490	88	3	1,009
2022	23	34	412	503	89	12	1,050
Jasper							
2024	124	283	2,856	5,846	6,503	301	15,789
2023	130	295	3,245	6,134	6,856	280	16,810
2022	142	324	3,476	6,023	7,956	167	17,946
Middleboro							
2024	210	290	5,820	12,673	14,868	256	33,907
2023	196	294	5,134	10,443	14,979	234	31,084
2022	190	273	5,244	10,936	14,902	240	31,595
Mifflenville							
2024	58	81	1,511	3,869	2,892	60	8,413
2023	54	90	1,534	3,427	2,745	45	7,841
2022	54	93	1,655	3,245	2,644	27	7,664
Minortown							
2024	13	290	412	486	367	12	1,567
2023	13	287	439	480	401	9	1,616
2022	15	276	512	534	428	34	1,784
Statesville							
2024	33	72	2,296	1,280	143	14	3,805
2023	31	80	2,193	1,320	140	12	3,745
2022	33	83	2,267	1,645	147	18	4,160
Total							
2024	478	1,057	13,620	24,771	24,958	657	65,063
2023	462	1,100	13,263	22,510	25,308	590	62,771
2022	476	1,115	13,888	23,106	26,270	500	64,879

Note: HH: home health; LPN: licensed practical nurse; PCA: personal care attendant; RN: registered nurse.

Community Health	Ante/ Postpartum Visits	Child Health Visits	Prenatal Class Enrollees	Children Seen	High Blood Pressure Screened	High Blood Pressure Referrals	Senior Health Clinics: Clients
Boalsburg							
2024	10	14	0	0	28	4	0
2023	9	13	0	0	36	4	0
2022	15	18	0	0	34	3	0
Carterville							
2024	10	28	0	0	74	9	0
2023	12	21	0	0	77	5	0
2022	12	22	0	0	73	8	0
Harris City							
2024	19	27	0	0	74	13	0
2023	12	21	0	0	63	12	0
2022	17	19	2	0	69	9	0
Jasper							
2024	95	78	28	145	2,430	112	209
2023	93	101	33	217	3,066	143	207
2022	90	124	42	312	3,378	168	243
Middleboro							
2024	145	131	79	571	4,133	207	882
2023	134	142	66	580	4,025	210	834
2022	123	135	73	528	3,997	212	956
Mifflenville							
2024	32	6	2	0	23	9	0
2023	26	12	0	0	44	6	0
2022	23	15	4	0	65	8	0
Minortown							
2024	6	8	0	0	31	9	0
2023	7	8	0	0	47	7	0
2022	9	10	0	0	44	9	0
Statesville							
2024	32	53	4	0	310	21	0
2023	48	44	4	0	446	34	0
2022	47	40	7	0	478	52	0
Total							
2024	349	345	113	716	7,103	384	1,091
2023	341	362	103	797	7,804	421	1,041
2022	336	383	128	840	8,138	469	1,199

Table 2.2C
Hillsboro Home Health Utilization by Town: Community Health

Table 2.2D
Hillsboro Health
Utilization by
Town: Hospice
and Palliative
Care

Hospice and Palliative Care	Palliative Care Clients	Veterans Served	Percent Palliative Care Who Died*	Hospice Care Clients	Home Nursing and Aide Visits	Home Social Work and Chaplain Visits	Bereavement Hours for Families and Friends
Boalsburg							
2024	0	0	0.0%	1	21	0	19
2023	0	0	0.0%	0	0	0	0
2022	0	0	0.0%	3	67	9	13
Carterville							
2024	0	0	0.0%	0	0	0	0
2023	0	0	0.0%	1	17	2	14
2022	0	0	0.0%	2	31	0	26
Harris City							
2024	0	0	0.0%	2	47	19	26
2023	0	0	0.0%	2	43	14	35
2022	0	0	0.0%	4	89	18	34
Jasper							
2024	36	3	58.2%	61	977	176	201
2023	34	3	60.2%	73	856	146	243
2022	33	2	65.1%	84	1144	114	256
Middleboro							
2024	56	12	54.7%	189	3024	400	504
2023	68	9	61.9%	172	2955	392	476
2022	62	5	61.8%	169	2787	398	449
Mifflenville							
2024	7	3	58.0%	7	102	8	4
2023	4	2	54.0%	7	90	9	7
2022	9	2	61.3%	5	81	12	12
Minortown							
2024	0	0	0.0%	3	41	12	0
2023	2	0	0.0%	6	80	14	0
2022	2	1	0.0%	4	56	10	9
Statesville							
2024	12	1	24.5%	4	46	56	16
2023	15	2	33.0%	10	104	63	14
2022	14	2	0.0%	9	101	87	0
Total							
2024	111	19	n/a	267	4,258	671	770
2023	123	16	n/a	271	4,145	640	789
2022	120	12	n/a	280	4,356	648	799

Note: * Three-year average, % palliative care patients who died, died at home.

Principal Diagnosis	Percentage of All Cases			
	2024	2023	2022	2021
Diseases of the Circulatory System	25.5	27.4	28.5	26.3
Heart Disease	12.6	14.4	16.4	13.2
Diseases of the Musculoskeletal System and Connective Tissue	12.6	11.8	11.2	10.4
Diabetes Mellitus	10.8	10.7	10.5	10.6
Diseases of the Respiratory System	8.6	8.6	8.4	8.0
Essential Hypertension	7.0	7.2	7.2	6.9
Injury and Poisoning	6.6	6.3	5.5	6.5
Diseases of the Skin and Subcutaneous Tissue	6.2	6.3	6.9	6.8
Neoplasm	4.5	4.7	4.3	5.2
Total	**94.4**	**97.4**	**98.9**	**93.9**

Table 2.3
Hillsboro Health Home Care Utilization by Principal Diagnosis

Principal Diagnosis	Percentage of All Cases			
	2024	2023	2022	2021
Cancer	36.7	33.0	35.4	35.1
Heart Disease	32.7	35.9	32.5	30.0
Parkinson's Disease	6.3	6.4	7.8	9.2
Lung Disease	6.3	6.0	8.2	9.0
Debility Unspecified	3.2	3.0	3.3	3.8
Renal Failure	3.1	3.4	3.4	3.1
Alzheimer's Disease	3.1	3.6	3.4	3.1
Other	8.6	8.7	6.0	6.7
Total	**100.0**	**100.0**	**100.0**	**100.0**

Table 2.4
Hillsboro Health Hospice Admission by Principal Diagnosis

Table 2.5
Hillsboro Health
Hospice Patient
Age at Time of
Admission

Age (Years)	Percentage of All Admissions			
	2024	2023	2022	2021
Under 35	1.0	0.0	0.0	2.0
35–64	11.8	12.3	12.2	11.4
65–74	18.4	18.1	17.0	17.1
75–84	25.9	26.4	26.3	25.9
85 or older	42.9	43.2	44.5	43.6
Total	**100.0**	**100.0**	**100.0**	**100.0**

Table 2.6
Hillsboro
Health Hospice
Services by
Level of Care

Level of Care	Percentage of All Admissions			
	2024	2023	2022	2021
Routine Care	91.0	92.2	93.2	94.1
General—Inpatient	3.7	2.5	2.2	1.9
Continuous Care	4.3	3.8	3.7	3.5
Respite Care	1.0	1.5	0.9	0.5
Total	**100.0**	**100.0**	**100.0**	**100.0**

	2024	2023	2022	2021
Revenues				
Home Care Division				
Medicare—Net	5,045,223	4,293,252	4,999,224	4,953,229
Medicaid—Net	149,924	129,230	143,204	142,335
Other—Net	86,340	83,465	90,365	93,226
Subtotal	**5,281,487**	**4,505,947**	**5,232,793**	**5,188,790**
Private Duty Division				
Revenue—Gross	5,356,007	4,242,443	4,967,242	4,734,561
Bad Debt—Less	48,223	53,451	41,340	41,796
Allowances—Less	9,145	8,539	8,956	8,677
Subtotal	**5,298,639**	**4,180,453**	**4,916,946**	**4,684,088**
Community Health Division				
From State and Towns	252,559	203,446	232,445	254,300
United Way	80,000	60,000	80,000	40,000
Other	25,256	5,089	5,634	4,356
Subtotal	**357,815**	**268,535**	**318,079**	**298,656**
Hospice and Palliative Care Division				
Medicare	2,703,450	2,401,470	2,604,385	2,659,223
Other	515,330	493,274	462,349	412,550
Subtotal	**3,218,780**	**2,894,744**	**3,066,734**	**3,071,773**
Total Revenue	**14,156,721**	**11,849,679**	**13,534,552**	**13,243,307**
Expenses				
Salaries and Wages	8,919,091	7,602,464	8,129,089	7,935,227
Benefits	2,943,300	2,504,117	2,682,599	2,539,273
Supplies	615,239	412,556	601,529	602,437

Table 2.7
Hillsboro Health Statement of Operations: January 1–December 31, in USD $

continued

	2024	2023	2022	2021
Equipment—Medical	412,443	128,464	435,223	467,223
Equipment—Office	3,067	2,022	4,250	9,341
Rental—Middleboro	410,336	375,200	375,200	328,400
Rental—Other	0	0	65,250	95,250
Computer Systems	184,230	192,000	192,000	192,556
Travel	166,848	143,220	183,236	177,360
Computer Services	135,202	135,202	130,282	130,023
Consulting	500	0	1,200	1,000
Insurance	59,800	59,800	59,800	59,710
Advertising and PR	55,868	55,339	54,939	58,359
Legal/Audit	42,839	42,100	46,223	45,230
Telecommunications	19,239	20,445	19,337	22,430
Printing and Postage	5,150	7,345	10,439	13,450
Board Expenses	21,300	16,465	21,450	21,500
Memberships	10,200	9,200	10,200	10,200
Depreciation Expense	163,252	161,430	154,230	152,302
Total Expenses	**14,167,904**	**11,867,369**	**13,176,476**	**12,861,271**
Gain or (Loss) from Operations	**–11,383**	**–17,690**	**358,076**	**382,036**

Table 2.7
Hillsboro Health
Statement of
Operations:
January 1–
December 31, in
USD $
(continued)

Note: PR: public relations.

	2024	2023	2022	2021
Current Assets				
Cash and Cash Equivalents	1,499,717	1,585,536	1,598,865	415,443
Accounts Receivable (Net)	2,312,327	2,034,574	1,945,303	2,284,345
Prepaid Insurance	21,883	20,476	21,463	20,456
Inventory	113,326	121,839	139,223	153,203
Total Current Assets	3,947,253	3,762,425	3,704,854	2,873,447
Property/Equipment				
Gross, Property, and Equipment	2,644,309	2,744,530	3,051,324	3,264,667
(Less Accum. Depreciation)	1,322,758	1,078,345	993,284	912,466
Net Property and Equipment	1,321,551	1,666,185	2,058,040	2,352,201
Other Assets				
Investments (at Market)	9,785,337	9,641,086	9,406,166	9,665,403
Total Assets	15,054,141	15,069,696	15,169,060	14,891,051
Liabilities and Net Assets				
Current Liabilities				
Accounts Payable	693,440	645,223	701,774	745,230
Salaries Payable	160,778	169,460	173,443	165,324
Accrued Items	198,364	193,557	201,739	205,377
Current Portion of Long-Term Debt	84,500	84,500	84,500	91,600
Total Current Liabilities	1,137,082	1,092,740	1,161,456	1,207,531
Noncurrent Liabilities				
Loan Payable	923,870	972,384	985,342	1,019,334
Total Liabilities	2,060,952	2,065,124	2,146,798	2,226,865
Net Assets				
Restricted Funds	9,565,680	9,468,771	9,637,404	8,924,882
Unrestricted Funds	3,739,304	3,739,304	3,739,304	3,739,304
Total Net Assets	12,993,189	13,004,572	13,022,262	12,664,186
Total Net Assets + Liabilities	15,054,141	15,069,696	15,169,060	14,891,051

Table 2.8
Hillsboro Health
Balance Sheet
as of December
31, in USD $

Table 2.9
Hillsboro Health
Agency Staffing

Position	2024			2023			2022		
	Salary	FTE	Total	Salary	FTE	Total	Salary	FTE	Total
Administration									
Chief Executive Officer	180,660	1.0	180,660	180,660	1.0	180,660	172,343	1.0	172,343
Chief Operating Officer	139,226	1.0	139,226	139,226	1.0	139,226	135,500	1.0	135,500
Chief Financial Officer	154,220	0.9	138,798	154,220	1.0	147,202	146,223	1.0	146,223
Chief QI Officer	79,450	0.8	63,560	79,450	0.9	71,505	79,450	1.0	79,450
Director of ISM	72,445	1.0	72,445	72,445	1.0	72,445	71,300	0.7	49,910
Medical Director	180,000	0.5	90,000	172,800	0.5	86,400	180,000	0.4	72,000
Director of Administration	48,320	1.0	48,320	47,230	1.0	47,230	45,220	1.0	45,220
Director of Marketing	68,937	1.0	68,937	64,294	0.9	57,865	62,445	0.7	43,712
Other Finance Staff	38,293	4.2	160,831	33,600	4.0	134,400	33,400	3.5	116,900
QI Staff	38,939	4.0	155,756	34,550	4.0	138,200	33,401	3.0	100,203
ISM Staff	65,337	1.8	117,607	65,900	1.5	98,850	65,229	1.0	65,229
Other Administration Staff	23,014	6.0	138,084	22,912	6.0	137,472	22,800	4.5	102,600
Subtotal		**23.2**	**1,374,223**		**22.8**	**1,311,455**		**18.8**	**1,129,290**
Home Care Program									
Program Director	82,450	1.0	82,450	82,450	1.0	82,450	75,986	1.0	75,986
RN	68,340	38.6	2,637,924	68,340	33.0	2,255,220	61,342	39.0	2,392,338
LPN	41,204	0.6	24,722	40,380	0.6	24,228	39,572	0.5	19,786
HH Aide	25,188	18.3	460,940	24,684	14.0	345,576	24,191	20.0	483,820
Physical Therapist	83,556	5.0	417,780	80,282	4.0	321,128	77,350	5.0	386,750
Occupational Therapist	88,738	1.0	88,738	89,339	1.0	89,339	89,340	1.0	89,340

continued

Position	2024			2023			2022		
	Salary	FTE	Total	Salary	FTE	Total	Salary	FTE	Total
Speech Therapist	58,340	0.5	29,170	53,848	0.5	26,924	51,220	0.7	35,854
Social Worker	73,563	1.0	73,563	69,149	1.0	69,149	64,024	1.0	64,024
Administrative Staff	32,200	3.5	112,700	31,556	3.0	94,668	30,925	3.0	92,775
Subtotal		**69.5**	**3,927,988**		**58.1**	**3,308,682**		**71.2**	**3,640,673**
Private Duty Services									
Program Director	79,484	1.0	79,484	79,484	1.0	79,484	70,346	1.0	70,346
RN	69,350	0.5	34,675	69,350	1.0	69,350	63,445	1.0	63,445
LPN	41,204	9.5	391,438	40,380	4.5	181,710	40,300	5.5	221,650
Occupational Therapist	88,738	0.5	44,369	86,963	1.0	86,963	85,224	1.0	85,224
PCA	24,197	24.8	600,086	22,546	20.5	462,193	21,474	28.2	605,567
Other	26,880	0.8	21,504	28,990	0.8	23,192	28,990	0.8	23,192
Administrative Staff	19,342	1.0	19,342	18,500	1.0	18,500	18,300	1.0	18,300
Subtotal		**38.1**	**1,190,898**		**29.8**	**921,392**		**38.5**	**1,087,724**
Community Health Program									
Program Director	83,252	1.0	83,252	83,252	1.0	83,252	80,120	1.0	80,120
RN	78,334	4.2	329,003	78,334	2.0	156,668	61,797	3.5	216,290
Administrative Staff	21,445	1.0	21,445	22,450	1.0	22,450	20,474	0.5	10,237
Subtotal		**6.2**	**433,700**		**4.0**	**262,370**		**5.0**	**306,647**
Hospice Program									
Program Director	78,200	1.0	78,200	78,200	1.0	78,200	74,620	1.0	74,620
RN	69,347	14.5	1,005,532	69,347	12.5	866,838	68,348	14.5	991,046
HH Aide	29,446	2.5	73,615	30,228	2.0	60,456	28,891	2.5	72,228
PCA	26,450	10.4	275,080	27,334	10.5	287,007	26,450	10.4	275,080
Occupational Therapist	90,137	0.5	45,069	90,337	0.5	45,169	89,363	0.5	44,682

Table 2.9
Hillsboro Health Agency Staffing *(continued)*

continued

Table 2.9
Hillsboro Health
Agency Staffing
(continued)

Position	2024			2023			2022		
	Salary	FTE	Total	Salary	FTE	Total	Salary	FTE	Total
Social Worker	65,430	5.0	327,150	69,149	4.0	276,596	65,000	5.0	325,000
Other	48,440	2.0	96,880	49,500	2.0	99,000	49,233	2.0	98,466
Administrative Staff	36,303	2.5	90,758	34,120	2.5	85,300	33,454	2.5	83,635
Subtotal		**38.4**	**1,992,283**		**35.0**	**1,798,565**		**38.4**	**1,964,756**
Total Salary and Wages		**175.4**	**8,919,091**		**149.7**	**7,602,464**		**171.9**	**8,129,089**

Notes: (1) Salaries are in US dollars. (2) Full-time equivalent (FTE) positions are paid for 2,080 hours per year. (3) All full-time employees work 1,896 hours per year and receive two weeks of paid vacation and 13 paid holidays. (4) All salaries are expressed as the average salary for that position. (5) Benefit costs are in addition to salary costs. (6) HH: home health; ISM: information systems management; LPN: licensed practical nurse; PCA: personal care attendant; QI: quality improvement; RN: registered nurse.

	Hillsboro Health Home Care	State Average	National Average
Managing Daily Activities			
How often patients improved at walking or moving around	80%	85%	79%
How often patients improved at getting in and out of bed	80%	87%	81%
How often patients improved at bathing	81%	86%	82%
Treating Symptoms			
How often patients' breathing improved	75%	82%	82%
How often patients' wounds improved or healed after an operation	95%	92%	91%
How often patients had pressure ulcers/ pressure injuries that are new or worsened	1%	1%	1%
Preventing Harm			
How often the home health team began their patient care in a timely manner	94%	97%	97%
How often the home health team taught patients (or their family caregiver) about their drugs	98%	99%	99%
How often patients got better at taking their drugs correctly by mouth	71%	80%	75%
How often the home health team checked patients' risk of falling	99%	99%	99%
How often the home health team checked patients for depression	98%	97%	96%
How often the home health team determined whether patients received a flu shot for the current flu season	74%	81%	78%
How often the home health team made sure that their patients have received a pneumo-coccal vaccine	84%	88%	85%

Table 2.10
Hillsboro Health
Home Care
Services Quality

continued

	Hillsboro Health Home Care	State Average	National Average
For patients with diabetes, how often the home health team got doctor's orders, gave foot care, and taught patients about foot care	93%	96%	96%
How often physician-recommended actions to address medication issues were completed timely	90%	97%	98%
Preventing Unplanned Hospital Care			
How often home health patients had to be admitted to the hospital	18%	15%	13%
How often patients receiving home health care needed any urgent, unplanned visit to the hospital emergency room, without being admitted to the hospital			
How often patients remained in the community after discharge from home health agency	79%	74%	76%
How often patients were readmitted to the hospital for a potentially preventable condition after discharge from home health agency	3%	5%	4%
Patient Survey Summary Ratings			
Number of surveys/response rate	689/39%		
How often the home health team gave care in a professional way	84%	88%	89%
How well did the home health team communicate with patients? (Good or Excellent)	87%	85%	87%
Did the home health team discuss medicines, pain, and home safety with patients? (yes)	87%	80%	81%
How did patients rate the overall care from the home health agency? (positive)	87%	87%	84%
Would patients recommend the home health agency to friends and relatives? (positive)	87%	80%	73%

	Hillsboro Health Hospice	National Average
Family Caregiver Experience		
Communicates (well) with family	83%	81%
Provided timely help	77%	78%
Treated patients with respect	90%	91%
Provided emotional and spiritual support	94%	90%
Provided help for pain and symptoms	78%	75%
Trained family to care for patient	79%	75%
Overall rating of this hospice	86%	80%
Willingness to recommend this hospice	90%	84%
Quality of Patient Care		
Percentage of patients getting at least one visit from a registered nurse, a physician, or a nurse practitioner, or a physician assistant in the last three days of life	92%	83%
Patients who got an assessment of all seven HIS quality measures at the beginning of hospice care to meet the HIS Comprehensive Assessment Measure requirements	100%	88%
Patients or caregivers who were asked about treatment preferences such as hospitalization and resuscitation at the beginning of hospital care	100%	98%
Patients or caregivers who were asked about their beliefs and values at the beginning of hospice care	100%	97%
Patients who were checked for pain at the beginning of hospice care	100%	96%
Patients who got a timely and thorough pain assignment when pain was identified as a problem	100%	92%
Patients who were checked for shortness of breath at the beginning of hospice care	100%	98%
Patients who got timely treatment for shortness of breath	100%	96%
Patients taking opioid medications who were offered care for constipation	100%	94%

Table 2.11
Hillsboro Health Hospice Services Quality Scorecard

Note: HIS: Hospice Item Set.

CASE 3

PHYSICIAN CARE SERVICES, INC.

Physician Care Services (PCS), Inc., was founded as a tax-paying corporation on January 1, 2000. Currently, three physicians each own 20 percent and one physician owns 40 percent of the stock. PCS offers urgent care and occupational health services in two locations—at the Alpha Center located in Mifflenville (just outside the city limits of Middleboro) and at the Beta Center located in Jasper (close to the Jasper Industrial Park and suburban neighborhoods). The Alpha Center opened in January 2000. Initially, it treated only occupational health clients, but this policy changed in 2004 when services began to be offered to private-pay (retail) clients. The Beta Center opened in January 2006 and treats private-pay and occupational health clients.

At these centers, ambulatory medical care is provided on a walk-in basis, but no emergency services are available. If an individual who needs emergency care arrives, the center calls an ambulance to transport the person to the nearest hospital emergency department (ED). Over the past two years, approximately 2 percent of PCS arrivals were immediately dispatched to a hospital. PCS refers people covered by Medicaid to other service providers.

PCS specializes in offering services deemed "convenient" by the general public. It does not provide continuing medical care. Its physicians refer to other physicians in the area if their patients need continuing or specialized medical care. Although clients often return to the centers for services, PCS does not offer chronic illness management. Client satisfaction is PCS's highest operational goal.

Client Services

Occupational Health Clients

Occupational health clients are employees sent to a PCS center by their employer for treatment of a work-related injury (which is usually covered by workers' compensation insurance) and for pre-employment or annual physicals and health testing (which are paid directly by the employer). Because they have special work conditions—usually involving the use of hazardous chemicals or materials—some local organizations contract with PCS to conduct comprehensive physicals in accordance with the US Department of Transportation (DOT) requirements and other federal and state laws and regulations. Local industries consider PCS a cost-effective and convenient alternative to a hospital ED and thus use PCS in lieu of employing an in-house physician. Corporate clients expect PCS to assist with all case management related to worker injury, and they hold PCS accountable for providing timely, appropriate, and cost-effective services.

Physicals for OSHA (Occupational Safety and Health Administration) compliance are currently priced between $300 and $500 per physical. Physicals for local police and fire include pulmonary function tests (PFTs), laboratory tests, and electrocardiograms (EKGs) and are currently priced between $250 and $350 per physical, depending on contractual volume. Pre-employment physicals include a urine dip test and are typically priced between $150 and $190 per physical. Charges for these services are billed directly to the employer.

Private-Pay Clients

PCS offers private-pay clients general medical care, except obstetrics and gynecology services. Private-pay clients are attracted to PCS because they do not need an appointment and they can pay with cash, check, or credit card at the time of service. PCS also works with four health insurance plans in the area: Statewide Blue Shield, American Health Plan, Cumberland River Health Plan, and Central State Good Health Plan.

At the time of service, private-pay clients with these insurance plans are screened by staff to verify their coverage and determine whether they have satisfied any required deductibles. If deductibles have been met, the clients pay just the copay amount and the full bill is electronically sent to their insurance plan. If deductibles have not been met, the clients pay the charge for the service and the amount is entered into the insurance company's system as partial fulfillment of any outstanding deductible. A recent study suggested that these four insurance companies and Medicare cover approximately 50–60 percent of PCS's private-pay clients. If clients are not covered by one of these four insurers, they are given a bill to claim reimbursement directly from their own insurance plan. In addition, PCS bills Medicare. Clients covered by Medicaid are referred to a nearby hospital ED. Clients with a history of bad debt at PCS or who are unable to pay at the time of service are not served. PCS maintains an aggressive credit and bad-debt collection policy.

Eighty percent of private-pay clients live within a 30-minute travel distance from a PCS center. Approximately 45 percent have a primary care provider (PCP). At the time of service, private-pay clients are asked whether a record of their care at PCS should be sent to their PCP. If authorized by clients, the staff sends an electronic record to the PCP.

ORGANIZATIONAL STRUCTURE AND MANAGEMENT TEAM

The Alpha Center is in a small shopping center on the main road between Middleboro and Mifflenville. The Beta Center is on the first floor of a new office building adjacent to a large shopping mall in Jasper. Ample parking is available in both locations, and attractive, visible signage helps visitors find their way in each center. Currently, each center is open 48 hours per week, from 8 a.m. to 5 p.m. on weekdays and from 9 a.m. to 12 p.m. on Saturdays. Prior to March 2019, the centers were open from 8 a.m. to 7 p.m. on weekdays and from 8 a.m. to 12 p.m. on Saturdays. They continue to be closed on Sundays and on some holidays, such as Memorial, Independence (July 4), Thanksgiving, Christmas, and New Year's days. Plans to begin Sunday hours were cancelled when the pandemic reached the area. Each center operates in 6,000 square feet of rental space and has four fully furnished patient examination rooms as well as a well-equipped imaging center.

Nine years ago, PCS made its imaging services available to all PCPs in the community. Using electronic ordering, a PCP can order an X-ray at PCS and choose whether to receive a radiologist's report within 12 hours or to directly receive the image electronically. PCS charges for the X-ray, and the patient is responsible for any additional charges such as the reading fee. This service was cancelled in December 2021.

For patient care, the minimum weekday staffing at each center is one receptionist, one registered nurse, and one physician. On Saturdays, minimum staffing is one nurse practitioner, one medical assistant, and one receptionist. The three radiographic technicians employed prior to January 2021 were discharged.

The central administrative and billing office is an additional 2,500 square feet and is located adjacent to the Alpha Center. The central office staff includes the president, medical director, director of nursing and clinical care, business manager, and receptionist/billing personnel.

CHARGES

Each center uses the same prices. The basic visit charge (CPT 99202) is currently $160. Current detailed prices are as follows; at PCS, the current procedural terminology (CPT) codes are also known as evaluation and management or E and M codes:

CPT Code	Description	Price ($)
99201	Office visit, brief, new	130
99202	Office visit, limited, new	160
99203	Office visit, intermediate, new	190
99204	Office visit, comprehensive, new	240
99211	Office visit, minimal, established	100
99212	Office visit, brief, established	120
99213	Office visit, limited, established	160
99214	Office visit, intermediate, established	190
99215	Office visit, comprehensive, established	210

Additional charges are levied for ancillary testing and specialized physician services, such as suturing. A client returning for a medically ordered follow-up is charged $100. PCS has raised its prices 25–30 percent since January 2020. In the past, as part of an advertising campaign to attract private-pay clients, PCS offered discounted physicals—such as $48 camp physicals for children and $69 family checkups. Discussions are underway to reinstate these services.

The following are PCS's 15 most common diagnoses:

ICD-10-CM Diagnostic Code	Description
J01.00	Sinusitis, acute
J02.9	Pharyngitis, acute
J20.9	Bronchitis, acute
J06.0	Laryngopharyngitis, acute
N39.0	Urinary tract infection
R06.9	Respiratory, nonspecific
H66.009	Otitis media
R10.9	Abdominal pain, nonspecific
M48.00	Spinal stenosis
R55	Syncope and collapse
J30.1	Allergic rhinitis
H10.33	Conjunctivitis, acute

J02.0	Streptococcal sore throat
J40	Bronchitis, nonspecific
S93.409A	Ankle sprain

The following are PCS's most frequently performed procedures:

Current Procedure Terminology (CPT) Code	*Description*
12001	Simple wound repair, 2.5 cm
10060	Incision/drainage abscess, simple
29125	Short arm splint, static
12002	Simple wound repair body, 2.6–7.5 cm
29515	Short leg splint
10120	Foreign body removal

Some occupational health clients are charged a negotiated volume-based price for physicals. PCS's medical director negotiates fees for specific physicals and tests ordered by an employer. Typically, an employer approaches PCS in need of a specific type of physical (such as the annual physical required by the DOT for all operators of school buses) or lab test for its employees. PCS submits a bid to perform a certain number of physicals or tests for a flat rate.

INFORMATION SYSTEM

Urgent Care Plus is the corporation-wide electronic health record certified by the Centers for Medicare & Medicaid Services (CMS). It meets or exceeds all CMS Promoting Interoperability Programs (PIP) criteria. As an integrated business, financial, and medical information system, Urgent Care Plus is installed in the computer terminals in the reception areas and examination rooms at both Alpha and Beta centers as well as in the central office.

Clinically, it is used for storing and processing client records, which assist with treatment; physician order entry; prescription or pharmacy records (eRx); laboratory results; and radiographic services records. It is updated within four days of a client's visit to PCS, is available to the client electronically, and can communicate with the statewide immunization registry. Administratively, the system is used for bookkeeping and billing, appointment services, case management, staff scheduling, and data management. Financially, it captures, stores, and reports all CPT codes and links medical procedures with revenue and expense information. It has a direct online link with participating insurance companies and with Medicare.

Using Urgent Care Plus, all clients may register online before arriving at a center. Once they complete the registration, they are given a case number and one hour to arrive for their appointment. If clients do not register before coming to a center, they may do so using a computer terminal in the reception area. Displays in the waiting area indicate the case number currently being seen and the approximate wait time. In addition, Urgent Care Plus allows employees who have direct deposit with a local bank to receive their biweekly pay stubs (with accrued balance of vacation and sick time) and annual W-2s electronically. Billing clerks also use the system to prepare and electronically submit clinical documentation for reimbursement to participating health insurance companies and Medicare.

PCS leases its hardware and software, so vendors provide hardware maintenance, software updates, and technical assistance. Any paper medical records are retained in active files for ten years and then transferred to closed files.

Marketing and Advertising

PCS promotes its retail services primarily through newspaper advertisements and the Internet. Social media and search engine optimization direct potential clients to the PCS website, which allows clients to register for services and schedule appointments. Prior to April 2020, PCS also used direct mail advertising and sponsored a youth baseball team in Middleboro and an annual 5K road race in Jasper. The registration fees from the road race were donated to a charity selected by PCS's board of directors. Prior to 2021, each year in March, PCS distributed a coupon that could be applied to the cost of individual physicals or physicals for all children in any one family; coupons had to be redeemed by the end of June.

Occupational health services are promoted by direct contact. At least monthly, PCS contacts every company that uses its services to determine the company's satisfaction. Annually, PCS provides each corporate client with a comprehensive list of all the occupational health services PCS offers as a basis to meet with the company's leadership.

Board of Directors

The PCS board, composed of the four physician owners, meets quarterly to review operations. The annual board meeting occurs in December, at which time the officers are elected for the coming year. As majority stockholder, Dr. Stephen J. Tobias is chair of the board of PCS. The board secretary is Dr. Jay Smooth, and the other board members are Dr. Rita Hottle and Dr. Laura Cytesmath. The owners have the option of buying any available stock at the current book value. An outsider can purchase stock only if all the owners refuse to exercise this option and if all the owners approve the purchase. Except for 2020, PCS has distributed dividends to stockholders each year.

President, CEO, and Medical Director

In addition to being board chair, Dr. Tobias is the president/CEO and medical director of PCS. He graduated from Private University Medical School and completed postgraduate medical education in general internal medicine at Walter Reed National Military Medical Center. He also holds a master's in public health from State University and is board certified in general internal medicine, emergency medicine, and occupational health. As medical director, he is responsible for PCS's medical quality assurance programs and the recruitment and retention of qualified physician employees. Among his duties are securing professional services to read X-rays for occupational health clients, scheduling the other physicians and nurse practitioners, and seeing clients in the Alpha Center. Compensation for the medical director position began at PCS in 2008, so he receives a separate salary as medical director and as president/CEO. As president, he is responsible for the management of all resources and for strategic planning.

Dr. Tobias founded PCS. Before doing so, he was a full-time ED physician at MIDCARE. Originally, he tried to establish joint-venture urgent care centers with MIDCARE, but when those plans did not work, he recruited his colleagues—now the other PCS stockholders—to start PCS. On top of his PCS positions, he has consulting medical staff privileges in the department of medicine at MIDCARE and occasionally provides services in the hospital's ED.

A recent state court decision, which is currently under appeal, declared that physicians who work in an urgent care corporation constitute "real and bona fide" competition to a hospital's ED. If this decision is upheld, Dr. Tobias and other PCS physicians who have an employment arrangement with MIDCARE may be violating the noncompete clause in their contracts with MIDCARE.

Clinical Staff

The PCS clinical staff comprises eight physicians and three nurse practitioners. All physicians are required to be board certified and are credentialed annually.

Staff Name	Medical Specialty	Certification
Physicians		
Bennet Casey, MD	Family Practice	Board Certified
Mark Welby, MD	Family Practice	Board Certified
Stephen Tobias, MD	Emergency Medicine	Board Certified
Jay Smooth, MD	Emergency Medicine	Board Certified
Rita Hottle, MD	Emergency Medicine	Board Certified
Michael Ferreira, DO	Emergency Medicine	Board Certified

| Regina Bodensky, DO | Emergency Medicine | Board Certified |
| Laura Cytesmath, MD | Emergency Medicine | Board Certified |

Nurse Practitioners

Carla Withers	Family and Adult Health
Jane Jones	Family and Adult Health
Gerri Mattox	Family and Adult Health

Before 2007, PCS physicians were retained as independent contractors and received no benefits outside of their hourly wage. In 2007, nurse practitioners were added to the staff and physicians, and all other employees—who worked more than 1,250 hours—began to receive comprehensive benefits. Today, full benefits coverage (with deductibles and copays) is provided to an employee who works 1,400 or more hours. Anyone who works a minimum of 20 percent to 70 percent of the time receives a prorated coverage with the option to purchase additional coverage. Benefits include the following:

◆ Malpractice insurance, including tail coverage

◆ Stipend for continuing medical education

◆ Health insurance

◆ Dental insurance

◆ Life insurance

◆ Short-term disability

◆ Long-term disability

To reduce operating costs, deductibles and co-pays on all insurance plans were increased in January 2021 and in January 2023.

Physicians are paid $150 per hour, while nurse practitioners receive $75 per hour. Medical assistants are paid $25 per hour. Receptionists are paid $15 per hour. These salary levels have been fixed since January 2021, although modest bonuses were paid in December 2023 and 2024. Drs. Smooth and Hottle work as ED physicians at MIDCARE.

Dr. Casey also serves as an occupational health consultant to companies in the region and as an expert witness in occupational health cases in the state. Dr. Welby works at Convenient Medical Care, Inc., in Capital City. Dr. Ferreira works for Webster Hospital. Dr. Bodensky also works for Webster Hospital and as an ED physician in Capital City.

Once a month, Dr. Tobias creates a schedule for all clinical staff with the understanding that, if a physician is unable to work, in consultation with Dr. Tobias he or she is responsible for securing a replacement from the qualified medical staff. Physicians and nurse practitioners work an entire shift. Saturdays are assigned to the nurse practitioners.

In 2014, PCS changed its protocol involving radiographic images. Currently, the physician on duty can waive having the X-ray read by a radiologist and instead include the physician's notes on the X-ray in the client's chart. In January 2021, PCS introduced the policy that all X-rays requiring review by a radiologist be approved by Dr. Tobias. If the X-ray is referred to a radiologist for reading, a report is received in 12 hours or sooner. Nurse practitioners, however, are required to refer all X-rays they order for professional interpretation by either Dr. Tobias or a radiologist.

The clinical staff meets quarterly to review areas of concern. Dr. Tobias does random reviews of medical records to ensure compliance with standards of clinical practice. He is also responsible for all clinical staff credentialing issues.

Medical assistants are trained to take limited X-rays, draw specimens for laboratory testing, do EKGs, and conduct simple vision and audiometric examinations. Each center is equipped to do the following:

- On-site X-ray
- PFT
- EKG
- Vision and audiometric testing
- Some laboratory testing (e.g., streptococcal screen, urine dip)
- Drug and breath alcohol testing

A regional laboratory processes more advanced laboratory work.

CENTRAL OFFICE STAFF

Dr. Tobias is responsible for the overall management of PCS. Joan Washington, RN, is the director of nursing and clinical care. She trains, supervises, and schedules the nurses and medical assistants as well as orders medical supplies, meets with occupational health employers as needed, and performs general administrative duties as assigned by Dr. Tobias. If needed, she substitutes as a staff RN at a center or in lieu of a medical assistant. Beginning in January 2021, her position became a part-time appointment.

Hannah Coin is the business manager and supervises full- and part-time time staff members. She schedules the receptionists at each center, who also serve as billing clerks. Ms. Coin also manages all insurance billing and the general ledger, including accounts payable and accounts receivable. If needed, she or a member of her staff substitutes for a receptionist. Central office maintains a list of available (and trained) fill-in receptionists to cover absences and other needs.

RECEPTION STAFF

One full-time (35 hours per week) front-desk receptionist works in each center Monday through Friday. Aside from answering phones, greeting visitors, and helping clients with registration, the receptionist is also responsible for setting appointments, billing, creating and maintaining records for occupational health clients, and managing cash receipts. Other hours are covered by part-time staff.

THREATS AND OPPORTUNITIES

Prior to the pandemic, PCS planned to expand. PCS was considering opening a third— and even a fourth—center. It was also considering purchasing buildings to house its Alpha and Beta centers and add some services to better serve all its clients. Dr. Tobias explained, "We were a debt-free corporation that was beginning to earn serious profits. We distinguished ourselves by the high quality of care we provide. Our clients are delighted with our deep commitment to patient care, convenience, and affordability. Even today we have every reason to believe we will continue to recover from the impact of the pandemic and prosper and expand."

The original real estate leases on the Alpha and Beta centers expired in 24 months. Each current lease has a renewal clause for up to 36 months, with an escalation clause so that rents do not increase any more than 15 percent per year. Dr. Tobias named "patient waiting time" as an important issue that warrants ongoing study. At the most recent annual meeting of the board, he committed to hiring a consultant to address this issue.

Although Dr. Tobias was very pleased that PCS occupational health clients generally report "complete satisfaction" with the quality of care provided at the centers— for which he repeatedly credited the competent clinical and administrative staff—he was concerned about the occupational health business. "Our early success with occupational health changed in 2020 and 2021," he said. "If we continue to lose a significant amount of manufacturing in this region, we potentially lose our major occupational health clients. Our future in occupational health will follow the local economy."

Unemployment in the region has already affected the demand for occupational health. Fewer people are being hired, and the unemployed lack health insurance. Beginning in 2021, fees paid by the workers' comp program were fixed for 48 months.

For years, PCS physicians have expressed concern about how Dr. Tobias schedules them. In 2021, Dr. Tobias developed a permanent schedule for each physician or nurse practitioner indicating when and where they work. Records suggest, however, that physicians have revenue profiles. For example, on "busy days," revenue per visit tends to drop, a trend that suggests that physicians do less ancillary testing when they are busy. The target for physicians and nurse practitioners is to see three to four clients per hour. Two physicians have also requested extra compensation for "very busy days," arguing that they receive the same hourly pay as physicians who work on slow days. Two (nonowner) physicians also indicated that, because they are paid by the hour, they should be paid for treating clients who arrive right before closing time. Currently, all staff members are paid only for the hours in their shift, which is sometimes fewer than the actual number of hours worked. Employees are expected to treat all clients who arrive during work hours, even if this extends their work time beyond closing time. Physicians have also questioned when the wage freeze enacted during the early phases of the pandemic will be removed.

Six occupational health nurses at local corporations indicated they were satisfied with PCS's clinical staff. Several clients said they appreciated PCS for keeping them informed about certain employees and the physicians for being creative in explaining restrictions and suggesting "light duty," which is medically appropriate work an injured worker could perform for the employer until the worker is ready to resume regular duties.

At the last board meeting, Dr. Tobias reported that despite the decline experienced during the pandemic, PCS is again on track to report positive financial performance. He indicated that current trends may make it possible for PCS to consider new plans and strategies. At a recent board meeting, one member asked whether PCS will ever be for sale and, if so, how it can be best positioned for sale. He believes the corporation cannot be a long-term successful player in its increasingly competitive medical marketplace. "I am very concerned that the big-box stores will add walk-in services to go along with their pharmacies," he said. "I just do not see how we can compete for the private-pay patients. Our market area is just too small and volatile!" Dr. Tobias has always indicated that he would be willing to sell PCS for "the right price." He has also stated that when the economy and manufacturing in the region picks up, PCS's occupational health business, along with its overall profits, should rebound to pre-pandemic levels.

Board Member Dr. Laura Cytesmath raised the issue of board member retirement. She herself "retired" from providing medical care in 2020 but retains her stock in PCS. "I note with some concern the potential changes that lie ahead for our board. Should we have mandatory retirement ages or terms for board members? Who determines the 'appropriate time' for our physicians to retire from active practice?"

When asked to reflect on the pandemic's impact on PCS, Dr. Tobias explained that "our primary management plan was to lower PCS expenses to better correspond with our reduction in revenue." Dr. Tobias summarized the plans to further restore PCS to its position before the pandemic. He stated that "once we realized the impact of the pandemic on PCS, we made every attempt to lower our costs, especially our fixed costs, including the cost of personnel. We froze all compensation and reduced staff in keeping with our core mission. We also reevaluated every contract and renegotiated many of them. For example, we redesigned our supply chain and changed many of our service providers (e.g., laundry, housekeeping, insurance). The hardest decisions were to reduce our hours of operation and to not offer services on Sundays. These reductions were driven by our need to reduce our costs in keeping with the demand during these trying times. Whether we will be able to return to the service levels we achieved before the pandemic is still an open question." Dr. Tobias credited the board and especially PCS's business manager for their leadership. He said, "I hope the years of service reduction are now behind us. While we have not as yet totally recovered financially, we are in a stronger position to consider how we can return to our position of leadership in Hillsboro County."

Table 3.1
PCS Utilization
Report

	Total Visits	Alpha Center PP Visits	Alpha Center OH Visits	Beta Center PP Visits	Beta Center OH Visits	Alpha Center Gross Charges ($)	Beta Center Gross Charges ($)	Total Gross Charges ($)
2024								
January	884	415	28	201	240	80,803	100,989	181,792
February	774	378	40	154	202	76,243	81,524	157,767
March	843	401	37	104	301	79,891	92,745	172,636
April	887	438	39	209	201	87,005	93,890	180,895
May	917	401	40	256	220	80,438	109,004	189,442
June	877	426	51	170	230	87,005	91,600	178,605
July	833	380	31	215	207	74,966	96,638	171,604
August	853	390	39	230	194	78,250	97,096	175,346
September	1,000	467	48	207	278	93,936	111,065	205,001
October	958	460	25	180	293	88,464	108,317	196,781
November	1,064	530	26	254	254	101,414	116,332	217,746
December	852	401	30	200	221	78,614	96,409	175,023
Total	**10,742**	**5,087**	**434**	**2,380**	**2,841**	**1,007,030**	**1,195,609**	**2,202,639**
2023								
January	833	407	41	200	185	76,810	80,850	157,660
February	711	280	23	205	203	51,949	85,680	137,629
March	891	345	45	212	289	66,866	105,210	172,076
April	914	401	50	203	260	77,324	97,230	174,554
May	889	356	41	246	246	68,066	103,320	171,386
June	967	423	70	267	207	84,525	99,540	184,065
July	797	322	45	250	180	62,922	90,300	153,222
August	729	402	20	202	105	72,352	64,470	136,822
September	830	366	67	230	167	74,238	83,370	157,608
October	869	408	40	256	165	76,810	88,410	165,220
November	1,021	490	46	240	245	91,897	101,850	193,747
December	776	415	35	218	108	77,153	68,460	145,613
Total	**10,227**	**4,615**	**523**	**2,729**	**2,360**	**880,910**	**1,068,690**	**1,949,600**
2022								
January	612	312	40	120	140	56,327	50,960	107,287
February	595	280	31	101	183	49,766	55,664	105,430
March	722	345	43	145	189	62,088	65,464	127,552
April	592	301	56	101	134	57,127	46,060	103,187
May	687	356	51	102	178	65,128	54,880	120,008
June	658	321	60	110	167	60,968	54,292	115,260

continued

Table 3.1
PCS Utilization
Report
(continued)

	Total Visits	Alpha Center PP Visits	Alpha Center OH Visits	Beta Center PP Visits	Beta Center OH Visits	Alpha Center Gross Charges ($)	Beta Center Gross Charges ($)	Total Gross Charges ($)
July	674	323	45	143	163	58,887	59,976	118,863
August	730	402	28	156	144	68,809	58,800	127,609
September	811	380	51	189	191	68,969	74,480	143,449
October	837	378	58	106	295	69,769	78,596	148,365
November	678	390	39	104	145	68,649	48,804	117,453
December	629	315	38	167	109	56,487	54,096	110,583
Total	**8,225**	**4,103**	**540**	**1,544**	**2,038**	**742,973**	**702,072**	**1,445,045**
2021								
January	637	332	45	120	140	56,018	47,996	104,014
February	602	278	22	101	201	44,577	55,749	100,326
March	691	304	53	145	189	53,047	61,656	114,703
April	754	301	49	170	234	52,007	74,578	126,585
May	710	306	59	167	178	54,235	63,687	117,922
June	783	373	65	178	167	65,082	63,687	128,769
July	763	304	72	194	193	55,870	71,440	127,310
August	682	298	43	187	154	50,669	62,949	113,618
September	741	312	49	189	191	53,641	70,148	123,789
October	770	330	56	189	195	57,356	70,886	128,242
November	782	378	59	190	155	64,934	63,687	128,621
December	600	215	40	178	167	37,890	63,687	101,577
Total	**8,515**	**3,731**	**612**	**2,008**	**2,164**	**645,326**	**770,151**	**1,415,478**

Note: OH: occupational health; PP: private-pay.

	Monday	Tuesday	Wednesday	Thursday	Friday	Saturday
Alpha Center						
August				19	12	10
	21	20	12	14	17	12
	22	23	19	12	16	13
	24	22	12	12	10	16
	21	17	15	15	12	11
September	H	29	23	22	22	15
	29	23	18	20	25	12
	28	22	20	22	21	10
	29	28	19	24	21	12
	21					
October		26	19	13	15	8
	23	20	20	14	11	13
	28	22	14	20	12	13
	26	25	21	15	10	12
	29	17	20	19		
November					19	12
	29	22	25	28	19	11
	26	23	25	27	22	12
	23	24	26	H	29	18
	28	28	27	23	20	10
Beta Center						
August				17	19	9
	20	16	14	16	21	12
	19	20	18	10	19	9
	18	15	15	14	21	13
	22	14	18	15	20	11
September						
	H	33	18	17	13	6
	42	17	15	16	18	9
	33	26	22	12	18	10
	29	27	26	13	19	11
	24					
October		23	18	15	12	11
	26	24	14	15	10	10
	26	20	22	21	14	9
	27	22	20	17	12	9
	22	25	11	18		
November				18	12	17
	31	29	18	23	9	12
	28	21	17	20	12	14
	38	17	20	H	26	28
	31	17	15	22	13	

Table 3.2
PCS Monthly Detailed Utilization: August 1–November 30, 2024

Note: H: holiday.

Table 3.3
PCS Alpha Center Client Records, August 26–31, 2024

Day	Num	Art	Age	Town	Sex	First	Ins	Phy
1	1	815	23	1	2	1	1	2
1	2	817	64	2	2	2	1	2
1	3	819	34	1	2	3	1	2
1	6	822	56	4	1	3	2	2
1	7	830	19	6	1	3	2	2
1	8	915	23	1	2	1	2	2
1	9	925	21	7	2	2	2	2
1	10	1000	54	6	1	3	1	2
1	11	1012	51	1	1	1	2	2
1	12	1025	56	1	2	2	1	2
1	13	1215	71	1	1	2	3	2
1	14	1330	44	2	1	1	2	2
1	15	1510	58	8	1	1	2	2
1	16	1545	60	2	1	1	2	2
1	17	1605	18	2	2	2	1	2
1	18	1645	28	1	1	1	2	2
1	19	1650	34	2	1	1	2	2
1	20	1710	21	1	2	1	2	2
1	21	1712	54	1	1	2	1	2
2	1	800	57	4	2	1	1	2
2	2	805	42	1	2	2	1	2
2	3	910	40	1	1	1	1	2
2	4	1015	34	2	1	2	2	2
2	5	1100	45	4	1	2	9	1
2	6	1215	23	1	2	1	1	2
2	7	1350	35	8	1	1	8	2
2	8	1420	23	1	2	2	2	2
2	9	1430	55	1	2	2	2	2

continued

Day	Num	Art	Age	Town	Sex	First	Ins	Phy
2	10	1445	19	1	1	2	1	2
2	11	1500	21	4	2	2	1	2
2	12	1520	33	2	1	1	9	1
2	13	1545	33	1	2	2	2	2
2	14	1610	33	2	1	1	2	1
2	15	1630	68	2	1	2	3	2
2	16	1645	61	1	2	2	2	2
2	17	1715	35	1	1	1	2	2
3	1	805	24	2	1	1	1	2
3	2	930	45	1	1	2	8	2
3	3	1000	2	4	1	1	1	2
3	4	1015	34	1	1	1	1	2
3	5	1100	66	1	2	2	3	2
3	6	1215	44	1	1	3	2	1
3	7	1330	37	1	1	1	1	2
3	8	1345	50	2	2	1	2	2
3	9	1350	56	2	2	2	1	2
3	10	1420	32	4	1	2	1	2
3	11	1500	25	1	2	1	9	1
3	12	1515	7	1	1	3	2	2
3	13	1605	36	8	2	1	9	1
3	14	1650	44	2	2	1	2	2
3	15	1710	24	1	2	1	2	2
4	1	845	18	2	1	1	1	2
4	2	915	28	2	1	2	1	2
4	3	1015	34	1	2	1	1	2
4	4	1100	32	1	2	1	2	2

Table 3.3
PCS Alpha
Center Client
Records, August
26–31, 2024
(continued)

continued

Table 3.3
PCS Alpha Center Client Records, August 26–31, 2024 *(continued)*

Day	Num	Art	Age	Town	Sex	First	Ins	Phy
4	5	1215	9	2	2	1	1	2
4	6	1235	44	1	2	1	8	2
4	7	1245	47	1	2	1	2	2
4	8	1250	34	4	1	1	8	2
4	9	1310	29	6	2	2	2	2
4	10	1340	28	1	2	3	2	2
4	11	1420	44	1	2	1	2	2
4	12	1530	12	1	1	2	1	2
4	13	1545	50	2	2	2	1	2
4	14	1545	26	1	2	3	2	1
4	15	1650	39	2	2	2	2	1
5	1	1000	45	2	1	1	9	1
5	2	1000	23	2	1	2	9	1
5	3	1045	60	1	1	3	3	2
5	4	1130	59	1	2	2	1	2
5	5	1215	52	4	1	1	2	2
5	6	1230	35	4	2	3	2	2
5	7	1240	21	7	2	1	1	2
5	8	1250	66	2	2	2	3	2
5	9	1310	45	2	2	1	8	2
5	10	1320	23	1	1	1	1	2
5	11	1350	21	1	2	1	3	2
5	12	1440	37	1	1	2	9	1
6	1	910	23	3	1	1	1	2
6	2	930	19	2	2	2	2	1
6	3	1015	7	7	2	2	2	2
6	4	1045	70	9	1	1	3	2

continued

Day	Num	Art	Age	Town	Sex	First	Ins	Phy
6	5	1050	24	8	1	1	1	1
6	6	1100	17	9	2	3	2	2
6	7	1120	19	2	2	3	1	2
6	8	1130	24	1	1	1	2	2
6	9	1145	16	2	2	2	2	2
6	10	1215	44	8	1	1	2	2
6	11	1230	48	2	2	3	2	2

Table 3.3
PCS Alpha Center Client Records, August 26–31, 2024 *(continued)*

Notes:

Day: 1 = Monday, 2 = Tuesday, 3 = Wednesday, 4 = Thursday, 5 = Friday, 6 = Saturday

Num: Arrival order (1 = first person to arrive)

Art: Arrival time

Town:

1   Middleboro   5   Statesville   9   Other
2   Mifflenville   6   Carterville
3   Jasper   7   Boalsburg
4   Harris City   8   Minortown

Sex:
1 = male,
2 = female

First: Is this your first ever visit to a PCS center?
1 = Yes
2 = No
3 = No, this is a medically ordered return visit

Ins: Insurance coverage/payment

1   Commercial insurance   3   Medicare   9   Employer pays
2   Cash, check, or credit card 8   Workers' comp

Phy: Physical?
1 = Yes
2 = No

Table 3.4
PCS Beta Center
Client Records,
August 26–31,
2024

Day	Num	Art	Age	Town	Sex	First	Ins	Phy	Charge
1	1	800	44	3	2	2	8	2	385
1	2	810	32	3	1	1	9	2	305
1	3	810	45	3	2	1	8	2	270
1	4	945	66	3	1	2	3	2	160
1	5	1015	21	5	1	1	8	2	180
1	6	1130	7	9	2	2	1	2	180
1	7	1200	34	3	2	1	2	2	180
1	8	1215	51	3	2	1	8	2	350
1	9	1215	59	3	2	1	1	2	180
1	10	1320	40	3	1	1	8	2	390
1	11	1350	23	5	1	2	9	1	375
1	12	1430	32	3	2	1	8	2	280
1	13	1520	40	5	2	2	9	2	245
1	14	1530	75	5	2	2	1	2	220
1	15	1545	22	3	1	1	9	1	350
1	16	1550	30	3	2	1	1	2	160
1	17	1605	36	3	2	1	9	2	245
1	18	1620	50	3	1	1	2	2	145
1	19	1630	67	9	2	1	3	2	150
1	20	1700	23	3	1	1	2	2	160
1	21	1710	54	3	2	2	8	2	275
1	22	1720	19	3	1	1	2	2	220
2	1	815	40	3	1	1	8	2	325
2	2	930	23	3	1	1	1	2	190
2	3	1045	19	3	2	1	9	1	300
2	4	1050	25	4	1	1	9	1	275
2	5	1115	45	3	2	2	2	2	190
2	6	1130	50	3	1	1	2	2	160
2	7	1145	27	9	1	1	9	1	270
2	8	1300	29	3	2	2	1	2	190
2	9	1430	30	9	2	2	9	1	300

continued

Day	Num	Art	Age	Town	Sex	First	Ins	Phy	Charge
2	10	1520	47	3	1	1	9	1	300
2	11	1640	56	3	2	2	9	1	310
2	12	1700	23	9	2	1	1	2	165
2	13	1710	58	5	2	2	9	1	275
2	14	1720	47	3	1	1	2	1	160
3	1	830	12	3	1	1	1	2	175
3	2	915	40	3	2	1	8	2	375
3	3	1020	39	5	1	2	8	2	250
3	4	1040	50	5	1	1	9	1	375
3	5	1120	46	5	2	1	9	1	375
3	6	1215	45	3	2	1	8	2	325
3	7	1245	23	3	1	2	9	2	375
3	8	1305	48	3	1	2	8	2	325
3	9	1320	32	3	1	2	1	2	160
3	10	1350	23	3	1	1	9	1	350
3	11	1405	19	3	1	1	8	2	300
3	12	1430	44	3	2	2	8	2	290
3	13	1445	32	3	1	2	2	1	350
3	14	1500	50	5	1	2	2	2	350
3	15	1545	45	3	2	1	8	2	215
3	16	1605	56	9	1	1	2	2	210
3	17	1650	69	3	1	1	3	2	175
3	18	1710	34	9	1	1	9	2	190
4	1	800	43	3	2	2	9	1	375
4	2	845	50	5	1	1	8	2	400
4	3	915	9	3	2	3	2	2	160
4	4	930	45	3	2	1	1	2	190
4	5	950	56	3	1	1	9	1	300
4	6	1015	75	3	1	2	3	2	175
4	7	1120	46	3	1	2	8	2	300
4	8	1145	48	3	1	1	9	1	300

Table 3.4
PCS Beta Center Client Records, August 26–31, 2024 *(continued)*

continued

Table 3.4
PCS Beta Center
Client Records,
August 26–31,
2024
(continued)

Day	Num	Art	Age	Town	Sex	First	Ins	Phy	Charge
4	9	1205	40	3	1	1	9	1	300
4	10	1230	50	9	1	1	8	2	425
4	11	1315	23	3	1	2	2	2	180
4	12	1430	50	3	1	1	1	2	160
4	13	1620	27	5	1	1	8	2	280
4	14	1640	22	9	1	1	2	2	180
4	15	1645	18	3	1	1	9	1	300
5	1	800	64	9	2	1	8	2	260
5	2	810	45	9	1	2	9	1	300
5	3	815	23	3	2	2	1	2	160
5	4	905	12	3	2	2	8	2	260
5	5	945	35	5	2	2	9	1	300
5	6	1005	23	5	1	2	9	1	300
5	7	1100	29	3	2	1	1	2	175
5	8	1145	40	3	2	1	9	1	300
5	9	1220	35	3	2	1	2	2	180
5	10	1245	46	3	2	2	2	2	180
5	11	1330	24	9	1	1	1	2	210
5	12	1345	59	9	1	1	9	1	300
5	13	1350	60	3	1	1	8	2	325
5	14	1430	45	2	1	1	8	2	240
5	15	1550	33	3	2	3	8	2	170
5	16	1620	68	9	2	1	3	2	180
5	17	1640	19	5	2	1	1	2	200
5	18	1645	34	3	1	2	8	2	240
5	19	1700	45	3	1	2	2	2	170
5	20	1710	34	3	2	1	9	1	300
6	1	800	34	1	2	1	1	2	180
6	2	805	55	3	2	2	1	2	170
6	3	915	45	3	2	2	2	2	170

continued

Day	Num	Art	Age	Town	Sex	First	Ins	Phy	Charge
6	4	940	60	3	1	2	1	1	215
6	5	950	55	3	2	1	2	2	170
6	6	1005	14	9	2	1	1	2	160
6	7	1030	23	9	1	1	2	2	205
6	8	1100	50	3	1	2	1	2	185
6	9	1110	38	3	1	2	1	2	170
6	10	1200	61	3	1	2	1	2	180
6	11	1205	18	9	2	1	2	2	210

Table 3.4
PCS Beta Center Client Records, August 26–31, 2024 *(continued)*

Notes:

Day: 1 = Monday, 2 = Tuesday, 3 = Wednesday, 4 = Thursday, 5 = Friday, 6 = Saturday
Num: Arrival order (1 = first person to arrive)

Art: Arrival time

Town:
1   Middleboro   5   Statesville   9   Other
2   Mifflenville   6   Carterville

3   Jasper   7   Boalsburg
4   Harris City   8   Minortown

Sex:
1 = male, 2 = female

First: Is this your first ever visit to a PCS center?
1 = Yes
2 = No
3 = No, this is a medically ordered return visit

Ins: Insurance coverage/
payment
1   Commercial insurance   3   Medicare   9   Employer pays
2   Cash, check, or credit card   8   Workers' comp

Phy: Physical?
1 = Yes
2 = No

Charge: Gross billed charges ($)

	Record	Date	Day	MD/ARNP	Revenue ($)	Visits
Table 3.5 PCS Alpha Center Revenue Generation by Day of Week and Provider		**August**				
	1	1	4	3	3,458	19
	2	2	5	6	2,956	12
	3	3	6	7	1,945	10
	4	5	1	1	3,801	21
	5	6	2	1	3,467	20
	6	7	3	4	2,656	12
	7	8	4	3	2,310	14
	8	9	5	6	2,937	17
	9	10	6	7	2,078	12
	10	12	1	1	4,001	22
	11	13	2	1	3,835	23
	12	14	3	4	3,367	19
	13	15	4	3	2,194	12
	14	16	5	6	2,812	16
	15	17	6	7	2,167	13
	16	19	1	1	3,967	24
	17	20	2	1	3,988	22
	18	21	3	4	2,184	12
	19	22	4	3	2,109	12
	20	23	5	6	1,933	10
	21	24	6	7	2,690	16
	22	26	1	1	3,575	21
	23	27	2	1	3,415	17
	24	28	3	4	2,990	15
	25	29	4	3	2,765	15
	26	30	5	6	2,500	12
	27	31	6	7	2,150	11
		September				
	28	2	1	H	H	H
	29	3	2	1	5,173	29
	30	4	3	4	4,103	23

continued

Record	Date	Day	MD/ARNP	Revenue ($)	Visits
31	5	4	3	3,589	22
32	6	5	6	3,189	22
33	7	6	7	1,834	15
34	9	1	1	5,224	29
35	10	2	1	4,380	23
36	11	3	4	2,944	18
37	12	4	3	4,278	20
38	13	5	6	4,992	25
39	14	6	7	2,056	12
40	16	1	1	5,134	28
41	17	2	1	5,061	22
42	18	3	4	4,089	20
43	19	4	3	4,067	22
44	20	5	6	4,450	21
45	21	6	7	1,690	10
46	23	1	1	5,278	29
47	24	2	1	5,099	28
48	25	3	4	3,270	19
49	26	4	3	4,756	24
50	27	5	6	4,046	21
51	28	6	7	2,067	12
52	29	1	1	3,167	21
	October				
53	1	2	1	4,623	26
54	2	3	4	3,256	19
55	3	4	3	2,340	13
56	4	5	6	2,918	15
57	5	6	7	1,305	8
58	7	1	1	4,004	23
59	8	2	1	3,451	20
60	9	3	4	3,675	20
61	10	4	3	2,306	14

Table 3.5
PCS Alpha Center Revenue Generation by Day of Week and Provider *(continued)*

continued

Record	Date	Day	MD/ARNP	Revenue ($)	Visits
62	11	5	6	2,308	11
63	12	6	7	2,140	13
64	14	1	1	4,856	28
65	15	2	1	5,720	32
66	16	3	4	2,549	14
67	17	4	3	3,970	20
68	18	5	6	2,180	12
69	19	6	9	2,250	13
70	21	1	1	4,480	26
71	22	2	1	4,367	25
72	23	3	4	3,570	21
73	24	4	3	2,801	15
74	25	5	6	2,485	10
75	26	6	9	2,080	12
76	28	1	1	4,960	29
77	29	2	1	3,001	17
78	30	3	4	3,601	20
79	31	4	3	3,268	19
November					
80	1	5	6	3,276	19
81	2	6	7	2,049	12
82	4	1	1	4,989	29
83	5	2	1	3,805	22
84	6	3	4	4,145	25
85	7	4	3	5,090	28
86	8	5	6	4,308	19
87	9	6	9	1,845	11
88	11	1	1	4,502	26
89	12	2	1	3,950	23
90	13	3	4	4,430	25
91	14	4	3	5,820	27
92	15	5	6	5,037	22

continued

Record	Date	Day	MD/ARNP	Revenue ($)	Visits
93	16	6	7	1,956	12
94	18	1	1	3,940	23
95	19	2	1	4,160	24
96	20	3	4	4,456	26
97	21	4	3	H	H
98	22	5	6	5,601	29
99	23	6	9	2,980	18
100	25	1	1	4,831	28
101	26	2	1	4,734	28
102	27	3	4	4,496	27
103	28	4	3	5,098	23
104	29	5	6	4,296	20
105	30	6	9	1,620	10

Table 3.5
PCS Alpha Center Revenue Generation by Day of Week and Provider *(continued)*

Notes:

Code	MD/ARNP	Day
1	Casey, MD	Monday
2	Welby, MD	Tuesday
3	Tobias, MD	Wednesday
4	Smooth, MD	Thursday
5	Hottle, MD	Friday
6	Ferreira, DO	Saturday
7	Withers, ARNP	
8	Jones, ARNP	
10	Bodensky, DO	
11	Mattox, ARNP	

Revenue: Total gross billed charges
Visits: Number of paying patients
H: Holiday

Table 3.6
PCS Beta
Center Revenue
Generation by
Day of Week
and Provider

Record	Date	Day	MD/ARNP	Revenue ($)	Visits
	August				
1	1	4	10	4,222	17
2	2	5	5	4,956	19
3	3	6	9	1,855	9
4	5	1	2	4,176	20
5	6	2	2	3,174	16
6	7	3	3	2,967	14
7	8	4	10	3,864	16
8	9	5	5	4,892	21
9	10	6	9	2,227	12
10	12	1	2	4,105	19
11	13	2	2	3,896	20
12	14	3	3	3,856	18
13	15	4	10	2,055	10
14	16	5	5	3,590	19
15	17	6	9	1,570	9
16	19	1	2	3,888	18
17	20	2	2	3,355	15
18	21	3	3	3,180	15
19	22	4	10	4,008	14
20	23	5	5	4,105	21
21	24	6	8	2,385	13
22	26	1	2	5,405	22
23	27	2	2	3,410	14
24	28	3	3	5,165	18
25	29	4	10	4,025	15
26	30	5	5	4,750	20
27	31	6	8	2,015	11
	September				
28	2	1	H	H	H
29	3	2	2	7,428	33
30	4	3	3	3,926	18

continued

Record	Date	Day	MD/ARNP	Revenue ($)	Visits
31	5	4	10	5,922	17
32	6	5	5	4,099	13
33	7	6	8	1,162	6
34	9	1	2	8,270	42
35	10	2	2	3,464	17
36	11	3	3	3,467	15
37	12	4	10	5,265	16
38	13	5	5	5,389	18
39	14	6	8	2,004	9
40	16	1	2	6,430	33
41	17	2	2	5,289	26
42	18	3	3	4,377	22
43	19	4	10	5,278	12
44	20	5	5	4,902	18
45	21	6	8	2,080	10
46	23	1	2	6,128	29
47	24	2	2	5,812	27
48	25	3	3	6,112	26
49	26	4	10	3,290	13
50	27	5	5	4,083	19
51	28	6	8	1,870	11
52	29	1	2	5,018	24
	October				
53	1	2	2	4,689	23
54	2	3	3	3,656	18
55	3	4	10	4,966	15
56	4	5	5	3,487	12
57	5	6	8	2,008	11
58	7	1	2	5,061	26
59	8	2	2	4,892	24
60	9	3	3	3,202	14
61	10	4	10	4,840	15

Table 3.6
PCS Beta
Center Revenue
Generation by
Day of Week
and Provider
(continued)

continued

Table 3.6
PCS Beta
Center Revenue
Generation by
Day of Week
and Provider
(continued)

Record	Date	Day	MD/ARNP	Revenue ($)	Visits
62	11	5	5	1,920	10
63	12	6	8	1,890	10
64	14	1	2	5,085	26
65	15	2	2	3,955	20
66	16	3	3	4,033	22
67	17	4	10	6,980	21
68	18	5	5	2,955	14
69	19	6	8	1,652	9
70	21	1	2	5,644	27
71	22	2	2	4,467	22
72	23	3	3	4,080	20
73	24	4	10	6,122	17
74	25	5	5	2,748	12
75	26	6	8	1,592	9
76	28	1	2	5,072	22
77	29	2	2	5,085	25
78	30	3	3	3,680	11
79	31	4	10	4,556	18
November					
80	1	5	5	3,825	12
81	2	6	8	2,877	17
82	4	1	2	7,355	31
83	5	2	2	6,492	29
84	6	3	3	4,412	18
85	7	4	10	5,888	23
86	8	5	5	2,097	9
87	9	6	8	2,277	12
88	11	1	2	6,484	28
89	12	2	2	4,506	21
90	13	3	3	4,249	17
91	14	4	10	6,581	20
92	15	5	5	3,288	12

continued

Table 3.6
PCS Beta Center Revenue Generation by Day of Week and Provider *(continued)*

Record	Date	Day	MD/ARNP	Revenue ($)	Visits
93	16	6	8	2,655	14
95	18	1	2	7,932	38
96	19	2	2	4,122	17
97	20	3	3	4,806	20
98	21	4	H	H	H
99	22	5	5	4,691	26
100	23	6	8	6,012	28
101	25	1	2	7,145	31
102	26	2	2	4,170	17
103	27	3	3	4,581	15
104	28	4	10	6,469	22
105	29	5	5	3,418	13

Notes:

Code	MD/ARNP	Day
1	Casey, MD	Monday
2	Welby, MD	Tuesday
3	Tobias, MD	Wednesday
4	Smooth, MD	Thursday
5	Hottle, MD	Friday
6	Ferreira, DO	Saturday
7	Wither, ARNP	
8	Jones, ARNP	
10	Bodensky, DO	
11	Mattox, ARNP	

Revenue: Total gross billed charges
Visits: Number of paying patients
H: Holiday

Table 3.7
PCS Statement
of Operations,
USD $

	2024	2023	2022	2021
Revenue				
Client Services—Gross	2,202,639	2,190,454	2,023,428	1,852,226
Contractual Allowances	43,887	53,901	54,230	65,334
Patient Revenue—Net	2,158,752	2,136,553	1,969,198	1,786,892
Other Revenue	10,430	8,739	7,430	7,236
Total Revenue	**2,169,182**	**2,145,292**	**1,976,628**	**1,794,128**
Expenses				
Salaries and Wages	1,300,650	1,256,222	1,297,334	1,301,556
Staff Benefits	320,907	315,229	363,254	364,436
Administrative Expenses	2,462	3,972	4,033	4,836
Advertising	9,500	9,500	3,100	3,000
Collection Fees	601	992	958	922
Computer Support	46,202	46,202	44,870	44,560
Consultants	1,203	2,858	735	600
Equipment Leases	19,500	19,500	11,200	11,200
Insurance	25,336	34,200	34,200	34,002
Laboratory	64,289	68,420	68,736	68,553
Laundry and Housekeeping	10,565	16,440	13,670	12,045
Legal/Audit	7,000	9,000	8,500	8,100
Medical Supplies	59,349	64,220	60,363	61,320
Office Supplies	16,725	19,334	19,560	19,440
Printing and Postage	10,403	2,278	2,654	3,133
Professional Fees	14,103	14,392	15,340	15,330
Rent	84,250	84,250	84,250	78,500
Repairs and Maintenance	586	988	3,289	4,327
Telephone	3,057	3,506	2,877	2,845
Utilities	19,445	21,436	20,134	19,452
Interest	279	766	893	488
Depreciation	30,191	31,670	22,500	22,500
Bad Debt Expenses	1,002	1,439	2,478	2,256
Total Expenses	**2,047,605**	**2,026,814**	**2,084,928**	**2,083,401**
Income (Loss) Before Taxes	**121,577**	**118,478**	**−108,300**	**−289,273**
Federal Tax	−31,610	−30,804	0	0
State Tax	−948	−924	0	0
Income (Loss) After Taxes	**89,019**	**86,750**	**−108,300**	**−289,273**

	2024	2023	2022	2021
Assets				
Current Assets				
Cash, Operating	236,754	213,418	94,918	62,303
Accounts Receivable—Net	112,642	116,318	134,293	116,363
Inventory	4,100	4,823	3,023	3,389
Prepaid Expenses	423	946	835	4,033
Total Current Assets	**353,919**	**335,505**	**233,069**	**186,088**
Investments	1,206,042	1,118,820	1,074,355	738,179
Property, Plant, and Equipment (PPE)				
Equipment—Gross	249,034	240,262	196,445	218,445
Leasehold Improvements—Gross	449,150	456,434	499,284	473,995
Less Accumulated Depreciation	350,283	344,505	312,835	290,335
Equipment and Leasehold Improvements—Net	228,910	233,771	382,894	402,105
Total Assets	**1,788,871**	**1,688,096**	**1,690,318**	**1,326,372**
Liabilities and Net Assets				
Current Liabilities				
Accounts Payable	73,304	61,343	58,447	51,332
Accrued Expenses	17,336	18,336	30,549	38,556
Accrued Payroll Taxes	20,191	17,349	18,330	24,301
Total Current Liabilities	**110,831**	**97,028**	**107,326**	**114,189**
Notes Payable	52,878	60,663	66,349	12,445
Total Liabilities	**163,709**	**157,691**	**173,675**	**126,634**
Net Assets				
Common Stock Issued	720,000	720,000	720,000	720,000
Retained Earnings	905,162	810,405	796,643	479,738
Total Net Assets	**1,625,162**	**1,530,405**	**1,516,643**	**1,199,738**
Net Assets + Liabilities	**1,788,871**	**1,688,096**	**1,690,318**	**1,326,372**

Table 3.8
PCS Balance Sheet as of December 31, USD $

Table 3.9
PCS Compensation Budget: January–December 2025

	Alpha Center			Beta Center			Total		
	Salary	Benefits	Total	Salary	Benefits	Total	Salary	Benefits	Total
Physicians (M–F)	351,000	98,280	449,280	351,000	98,280	449,280	702,000	196,560	898,560
ARNP (Sat)	15,210	4,259	19,469	15,210	4,259	19,469	30,420	8,518	38,938
RN (M–F)	117,500	32,900	150,400	117,500	32,900	150,400	235,000	65,800	300,800
MA (Sat)	7,020	1,966	8,986	7,020	1,966	8,986	14,040	3,931	17,971
Receptionists (M–Sat)	38,610	9,266	47,876	38,610	9,266	47,876	77,220	18,532	95,752
Business Manager (1 FTE)							62,500	21,875	84,375
Business Staff (3.7 FTE)							92,000	22,080	114,080
Director of Clinical Care							68,000	20,400	88,400
Medical Director							20,000	2,000	22,000
President							25,000	2,500	27,500
Total	529,340	146,671	676,011	529,340	146,670	676,010	1,326,180	362,196	1,688,376

Notes: (1) Numbers are in US dollars. (2) ARNP: advanced registered nurse practitioner; FTE: full-time equivalent; MA: medical assistant; PB: partial benefits; RN: registered nurse.

	2024	2023	2022	2021
MIDCARE Emergency Department, Middleboro	250	250	240	240
Webster Hospital Quick Med, Middleboro*	180	170	160	150
Convenient Medical Care, Capital City*	130	130	130	130
Capital City General, Emergency Department	225	225	215	215
Medical Associates Express, Jasper*	130	130	125	125
Physician Care Services*	160	160	150	140

Table 3.10
PCS Market Analysis of Basic Visit Charges

Notes: (1) Charges in US dollars. (2) * Comparisons based on CPT 99202.

MIDDLEBORO COMMUNITY MENTAL HEALTH CENTER

Middleboro Community Mental Health Center (MCMHC) was founded in 1964 as a 501(c)(3) nonprofit organization and funded in part by the Community Mental Health Act of 1963. Today, it provides a comprehensive menu of mental health services and programs—including emergency and education—for adults and children and their families. It also runs a central office called Gardner Place as well as a four-bed group home called Justin Place in northwest Middleboro.

As a state-designated facility, MCMHC is required to offer an array of services, including 24-hour emergency services, assessment and evaluation, intake and referral, therapy, case management, community-based rehabilitation, outpatient psychiatric care, and disaster mental health support. The state designates catchment areas for community mental health centers, and the area for MCMHC—and for another center located between Jasper and Capital City—is Hillsboro County. Services provided outside the catchment area, other than emergency services, may reduce the resources used to treat residents within the catchment area. Every five years, the state conducts an assessment for redesignation, and MCMHC is due for its review in two years. In addition, a recent state Supreme Court decision ruled that hospitals could no longer retain individuals in need of behavioral health services in the emergency room for longer than three days due to a lack of inpatient space. This ruling is likely to have an impact on relationships between MCMHC and local hospitals as well as on the behavioral health system as a whole.

MCMHC maintains contracts with several private insurance carriers. It also receives reimbursement for serving Hillsboro County residents covered by Medicaid. To be eligible for the Medicaid program, a person must be determined to have conditions and circumstances that contribute to a mental health diagnosis.

HISTORY

Using federal funds, MCMHC began operations in 1964 in a small rental office in Middleboro. Its aim was to provide mental health services primarily to children and families who were unable to obtain such care elsewhere. Previously, mental health services in and around the city were delivered in a noncoordinated manner by area hospitals and by Swift River Psychological Services, which MCMHC acquired in 1967.

MCMHC purchased a building on the north side of Middleboro in 1971. It owes the expansion of its programs and services to changes in mental health legislation through the 1970s, which culminated in the passage of the Mental Health Systems Act (Public Law 96–398) in 1980. This act strengthened the linkages among mental health programs and services; awarded grants for serving specific populations, including the severely mentally ill and severely emotionally disturbed; and expanded mental health education. Just one year later—in 1981—under the Reagan administration, the act was repealed and replaced by a block grant program. These block grants sharply decreased federal funding for mental health services.

Amendments to the Medicare program in 1987 increased outpatient mental health benefits for the first time in more than two decades, enabling MCMHC to introduce programs for severely mentally ill adults. Service delivery remained at a steady level for many years, until President Clinton signed the Children's Health Act (Public Law 106–310) into law in 2000. This act established standards for the care and treatment of children and youth in community-based facilities. As a follow-up to this act, President George H. W. Bush called for the expansion of community health centers, including mental health services, in 2002.

Since 2002, MCMHC has continued to develop its programs and services, albeit modestly. In 2015, it moved its offices into Gardner Place, located in the central business district of Middleboro. In 2017, it purchased Justin Place, located on the northwest side of the city.

Inpatient behavioral healthcare across the state is extremely limited. Only one such facility exists in the state—the 154-bed State Behavioral Health Hospital situated nearly 150 miles northeast of Middleboro. This dearth of inpatient beds is particularly problematic given the recent state Supreme Court case limiting prolonged stays in the emergency department.

MISSION

The mission of MCMHC is as follows:

Our mission is to provide an array of appropriate mental and behavioral programs and services to residents of Hillsboro County. Our programs and services promote the well-being and quality of life of our community by preventing and managing the challenges to mental and behavioral health.

GOVERNANCE

MCMHC is licensed as a nonprofit community mental health center. Under its corporate umbrella are all of its programs and services as well as its two properties—Gardner Place and Justin Place.

The organization is governed by a board of directors that comprises 17 members. Members are elected to four-year terms and may serve a maximum of three consecutive terms. The board as a whole meets monthly, and its subcommittees meet on a separate schedule. The executive committee meets with the executive director every two weeks, while the other committees meet at least quarterly. Current members of the MCMHC board are as follows; the (number)* indicates the number of years remaining on the current board term:

MCMHC Board of Directors

Members	*Residence*
John Regis, JD (1)*, *Chair*	
Attorney	Middleboro
Juanita Crawford, PhD (2), *Vice Chair*	
Clinical psychologist	Statesville
Blanche Stacy, LCSW (3), *Secretary*	
Retired social worker	Middleboro
George Blanchford, CPA (2), *Treasurer*	
President, Blanchford Public Accountants	Jasper
Althea Actor, MD (1)	
Psychiatrist	Middleboro
Kayla Connelly (3)	
Management consultant	Jasper
William Dawson, Jr. (1)	
President, Hyland Motors	Middleboro

Amoli Doshi (4)	
Dental assistant	Mifflenville
Sadie Grant, CISSP (2)	
Manager, Information Technology, River Industries	Middleboro
Bennett Hauser (2)	
Human resources manager, Jersey Products	Jasper
Jackson Ang (1)	
Senior account executive, TV Channel 32	Boalsburg
Stephanie Jervis-Washburn	
Executive director, MCMHC	Middleboro
Stephen Rodgers, JD (4)	
Attorney	Middleboro
Penelope Sanchez-Rosario, NCC AP (3)	
Substance abuse counselor	Statesville
Virginia Aarons, PsyD (3)	
Pediatric clinical psychologist	Jasper
Joan Stemsrud, RN (4)	
Retired nurse	Carterville
Martha Washington, RN (2)	
CEO, Hillsboro Health	Middleboro
Bertram Yang (2)	
Vice principal, Middleboro High School	Middleboro

Assignments to the board's standing committees are as follows:

- Executive (Regis, Crawford, Stacy, Blanchford)

- Finance (Connelly, Ang, Blanchford, Regis)

- Nominating (Doshi, Grant, Hauser, Aarons)

- Quality and Compliance (Yang, Regis, Actor, Washington, Stemsrud)

- Planning (Actor, Dawson, Sanchez-Rosario, Ang, Rodgers)

- Development (Regis, Crawford, Stacy, Blanchford, Dawson, Connelly)

According to the term-limit clause of the organization, the following members are now serving their final term: Regis, Actor, Dawson, and Ang. In addition, Blanchford has indicated he will not serve beyond his current term when it ends in two years. All other members are eligible to serve at least one more term and have not voiced a plan to step down. MCMHC is considering increasing the size of the board and adding another term to the current limit of three. Dr. Crawford, vice chair of the board, explained the reasoning behind this idea: "It really takes two or three terms to understand the organization, and then it's time to leave. It's important that we retain continuity on the board. Also, it would be nice to have more board members from smaller towns outside of Middleboro. Some of the most serious mental health issues can be found in rural areas, so it's important for us to address those needs. After all, we are here for the entire county, not just Middleboro."

Development or fundraising is an area of increasing concern for MCMHC. Historically, it has been able to manage healthy total margins mostly because of substantial contributions from two Middleboro families. One of those families informed the board three years ago that it has shifted its charitable priorities and the coming year will mark the end of its generous donations. MCMHC's governance has yet to develop a strategy to make up for this financial loss. The recent pandemic provided additional needed government funding to the organization, but that funding was meant to serve as a stopgap measure given the extent of the pandemic challenge.

MANAGEMENT TEAM AND ORGANIZATIONAL STRUCTURE

Stephanie Jervis-Washburn has been the executive director of MCMHC since 2020. She holds a master's in marriage and family therapy (MFT) from an East Coast university and obtained her master's in healthcare administration from State University. Prior to joining MCMHC, she worked for ten years as a marriage and family therapist in a small private group in Capital City. She also served as a marriage mediator for three years. Active in professional organizations, she serves on the education subcommittee and the executive committee of the American Association for Marriage and Family Therapy as well as the executive committee of the Governor's Blue Ribbon Commission for Child Mental Health. She has extensive lobbying experience and is well-regarded in her profession.

Since arriving at MCMHC, Jervis-Washburn has focused on reorganizing the management structure and offering new service and educational programs for the community. Her background in MFT has, not surprisingly, led to the development of robust MFT programs, which are considered models in the state. She is frequently asked to consult with other organizations that are pursuing similar initiatives. Although the MFT programs have been popular and successful, they have caused concern among some board members and senior staff, who think her laser focus on MFT could diminish the quality of other MCMHC programs and services.

Another area of attention for Jervis-Washburn has been strengthening the administrative foundation of the organization, including finance and information technology. As she noted, "An organization such as ours must be incredibly sensitive to changes in reimbursement. We have survived because of our ability to respond to—I dare say, predict—the changes coming down the road in, for example, Medicaid reimbursement, which accounts for a large portion of our revenue. Programs like Medicaid are becoming more difficult to predict, given the current political environment locally and nationally. We need to be alert to opportunities that may expand our payer mix to nongovernmental sources, although many private and commercial payers do not compensate well—if at all—for community-based services such as ours. It's an ongoing struggle. During the pandemic, demand for our programs and services increased, and the financial challenges were particularly severe. Fortunately, we received governmental assistance to help support some of our program efforts. Now that the worst of the pandemic is essentially behind us, meeting the increased community demand without supplemental funds will be tough."

To this end, and at the board's instruction, Jervis-Washburn has been working to secure external or nonstate funding, such as federal and private grants. Small grants, usually obtained from the state, have always represented a portion of MCMHC's financial base. Typically, such grants are allocated for a particular program or service and are generally non-competitive, given that they are awarded to all designated community mental health centers. Last year, she submitted the organization's first grant application to the Substance Abuse and Mental Health Services Administration (SAMHSA), aiming to design and implement a countywide program to address the growing adolescent opioid epidemic. Unfortunately, the proposal was declined. Jervis-Washburn is undeterred, however, and intends to submit the proposal to other funders and to be more proactive with grant writing in general.

Rodgers, a member of the board, urged her to explore the possibility of MCMHC taking on some aspects of the Drug Court for Hillsboro County. While not necessarily a financially attractive venture, the organization's involvement in the court can have a positive impact on the county and will be consistent with MCMHC's mission.

Giving priority to information technology has paid off, as the organization's transition to the *Diagnostic and Statistical Manual of Mental Disorders*, 5th edition (DSM-5), has gone relatively smoothly. "Like most centers, we are still struggling a bit with the fine points of DSM-5, but overall we are doing relatively well," Jervis-Washburn said. "Changes in the area of autism spectrum disorders are still somewhat controversial for some of our clinicians, but this is not a problem unique to our organization. The autism spectrum is the one area we need to address more thoroughly."

In part because of its advanced information systems and its positive reputation for service provision, MCMHC has been approached by Swift Water Accountable Care Organization, based in Capital City, to enter into an affiliation agreement with the organization. "This is an opportunity we are definitely evaluating, although we may not be ready to assume the financial risk for our patient population," she admitted.

Within the past several years, Jervis-Washburn has substantially changed the organizational structure of MCMHC. She now has only one direct report—the senior director

Shanique Harrison, PhD. In addition, she meets regularly with Dr. Ivan Stanzl, the medical director, regarding clinical issues.

SENIOR DIRECTOR

Dr. Harrison was named senior director in 2019 when the previous clinical head retired after nearly 20 years in office. As a clinical psychologist with special training in dialectical behavior therapy for adolescents, she was a team leader in MCMHC's Adult Services Program, but before this she worked at a small mental health facility in Capital City for five years and was a faculty member in the psychology department at State University for seven years. She is active in the mental health community and has recently become a member of a regional committee—sponsored by the National Alliance on Mental Illness—that addresses the stigma of mental illness.

Dr. Harrison's appointment to senior director was somewhat divisive because several staff members who had worked for the organization longer than she had were passed over for the position. Although she is aware of the controversy, she has made deliberate efforts to be collaborative in her decision making. With direction from Jervis-Washburn and support from the board, she has made the following changes in her short tenure:

◆   Split MCMHC into two divisions—Administrative Services and Clinical Services—that are each headed by a director

◆   Combined all children and family programs into a single unit that is headed by a manager who reports to the director of Clinical Services (in the past, each of these programs had a direct reporting relationship to the clinical head)

DIRECTOR OF ADMINISTRATIVE SERVICES

Clement Gray, a longtime employee of MCMHC, is the director of the division. He received a bachelor of science degree in business administration from State University and is an active member of the Healthcare Financial Management Association.

The division of Administrative Services comprises Human Resources, Information Technology, Planning and Marketing, Properties, and Finance. Information Technology, Properties, and Finance are headed by a manager with specialized training and background in his area of responsibility. Human Resources is headed by an acting manager, and Gray has been acting as manager of Planning and Marketing. Given his experience and expertise, he is often called in to assist in Finance, a responsibility he enjoys but one that takes him away from his extensive assigned duties. As a result, he is "somewhat overwhelmed" and has frequently expressed to Dr. Harrison his difficulties.

The tacit discord between the two divisions is also a cause for frustration. "Everybody works really hard around here, but the clinical people believe they work just a little bit harder and what they do is more important than what we administration people do. Without us, there would be no resources and no information to get the clinical job done," he explained. "Many of our clinicians believe that their way of caring for a client is the only way to go. At times, they minimize the views of other staffers—who are as highly qualified but may not have gone through the same academic or theory-based training as the clinicians. People get pretty passionate about this."

Gray reported that maintaining a sustainable reimbursement structure is among the concerns that "keep him up at night," although he does meet with Dr. Harrison and the director of Clinical Services to commiserate and strategize. Another challenge is managing the human resources and professional needs of the large—and still growing—workforce that includes individuals with a wide variety of educational backgrounds and disciplines.

He thinks the organization does not pay enough attention to planning and marketing efforts, saying, "We get so focused on the clinical needs of our clients that we don't leave time as an organization to look ahead. Right now, that's working OK—mostly because we have dedicated people and because our IT system works so well. But I'm not sure how long that will last."

PROPERTY MANAGER

Three years ago, MCMHC hired Charles McKenny to handle all facility-related issues at both Gardner Place and Justin Place. A longtime, residential property manager, he maintains a small staff of one building engineer and three housekeepers; turnover has been high among the housekeepers. The board and Jervis-Washburn have instructed McKenny, who reports directly to Gray, to look for multiunit housing properties for possible purchase and conversion into condominiums for clients in the final phase of treatment. He believes many such properties are available in Middleboro and the northern communities of Hillsboro County but are limited in the southern area.

At Gardner Place, space is at a premium and the staff has been very adept at using the space creatively to adapt to the growing needs of the organization, but McKenny noted, "The building is out of space. It's not possible to double up any of the current offices or areas because of the confidential nature of what goes on in here, and it's not possible to add space. So we continue to apply Band-Aids to the place and make do with what we have."

DIRECTOR OF CLINICAL SERVICES

Simone Beauchamp, RN, has been an MCMHC employee for 14 years. Before she was promoted to director six months ago, she was the associate manager of Emergency Services.

Known for her high-energy, roll-up-your-sleeves attitude, she is passionate about making a difference in the lives of those with mental health needs. Dr. Harrison just asked her to conduct a thorough analysis of the programs under Clinical Services.

Although Beauchamp has six months to complete the assignment, she has already started and noticed some issues, such as duplication of services delivered by Adult Services and Child and Family Services. She wonders whether restructuring the programs by the type of service delivered—as opposed to by the client's age and family status—may eliminate or minimize the duplication. She also sees a need to work more closely with the director of Administrative Services to understand the financial implications of programs and services on MCMHC operations.

Clinical Services comprises five programs: Adult Services, Child and Family Services, Emergency Services, Quality and Compliance Services, and Education Services. Each program is headed by an associate manager who has skills, training, and experience appropriate for the role's tasks and responsibilities. The recent pandemic had a substantial impact on MCMHC, and the Clinical Services division was given responsibility for coordinating all related programs and services. These expanded responsibilities led to confusion and occasional conflict among the organization's departments. As Beauchamp noted, "The pandemic created enormous challenges for all of us. Utilization of several programs soared, and it was very difficult to coordinate everything. I think we did a good job for our clients, but it was not always smooth sailing for the staff. They did the best they could in very tough times, but conflicts definitely arose between programs. I don't know how much of this had to do with people 'protecting their turf' versus just the overall uncertainty of everything."

Adult Services

The adult program is designed for clients aged 18 years or older and provides a wide range of treatments and approaches as well as coordination of clinical and psychiatric rehabilitation. Services are offered at a variety of locations, depending on the needs of the client. Most clients are seen in Gardner Place, but care may also be delivered in the client's home or another healthcare facility. Among the most common services clients receive are counseling and therapy (individual or group), dialectical behavioral therapy, functional support (which assists with identifying and managing the use of community-based resources apart from MCMHC), illness management and recovery, psychiatric nursing, family support, mental health education, and vocational assistance. In addition, supported living services are provided in Justin Place.

Four standing interdisciplinary teams develop and deliver treatment plans to program clients. Every team includes one team leader-clinician and at least one other clinician. To maintain the greatest degree of flexibility, the teams do not specialize in a specific treatment modality, and the general approach followed for assessment is essentially the same for each team. On occasion, however, teams do "take on the clinical philosophy" of their respective team leader, which has created conflict among team members and complicated client transitions. Additional team members may be drawn from a rotating team, which is composed of clinicians with specific skills and experience that may augment those of the interdisciplinary teams.

Child and Family Services

This program is geared toward children aged 18 years and younger as well as their families. Like Adult Services, it has three standing interdisciplinary teams comprising a team leader-clinician and at least one other clinician; it also draws additional team members from a rotating team.

Services are provided in several settings, including Gardner Place, private homes, schools, and community-based facilities. In the past five years, the program has grown in schools because of the dramatic increase in substance abuse—opioid use in particular—among teenagers. MCMHC board and management have had frequent and ongoing conversations with state legislators to push for increased drug prevention and education as well as funding for such programming. At a recent board meeting, board members asked Jervis-Washburn to move youth substance abuse to the top of the organization's priorities.

Complicating this issue is that the federal government affords privacy protection to adolescents who seek treatment. Because providers may be prohibited from informing parents or guardians that their children are in treatment, they cannot bill for services rendered because parents or guardians may receive an Explanation of Benefits from their insurers if providers submit a claim.

Mental health services for children and their families are extremely limited in Hillsboro County. Communities ask their schools for an array of mental health counseling and education, and, in turn, schools seek help from MCMHC and the few providers in the county. Coordination of services between MCMHC and the schools has become increasingly problematic, however—although not necessarily because of the ongoing opioid crisis. Accommodating the goals and resource capabilities of both the schools and the organization remains a very serious challenge for MCMHC and its leadership.

Emergency Services

This program routinely maintains a four-person team responsible for providing services to individuals or organizations facing a crisis. However, this program was particularly stressed during the pandemic, as mental health services were in high demand. Telephone consultation services were greatly expanded as face-to-face assessment was reduced drastically. Telehealth services were generally very well received by both clients and providers, and it is likely that this modality will continue to constitute a significant portion of MCMHC's services. Phone and face-to-face assessment as well as referral and intervention are available on a 24/7 basis. Historically, about 50 percent of all assessments led to referrals, which are frequently directed to the hospital emergency department (ED), and about 10 percent of those referred to the ED are admitted into the hospital. About three-fourths of the hospital admissions are voluntary. In addition, the team provides counseling and other appropriate services to individuals who have experienced or are experiencing traumatic events.

Quality and Compliance Services

The team for this program is charged with ensuring that MCMHC is structured and operates in a way that is consistent with federal and state guidelines. Generally, compliance principles and standards exist for many areas, such as

◆ employee qualification, responsibilities, and credentialing;

◆ continuing professional education;

◆ professional sanctions;

◆ confidentiality, safety, and maintenance of documentation, records, and other information;

◆ clinical reviews;

◆ billing and financial reporting;

◆ conflict of interest;

◆ disclosure and reporting of employee misconduct; and

◆ employee and client rights.

Mental health is a heavily monitored and regulated sector of the healthcare industry, and the guidelines change frequently. As a response, MCMHC has increased the program's full-time staff from one to two individuals.

Developing behavioral health quality measures is a relatively new phenomenon influenced by the Affordable Care Act (ACA) of 2010. The ACA led to the publication of the National Quality Strategy (NQS), which "serves as a catalyst and compass for a nationwide focus on quality improvement efforts and approach to measuring quality." Part of the NQS pertains to behavioral health issues.

MCMHC believes strongly in creating and tracking appropriate measures of quality of care and has been working with SAMHSA's National Behavioral Health Quality Framework. This guideline focuses on the development of federal- and state-specific behavioral health barometers. Table 4.1 shows Hillsboro County's barometer as compared with that of the United States. Measuring and monitoring quality data enable MCMHC to develop a well-informed strategic plan.

Education Services

A staff of two health educators make up this program. These staff members develop and present behavioral health education customized for a client group or organization. For example, in 2021 at the request of three Middleboro-based employers, Education Services designed and then conducted for employees a four-hour educational session on the topic of stress management, substance abuse prevention strategies, and mindfulness. The training was well-received by both management and employees of the company. However, corporate clients are hard to secure and engage, and during the pandemic no such programs were developed.

Jervis-Washburn still believes the program as a whole is valuable and a market for it exists. More important, she believes educating the community is part of MCMHC's responsibility. She is particularly interested in expanding school-based education services—on the topics of alcohol and substance abuse, sexuality, and peer pressure—because schools do not have the expertise and dedicated staff to conduct such programs for students. Funding for this plan is nonexistent, however. During a discussion at a board meeting, a board member asked, "While we're on this issue, I've been wondering whether our education programs and services are organized in the most effective manner and whether these tasks shouldn't really fall to the schools, particularly when resources are so limited."

STAFFING

Table 4.2 displays MCMHC's staffing budget by program and position. In many cases, staff has the flexibility to work as needed in more than one division. The budget reflects the manner in which staff members are allocated among programs for accounting purposes.

MCMHC has a disadvantage in recruiting and retaining clinical staff for a number of reasons:

1.   Compensation levels are somewhat lower than market level for many positions, although few employment opportunities are available in Hillsboro County for mental health clinicians.

2.   Many positions can be filled adequately by an individual with a baccalaureate degree, but other positions—such as therapists—require graduate and even postgraduate degrees. Given the compensation shortfalls, attracting educationally qualified individuals is challenging. In addition, some positions require even a master's-level clinician to obtain two years of staff experience

prior to working independently. It has not been unusual for master's-level clinicians to work for MCMHC for two to three years to gain experience and then move out of the area to an organization that offers higher compensation.

3. Many healthcare organizations compete to hire individuals who are qualified to prescribe medications (e.g., nurse practitioners), but MCMHC has often not been successful at recruiting and retaining such staff because it offers low compensation.

The board has assigned Jervis-Washburn, Dr. Harrison, and Gray to develop a long-term strategy to address these ongoing problems.

Four psychiatrists work at least part-time for MCMHC, but only two of them—Dr. Stanzl (the medical director) and Dr. Actor (a board member)—have affiliations at MID-CARE. The other two psychiatrists have admitting privileges at Capital City General Hospital.

Two years ago, MCMHC implemented a tracking system that requires all staff members to log their time by activity, on 15-minute intervals. Although not a significant change for some clinicians, the logging requirement was initially resisted by many other staff. Jervis-Washburn had to spend a substantial amount of time explaining the importance of the procedure for cost-finding, which is a long-term goal of the organization, in anticipation of bundled-pricing initiatives. Still, the feeling among many employees—including clinicians—was that the change represented management's lack of trust in their professionalism. The tracking system also highlighted the US Department of Labor's requirement for organizations to pay for overtime work.

According to Jervis-Washburn, the relationship between MCMHC and private-practice mental health providers in the county is excellent: "They know we provide very good client services and are not reluctant to refer to us. We have worked very well to coordinate our care with theirs. At times, though, it appears they prefer to send to us the uninsured or Medicaid clients and keep the private-pay clients for themselves. We have been working with them to reach a more equitable arrangement, but frankly I'm not optimistic." These are the four private mental health practices in the county:

1. *Sockalexis Center.* Located in Jasper, this group is staffed by four PhD psychologists, three master's-level social workers, and three substance abuse counselors. It has the contract to provide services to Jasper schools and is developing a substance abuse program as well as an employee assistance program for some employers in Jasper. It also has contacted Physician Care Services, Inc., to explore a partnership to provide occupational health services.

2. *Royman Oaks, LLC.* Located in Statesville, the practice is staffed by two master's-level clinical social workers and four occupational therapists. It focuses on employment counseling and job-placement assistance.

3. *Grosvenor Arms.* Located in Jasper, this seven-bed adult group home is staffed by three residential counselors, one part-time clinical psychologist, one master's-level clinical social worker, and an MFT.

4. *Greenwood Group.* Located east of Jasper, the group is staffed by a psychiatrist with admitting privileges at MIDCARE, a psychiatrist with admitting privileges at Capital City General Hospital, two PhD clinical psychologists, one master's-level clinical social worker, one MFT, four substance abuse counselors, and several health-and-wellness personnel. The practice has been successful in penetrating the commercially insured substance abuse market and has a reputation for providing high-quality care in its "upscale" office.

FINANCE

Medicaid is the major payer at MCMHC. As shown in table 4.3, Medicaid accounts for approximately 75 percent of net client service revenue. This percentage has increased during the pandemic. Commercial insurance, such as Blue Cross/Blue Shield, is the second largest source of client service revenue, but this percentage has decreased slightly over the same time period. Table 4.4 displays the organization's published charges for the most common services. At MCMHC, charges for services are set on a sliding schedule, according to income. The minimum fee is charged for clients who are at or under the federal poverty level.

Internal Revenue Service Form 990 requires that salaries be released for the key employees of the organization. These are the key employees at MCMHC:

Name	Position	Current Salary ($)
Seymour Usher, MD	Psychiatrist	174,000
Birgitta Stanislavska, MD	Psychiatrist	160,000
Stephanie Jervis-Washburn	Executive Director	124,286
Ivan Stanzl, MD	Medical Director	122,250
Shanique Harrison, PhD	Senior Director	90,000
Jorge Ramirez, PhD	Clinical Psychologist	88,000
Elizabeth Gretsch, PhD	Clinical Psychologist	85,000
Simone Beauchamp, RN	Director, Clinical Services	82,500
Sophie Juarez, PMHNP-BC	Nurse Practitioner	82,000
Clement Gray	Director, Administrative Services	80,000
Grace Walker, ACNP-BC	Nurse Practitioner	80,000
Scott Burford	Director, Information Technology	70,000

Tables 4.5 and 4.6 are MCMHC's balance sheet and statement of revenues and expenses, respectively.

MARKETING

Table 4.7 displays the client volume by service for the past four years; the data reflect unduplicated client counts. Table 4.8 shows the results of a special study of the most frequently ordered services by program; psychotherapy takes that designation across all programs. As shown in table 4.9, the largest share of the organization's clients in all service areas comes from Middleboro; this is not surprising, given that MCMHC began and is still headquartered in the city. Jervis-Washburn has given Gray the task of drafting a strategic and marketing plan to enhance the organization's profile outside of Middleboro.

To date, the organization has never had a marketing program. It believed for a long time that its excellent reputation and long-standing history in the area would be enough to attract a solid client base. In addition, the board tended to favor good services over market share and profitability. Within the past five years, however, competitors have entered the area, bringing along with them aggressive marketing campaigns that target local employers and what Gray has called "the high-paying client who needs substance abuse help."

In addition to increasing penetration in existing markets, the board and management team are making plans to identify needs or demands that could catalyze new programs and services that will showcase the staff's strengths and expertise. As Jervis-Washburn put it, "We have done well through the years doing what we do, but potential programs, services, and clients are waiting for us to discover them. It is incumbent on us to find them and move forward on a select few."

Table 4.1
MCMHC
Behavioral
Health
Barometer,
Hillsboro
County

Factor	Hillsboro County (%)	United States* (%)
Marijuana Use for Year, Aged 12+ Years	16.4	15
Nonmedical Use of Pain Reliever for Past Year: Aged 12–17		
Female	9.4	5.4
Male	7.3	4
Illicit Drug Use for Past year, Aged 12+ Years		
Cocaine	0.7	0.1
Heroin	1.9	0.3
Prescription Drugs	7.1	4.5
Major Depressive Episode for Past Year, Aged 12–17 Years—Total	**14.3**	**13.3**
Female	22.8	20
Male	7.9	6.8
Treatment for Major Depressive Episode for Past Year, Aged 12–17 Years	37.5	41.5
Serious Thoughts of Suicide for Past Year, Aged 18–25 Years	11.3	10.5
Serious Mental Illness (SMI) for Past Year, Aged 18+ Years	8.3	4.5
Mental Health Treatment/Counseling for Past Year, Among Aged 18+ Years With SMI	57.9	68.5
Alcohol Dependence or Abuse for Past Year, Aged 12+ Years	6.5	6.4
Illicit Drug Dependence or Abuse for Past Year, Aged 12+ Years	3.4	2.7
Heavy Alcohol Use for Past Month, Aged 21+ Years	6.7	6.6
Substance Abuse Treatment (Alcohol) for Past Year, Aged 12+ Years	3.2	4.2
Substance Abuse Treatment (Illicit Drugs) for Past Year, Aged 12+ Years	15.3	13

*Source: Substance Abuse and Mental Health Services Administration (SAMHSA). *Behavioral Health Barometer: United States, Volume 6: Indicators as Measured Through the 2019 National Survey on Drug Use and Health and the National Survey of Substance Abuse Treatment Services*. HHS Publication No. PEP20-07-02-001. Rockville, MD: SAMHSA, 2020.

Position	FTE	Payroll ($)
Administrative Services		
Executive Director	1.0	124,286
Medical Director	0.8	122,250
Senior Director	1.0	90,000
Director, Clinical Services	1.0	82,500
Executive Assistant	1.0	48,500
Director, Admin. Services	1.0	80,000
Sr. Administrative Assistant	1.0	38,000
Assistants		
HR Assistant	1.0	43,500
IT Manager	1.0	70,000
IT Assistant Manager	1.0	50,000
Records Assistant	1.0	28,000
Finance Manager	1.0	60,000
A/R Assistant	1.0	45,000
Accountant	1.0	45,000
A/R Staff Reps.	2.0	58,000
Insurance Rep.	1.0	29,500
Facility Manager	1.0	48,000
Maintenance Staff	2.0	54,000
Housekeeping Staff	4.0	92,000
Facility Psychologist	0.4	40,000
Residential Counselors	3.0	93,000
Facility Assistant	0.5	18,500
Facility Therapist	0.5	18,500
Housing Coordinator	1.0	41,000
Subtotal	**29.2**	**1,419,536**
Adult Services		
Team Leaders	4.0	194,500
Records Assistant	1.0	29,000
Psychiatrist	0.8	174,000
Health/Wellness Mentors	5.0	178,000
Intake/Admission Staff	3.0	93,500
Receptionists	2.0	46,000
Psychiatric Nurse	0.4	37,500
Outreach Therapists	23.0	850,000
Other Therapists	12.0	435,000
Program Assistants	4.0	130,000

Table 4.2
MCMHC Staffing Budget, Fiscal Year 2024

continued

Position	FTE	Payroll ($)
Administrative Assistants	2.0	47,000
Transcriptionists	2.0	52,000
Senior Social Worker	1.0	49,000
QI Associate	0.8	37,000
Nurse Practitioner	1.0	82,000
Psychologist	1.0	85,000
Total	**63.0**	**2,519,500**
Quality and Compliance Services		
QI Coordinator	1.0	43,000
QI Assistant	1.0	38,000
Subtotal	**2.0**	**81,000**
Education Services		
Administrative Assistant	1.0	27,500
Health Educators	2.0	86,000
Subtotal	**3.0**	**93,500**
Child and Family Services		
Team Leaders	3.0	145,000
Outreach Therapists	14.0	515,000
Psychiatrist	0.8	160,000
Spectrum Specialists	4.0	130,000
Intake/Admission Staff	2.0	59,500
Administrative Assistants	1.2	32,000
Assistants		
Program Assistants	2.5	75,000
Transcriptionists	1.5	39,000
Psychologist	0.5	58,000
Records Assistants	1.0	28,900
Receptionists	2.0	46,000
School Therapists	2.0	96,000
Other Therapists	10.0	367,000
QI Associate	0.8	37,000
Subtotal	**45.3**	**1,788,400**
Emergency Services		
Intake/Admission Staff	3.0	90,000
Emergency Technicians	5.0	254,000
Psychiatrist	0.1	18,000
Records Assistant	0.5	15,000
Psychologist	1.0	88,000

continued

Position	FTE	Payroll ($)
Administrative Assistant	1.0	25,000
Transcriptionist	1.0	25,000
Therapists	3.0	97,000
Nurse Practitioner	1.0	80,000
QI Associate	0.2	9,500
Subtotal	**15.8**	**$701,500**
Summary		
Administrative	29.2	1,419,536
Child and Family	45.3	1,788,400
Adult	63.0	2,519,500
Emergency	14.8	701,500
Education	3.0	93,500
Quality/Compliance	2.0	81,000
Total	**157.3**	**6,603,436**

Table 4.2
MCMHC Staffing Budget, Fiscal Year 2024 *(continued)*

Notes: (1) For fiscal year ending December 31. (2) Numbers are in US dollars. (3) This table includes salary only. An additional 19% should be added to account for fringe benefits. (4) A/R: accounts receivable; FTE: full-time equivalent; HR: human resources; IT: information technology; QI: quality improvement.

	Programs			
Payer	Adult (%)	Child/Family (%)	Emergency (%)	Total (%)
Self-Pay	5.7	3.5	3.1	3.7
Commercial Insurance	15.9	9.6	13.6	14.5
Medicaid	69.1	86.9	80.4	76.5
Medicare	9.3	0	2.9	5.3
Total	**100**	**100**	**100**	**100**

Table 4.3
MCMHC Payer Mix and Percentage of Client Service Revenue by Program, Fiscal Year 2024

Table 4.4
MCMHC
Published
Charges for
Most Common
Services, 2024

Service	CPT Code	Rate ($)	Minimum Fee ($)
Intake/Diagnostic Evaluation	90781	185	10
Individual Psychotherapy	90834	125	8
Group Therapy	90853	50	3
Marriage/Family Therapy	90846	145	10
Emergency Treatment/Visit	Variable	400	20
Psychological Testing	Variable	110	8
PhD Psychologist Consultation	Hourly	250	15
Master's-Level Consultation	Hourly	150	12
Other Therapy	Variable	75	7
Educational Program	Variable	400	N/A
Nursing Services	Variable	150	12
Injection Administration	96372	25	5
Psychiatric Services			
New Patient—Level 1	99201	65	10
New Patient—Level 2	99202	80	12
New Patient—Level 3	99203	107	13
New Patient—Level 4	99204	205	14
New Patient—Level 5	99205	297	15
Established Patient—Level 1	99211	48	6
Established Patient—Level 2	99212	65	9
Established Patient—Level 3	99213	95	10
Established Patient—Level 4	99214	155	11
Established Patient—Level 5	99215	225	12

Notes: (1) A full fee is charged for clients at 200% of federal poverty level and above. Income verification is required before treatment (other than emergency).

(2) CPT: current procedural terminology; N/A: not applicable.

	2024	2023	2022	2019	2014
Assets					
Current Assets					
Cash	613,995	623,911	396,970	1,165,488	748,151
A/R Client Services	1,302,989	1,190,289	1,538,511	1,634,938	1,493,082
Less Allowances	−654,090	−601,289	−736,584	−763,088	−774,209
Net A/R Client Services	648,899	589,000	801,927	871,850	718,873
Other A/R	18,509	21,345	36,893	50,909	39,204
Inventory	13,209	13,409	15,903	13,084	15,689
Prepaid Accounts	70,209	67,809	79,888	43,892	56,356
Total Current Assets	1,364,821	1,315,474	1,331,581	2,145,223	1,578,273
Other Assets, Limited Use					
Restricted Building Fund	5,265,209	5,249,709	5,182,698	3,998,920	2,953,183
Halloway Fund	400,000	400,000	400,000	400,000	400,000
Total Other Assets	5,665,209	5,649,709	5,582,698	4,398,920	3,353,183
Property, Plant, and Equipment (PP&E)					
Furniture/Equipment	1,339,039	1,341,209	1,587,354	1,197,923	1,134,913
Computer Leasehold	450,000	450,000	450,000	400,000	400,000
Subtotal PP&E	1,789,039	1,791,209	2,037,354	1,597,923	1,534,913
Less Accum. Depreciation	−937,086	−888,058	−829,849	−746,849	−641,849
Total	851,953	903,151	1,207,505	851,074	893,064
Total Assets	**7,881,983**	**7,868,334**	**8,121,784**	**7,395,217**	**5,824,520**
Liabilities					
Current Liabilities					
Accounts Payable	150,309	145,609	150,258	146,903	69,384
Notes Payable	151,390	153,498	154,900	108,690	98,045
Accrued Benefits/Taxes	214,509	219,409	218,504	194,856	235,943
Contracts and Grant Payable	45,209	47,309	46,390	47,930	53,892
Other Accrued Expenses	258,309	254,590	294,830	248,594	210,392
Total Current Liabilities	819,726	820,415	864,882	746,973	667,656
Long-Term Debt	0	0	275,004	302,982	352,483
Total Liabilities	819,726	820,415	1,139,886	1,049,955	1,020,139
Net Assets					
Fund Balance—Unrestricted	1,328,948	1,355,421	1,289,200	1,946,342	1,451,198
Restricted Fund—Halloway	400,000	400,000	400,000	400,000	400,000
Restricted Building Fund	5,333,309	5,292,498	5,292,698	3,998,920	2,953,183
Total Net Assets	7,062,257	7,047,919	6,981,898	6,345,262	4,804,381
Net Assets + Total Liabilities	**7,881,983**	**7,868,334**	**8,121,784**	**7,395,217**	**5,824,520**

Table 4.5
MCMHC Balance Sheet as of December 31, 20XX

Note: (1) Numbers are in US dollars; (2) A/R = accounts receivable.

Table 4.6
MCMHC
Statement
of Revenues
and Expenses
for Fiscal
Year Ending
December 31,
20XX

	2024	2023	2022	2019	2014
Revenues					
Fees Billed	16,892,029	16,580,390	15,356,832	13,584,209	12,409,309
Less Adjustments	−6,883,961	−6,756,960	−5,221,323	−4,457,856	−3,970,979
Net Fees Billed	10,008,068	9,823,430	10,135,509	9,126,353	8,438,330
Grant 1	26,409	29,309	53,509	104,309	84,309
Grant 2	45,000	45,000	45,000	40,629	40,390
State Public Health	50,000	45,000	42,039	48,309	54,309
Towns/County	128,209	124,208	98,209	135,209	130,309
Federal Pandemic Funds	84,305	67,309	35,039	0	0
United Way	0	2,500	5,000	0	0
MIDCARE	21,409	25,209	38,509	41,489	45,980
Webster Hospital	6,927	6,353	6,309	4,309	5,609
Donations and Other	379,029	401,409	450,309	678,743	709,583
Total	**10,749,356**	**10,569,727**	**10,909,432**	**10,179,350**	**9,508,819**
Expenses					
Salaries/Wages	7,038,209	6,828,509	6,683,309	6,142,320	5,927,339
Benefits and Payroll Taxes	1,478,005	1,345,701	1,298,867	1,167,041	1,126,194
Rental	8,000	10,500	12,500	15,000	12,000
Insurance	150,000	145,000	142,000	150,000	145,000
Depreciation	49,028	58,209	64,000	83,000	105,000
Other	2,023,289	2,190,287	2,568,309	2,438,209	2,089,035
Total	**10,746,531**	**10,578,206**	**10,768,985**	**9,995,570**	**9,404,568**
Excess (Deficit) of Revenues over Expenses (Total)	**2,825**	**(8,479)**	**140,447**	**183,780**	**104,251**

Note: Numbers are in US dollars.

Program	2024	2023	2022	2019	2014	
Adult Services	4,389 *46%*	4,093 *45%*	3,927 *49%*	3,769 *53%*	3,734 *53%*	*17.5% ↑*
Child and Family Services	2,134 *22%*	1,979 *22%*	1,736 *21%*	1,490 *21%*	1,501 *21%*	*42% ↑ 2014 → 2024*
Crisis Calls	2,983 *31%*	2,876 *32%*	2,306 *29%*	1,847 *26%*	1,739 *25%*	*71% ↑*
	9506	*8948*	*7969*	*7106*	*6974*	

Table 4.7
MCMHC Clients by Program

Program	Percentage of Total Billed Hours
Adult Services	
Psychotherapy (Individual)	41.5
Family Support Services	26.5
Group Therapy	5.3
Psychiatric Evaluation/Management	7.8
Intake/Evaluation—Psychotherapy	9.9
Psychoeducation	1.8
Child and Family Services	
Psychotherapy (Individual)	55.5
Family Support Services	7.1
Intake/Evaluation—Psychotherapy	10.3
Family Therapy	18.1
Psychiatric Evaluation/Management	3.5
Psychological Testing	2.5
Emergency Services	
Crisis Psychotherapy	77.9
Emergency Services (Nonspecified)	7.1
Other	15.0

Table 4.8
MCMHC Special Study of Most Common Services by Program, 2024

Table 4.9
Percentage
of MCMHC
Program Clients
by Residence,
2024

Town/City	Child and Family (%)	Adult (%)	Emergency (%)	Total
From Hillsboro County				
Middleboro	40	40	64	46
Jasper	16	23	13	21
Harris City	15	9	5	8
Statesville	8	8	5	8
Mifflenville	8	7	4	6
Carterville	3	5	4	4
Minortown	1	2	1	1
Boalsburg	2	1	1	1
Others in Hillsboro County	3	2	1	2
Out of Hillsboro County	4	3	2	3
Total	**100**	**100**	**100**	**100**

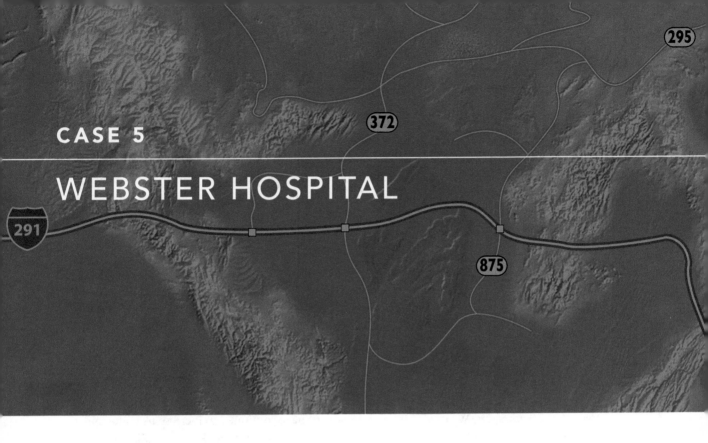

CASE 5

WEBSTER HOSPITAL

Webster Hospital, a 501(c)(3) corporation, is a fully accredited tax-exempt hospital located in Middleboro adjacent to the interstate highway. The hospital is accredited by The Joint Commission (TJC). Until 2020, it was an affiliate member of Capital City–based Osteopathic Hospitals of America, Inc. Webster is licensed to operate 115 inpatient beds. Since the pandemic began, it has reduced its inpatient capacity to 70 operational beds. It continues to meet all the conditions necessary for Medicaid, Medicare, and Blue Cross insurance coverage.

HISTORY

The original 1930s hospital was a three-floor brick structure built to accommodate 45 inpatient beds. Surrounding the facility were houses purchased by the hospital. Over the years, the building has undergone expansions and renovations. For example, in 1989, the space was reconfigured to increase the number of inpatient beds to 115, an addition that was later cut back to its current size. The most recent modernization program was completed seven years ago. It installed modern features that make the hospital more attractive and rearranged spaces to make operations and care delivery more efficient. It also expanded the maternity unit so that, when possible, all maternity services—including labor and delivery—are contained in the mother's private room. It also increased the number of private rooms. The homes next to the facility have been converted into offices for the members of the medical staff. All of the other land on the hospital campus remains undeveloped. The hospital and adjacent offices, each of which complies with current building standards and codes, sit on a 16-acre campus located in southeastern Middleboro next to the interstate highway. The campus is approximately four miles east of MIDCARE hospital.

Founded in 1930 by Dr. Edward W. Webster as a short-term, general acute care nonprofit organization, the hospital had very close ties with Osteopathic Medical Center (OMC) in Capital City even before Osteopathic Hospitals of America (OHA) was established. Dr. Webster was a senior osteopathic physician at OMC, and in 1929, upon arriving in Middleboro, he began a community campaign to found a hospital that would serve as an alternative to Middleboro Community Hospital. He was the first superintendent of Webster Hospital and was successful in establishing osteopathic medicine in Hillsboro County. The Webster Family Trust still financially supports Webster Hospital. In the past 20 years, Dr. Webster's sons and grandsons have continued to increase its endowment.

Since 1930, the hospital's relationship with MIDCARE—then called Middleboro Community Hospital—has been strained. Here are some examples:

◆   In 1996, Webster Hospital and Middleboro Community Hospital dissolved their more than 30-year joint venture corporation for shared laundry services. Middleboro Community Hospital elected a provision in the original 1965 agreement to buy Webster Hospital's share of the joint venture, even though Webster Hospital wished to retain the partnership. At the time of the forced sale, Middleboro Community Hospital indicated that its need for laundry services could only be met if it fully owned the laundry corporation. Middleboro Community Hospital did offer to provide laundry services to Webster Hospital on an annual contract, but Webster Hospital determined that establishing its own laundry service would be more efficient.

◆   In 1998, Webster Hospital terminated a joint education agreement with Middleboro Community Hospital. Under this agreement, staff members of both hospitals received continuing education at both institutions.

◆   In 1999, a formal joint committee of the boards of each hospital explored the possibility of a merger of the two organizations. Although supported by both CEOs, the merger was deemed not feasible by the committee. Since that time, the two entities have had minimal contact and have been increasingly competitive with each other.

◆ In 2000, when Webster Hospital signed the affiliation agreement with OHA and became Webster Health System (WHS), the president and board chair of Middleboro Community Hospital published an open letter in the *Middleboro Sentinel*. The letter indicated disappointment that a community hospital in Middleboro was now going to be "directed by a medical center based outside of the community" in Capital City. The letter went on to say, "We wish it had been obvious to us that Webster Hospital needed help to continue its operations. We would have assisted with providing quality care at a reasonable price for our community, as we do now."

Today, the sole remaining agreement between the two hospitals is compelled by state regulation. Under this agreement, Webster hospital patients and others under the care of an osteopathic physician may use MIDCARE for ambulatory cancer treatment. This provision was required by the state when it issued to MIDCARE the certificate of need for this service.

OSTEOPATHIC HOSPITALS OF AMERICA (OHA): 1990–2021

Established in 1990, OHA was developed to provide corporate direction and control for community osteopathic hospitals in the tristate region and foster osteopathic medicine. It was a nonprofit corporation with a regional network composed of 18 affiliated nonprofit osteopathic community hospitals. Affiliated hospitals paid Osteopathic Medical Center (OMC) a percentage of their patient revenue for specific services, including the following:

◆ *Medical credentialing.* All physicians holding active or consulting medical staff privileges at an affiliated hospital, including OMC, were granted, based on OHA review, similar privileges at all affiliated hospitals in the network.

◆ *Electronic medical record (EMR) system.* All affiliate hospitals participated in a common EMR.

◆ *Supply chain management.* Affiliates purchased all supply items (medical and nonmedical) and durable medical equipment through OHA.

◆ *Revenue and expense budget assistance.* Affiliated hospitals were required to submit their draft revenue and expense budget for the next fiscal year to OHA and bring to the hospital's board OHA's comments on the budget.

◆ First option to buy. An affiliated hospital was required to give OHA the first option for purchase if the hospital decided to change its ownership status.

◆ *OHA Tele-Med Services.* These services provided a high-speed voice and video communications link between attending physicians at an affiliated hospital and physicians at OMC.

◆ *Special services.* Under the affiliation agreement, a hospital could lease from OHA a CEO at cost; use OHA service-marked services, such as Quick Med; and book OMC Air Evac transportation at reduced cost.

◆ *OHA seminars* for board education, employee education, and continuing medical education

◆ *Technical assistance* related to the development of the hospital's strategic plan and quality assurance system.

◆ *Access to capital* for capital projects approved by OHA at the prime rate plus 0.2 percent.

◆ *Regional and community-specific advertising of the OHA brand.*

◆ *Other services* related to electronic health records, financial management, human resources administration, health benefit surveys, new service development, retirement planning, risk-management programs, outplacement and recruiting, meaningful use advisory, and data warehousing.

OHA ceased operation in 2021. Before its demise, 62 percent of all osteopathic hospitals in the tristate area were affiliated with OHA.

OHA VENTURES (RECENTLY CAPITAL CITY HEALTH CARE, INC.)

OHA Ventures was a for-profit corporation headed by Leroy Paige and specializing in managing medical groups. It also owned and operated medical office buildings. Seven years ago, OHA Ventures introduced a joint purchase and management program that enabled an OHA-affiliated hospital to co-purchase and co-manage individual medical practices with OHA Ventures. No physician practice affiliated with Webster Hospital elected to use OHA Ventures as a practice manager.

In the same period as the launch of the joint program, OHA Ventures independently began purchasing orthopedic, family practice, and cardiology practices of physicians affiliated with OHA-affiliated hospitals. As a result, all these physicians became employees of OHA Ventures and were granted consulting status at OMC. Capital City Health Care, Inc., acquired OHA Ventures in 2021 and manages 24 medical practices. In Hillsboro County, it manages three practices.

Osteopathic Medical Center (OMC)

Located in Capital City, OMC was a nonprofit, 210-bed medical center that provided a full range of acute and tertiary care services. It was a Level I trauma center as well as a designated teaching hospital that offered approved residencies in most medical specialties. Medical interns and residents visited Webster Hospital regularly as part of their community medicine training. Eight years ago, in collaboration with State University, OMC launched degree programs for physician assistants and advanced nurse practitioners, with numerous specialties for the latter.

OMC was sold to Valley Medical Center, Inc. (VMC) 15 months ago. At the time of sale, OMC was involved in Chapter 7 bankruptcy proceedings and secured the approval of the court for the sale of its assets and the disbursement of its proceeds. VMC is part of a national chain of investor-owned hospitals. One of VMC's first actions was to eliminate OMC's teaching missions and concentrate on patient care services. Based on the direction of the bankruptcy court, OMC was also required to recall all financial loans it had issued to OHA-affiliated hospitals and cease providing OHA with any services. OMC cancelled all contracts with OHA and billed OHA and affiliated hospitals for any services provided for 24 months prior to its declaration of its bankruptcy. OMC's bankruptcy led to the total collapse of the OHA network of affiliated osteopathic hospitals. Causes of OMC's bankruptcy include the impact of the recent pandemic as well as the debt structure OMC used to finance the development and operation of the OHA-affiliated hospitals.

Governance

Webster Hospital's board of trustees is composed of eight individuals. The hospital's 100 incorporators elect trustees on the basis of nominations by the board's nominating committee. Trustees are elected for four-year terms, with the stipulation that they may serve no longer than two consecutive terms. Current board trustees are as follows; the (number)* indicates the number of years remaining on the current board term, and the (number)+ indicates the trustee's second term:

Webster Hospital Board of Trustees

Daniel Will (2)* +, *Chair*

   Attorney, Will & Associates. Resident of Middleboro.

Harlan Crowe (3), *Vice Chair*

   President, Farmers and Merchants Bank. Resident of Mifflenville.

Yolanda Nice (4), *Secretary*

   Director of Human Resources, U.S. Parts. Resident of Jasper.

Belinda Bond (1)+, *Treasurer*

Retired stockbroker. Resident of Boalsburg.

Thomas Patrick (4), *At-Large*

Executive Manager, Big Box, Inc. Resident of Middleboro.

Juanita Melendez (2), *At-Large*

Vice president of Finance, River Industries. Resident of Middleboro.

Samuel Mudd, DO (3), *At-Large*

Retired physician. Resident of Middleboro.

Mike Webster (1), *At-Large*

Proprietor, Webster Family Farm. Resident of Statesville.

The standing committees of the board are as follows:

◆ Executive (Will, Crowe, Nice, Bond)

◆ Finance (Crowe, Bond, Patrick)

◆ Joint Conference (Will, Dr. Taff, Swisher)

◆ Long-Range Planning (All Trustees)

◆ Medical Manpower/Credentials (Dr. Mudd, Melendez, Webster)

◆ Nominating (Nice, Crowe, Patrick)

◆ Quality Assurance (Melendez, Will, Dr. Mudd)

The board meets monthly, the executive committee meets twice a month, and other committees meet as needed (usually monthly). Every December, the board—along with the hospital auxiliary—sponsors a hospital fundraising event called Holiday Ball at the Middleboro Golf Club.

MANAGEMENT TEAM AND ORGANIZATIONAL STRUCTURE

PRESIDENT AND CEO

Steve Swisher, CPA, was promoted to president and CEO in 2021. Prior to this appointment, he was vice president of Administrative Services and chief financial officer (CFO) at Webster Hospital for 14 years. He holds a bachelor's degree in accounting and a master of business administration from a midwestern university and is a member of the Healthcare Financial Management Association. Before coming to Webster Hospital, he was a senior fiscal analyst at Blue Cross and Blue Shield in Capital City.

The position of president and CEO became vacant when the well-loved and respected Edith Masterman retired from the job. Initially, the hospital used a national executive search firm to identify qualified candidates. The first search yielded no candidates acceptable to the board, but the second search resulted in the hiring of Stella MacArthur. Twelve months later, however, she reached a mutual agreement with the board and resigned from the post. The board offered no reason for her immediate departure. After another lengthy search, Swisher was appointed president.

When interviewed, Swisher noted the OMC bankruptcy and the demise of OHA as very significant and negative impacts on Webster Hospital. He also indicated that OHA's collapse caught everyone by surprise. Over many years, Webster Hospital had developed a strong reliance on OHA. Swisher explained, "In a 12-month period we had to adjust, including refinancing a great deal of our long-term debt and contracts involving our supply chain, information systems, and telehealth. Existing costs from OHA were much higher than we expected, and we are experiencing fiscal and operational issues due to the demise of OHA and OMC. Several of our physicians left the area, retired, or have been granted medical staff privileges at MIDCARE. Many of our affiliated physicians also had to develop new relationships with Capital City General Hospital in Capital City. Employee turnover, especially in nursing, continues to be an issue."

He reported long-standing board concerns regarding changing market dynamics, especially in Jasper; the need to recruit new physicians for Webster's primary markets; the potential addition of specialized services; the system's financial challenges; and the development of a regional accountable care organization. In reflecting on the impact of the pandemic, Swisher stated that Webster, "like so many other hospitals, initially faced this challenge almost totally unprepared. We lacked sufficient medical supplies, ICU [intensive care unit] beds, and ventilators. It took us longer than it should have to be able to meet the new needs and respond to the downturn in inpatient and outpatient utilization. We are still recovering. Our most significant 'change' traceable to the pandemic and demise of OHA and OMC is the number of our affiliated physicians who retired, left the area, and/or now have medical staff privileges at MIDCARE. To address gaps, we have begun recruiting new allopathic as well as osteopathic physicians to address our needs." He also added that given Webster's personnel reductions, operating fewer inpatient beds seems sufficient to meet current demands.

VICE PRESIDENT OF ADMINISTRATIVE SERVICES AND CFO

June Taylor, CPA, replaced Swisher in this position. She was promoted from the position of deputy chief fiscal officer, where she had been for ten years. She holds a bachelor's degree in accounting and a master of business administration from State University and is a member of the Healthcare Financial Management Association. As Swisher's direct report, she has extensive responsibilities, including overseeing the following departments: Admitting, Business Office, Central Supply, Housekeeping, Laundry, Maintenance, Medical Records, Personnel, Purchasing, Security, and Telecommunications. In addition, Taylor is in charge of a laundry service contract between Webster Hospital and the Hillsboro County Health Department. Several years ago, when Webster began searching for clients to use its excess laundry capacity (caused by the decrease in inpatient days), Taylor developed a contractual program that provides laundry services to Manorhaven, the long-term care facility owned and operated by Hillsboro County Health Department. She indicated that this contract, aside from being good business, helps the hospital's laundry service maintain an efficient operation with its current level of staffing.

Another one of her many duties is as chief personnel officer, which has become "an almost full-time job." She said, "Our staff have had recruiting challenges because there seems to be a lack of qualified and acceptable professionals in our area. We're working hard to attract them." Although Taylor remains optimistic about the future, she has concerns. She also indicated that "the hospital's inpatient capacity has gotten about as small as it should. Too much smaller, and it will become less efficient." As a result, she advocates a competitive strategy to recapture ambulatory and inpatient market share historically served by MIDCARE. Taylor explains, "With the demise of OHA, we lost our consulting contract for development and maintenance of our information systems. Nine years ago, based on this contract, we installed an electronic health record system. Whether we need to develop in-house expertise to fill this void is a question that management needs to address in the near future."

When asked to comment on the hospital's financial future, Taylor indicated that she and her staff continue to review all fixed costs and work with all departments to ensure adequate, but not excessive, staffing. "Over the last four years," she noted, "many dedicated and talented employees and physicians have left the area or retired. We have recruited replacements to meet anticipated demands, although we have not always been successful. I believe we are adequately positioned to recover from both the impact of the pandemic and the demise of OHA and OMC."

VICE PRESIDENT OF PROFESSIONAL SERVICES

Ellen Wilgus has been employed by Webster Hospital for 15 years and was director of Physical Therapy right before her appointment as vice president. She holds a bachelor's degree in physical therapy from State University. She has served as president of the state chapter of the American Physical Therapy Association and remains active in professional organizations related to physical therapy and rehabilitation.

Wilgus reports to the president and has responsibility for the following departments: Anesthesiology, Dietary, Laboratory, Pharmacy, Physical Therapy, Radiology, Respiratory

Therapy, and Social Services. The ever-increasing complexity of hospital management and the greater competition from MIDCARE are among her top concerns; she thinks Webster Hospital faces an uncertain future, especially given the demise of OHA and OMC. She indicated feeling supported by her hardworking department heads and especially proud that the most recent accreditation review found no significant deficiencies in any of the departments she oversees.

Years ago, Wilgus headed the management task force that implemented the maternity unit redesign and expansion. For her exemplary performance on the task force, she earned an official commendation from the medical staff as well as a special recognition from the board and the former president. Currently, she leads the continuous quality improvement team's effort to shorten the length of inpatient hospital stays per diagnosis-related group. After 20 years of service, she has informed senior management of her decision to retire in six months.

VICE PRESIDENT OF CLINICAL SERVICES

Greg Schmidt, RN, was hired nine years ago to replace a retiring vice president. Prior to coming to Webster Hospital, he held numerous nursing positions in military hospitals. He was born in Boalsburg and still has family in the area. He has a bachelor's and a master's in nursing from a public university in the southwest and is active in the state nursing association. Like the other vice presidents, Schmidt reports to the president and is in charge of multiple departments, including Clinical Education, Pediatrics, Intensive Care, Medical Surgical Unit I, Medical Surgical Unit II, Medical Surgical Unit III, Emergency and Outpatient Departments, and Staff Development. According to Schmidt, Webster has had to lower its nurse–patient ratio and delay achieving an all-RN (registered nurse) nursing staff, until "we clarify our mission and fiscal affairs." He also stated that the overall impact of the pandemic is still being felt at this hospital.

When interviewed, Schmidt was careful with his remarks about MIDCARE, stating, "I'm unsure about the real issues between MIDCARE and this hospital. I am very impressed, though, by the high clinical competence of the nursing staff here. Nurse turnover is not as big an issue here as it is at MIDCARE." He is equally complimentary of the professional relationship between physicians and nurses. He also said, "Although there is no formal joint practice program, most aspects of joint practice characterize the nurse–physician relationship at Webster Hospital."

VICE PRESIDENT OF MARKETING

David Story, who is from a prominent family in Middleboro, has been the marketing head at Webster Hospital for 24 years and, before that, was deputy director of marketing for a durable medical equipment firm in Capital City. He holds a liberal arts degree and a master of health administration from an eastern university and is a member of the American College of Healthcare Executives (ACHE). His noted accomplishments at Webster Hospital include recruiting a number of physicians, many of whom are still on the medical staff. He, along with Swisher, negotiated a long-term financial loan with OMC to finance many hospital projects. Currently, he is working with Schmidt and the medical staff to examine the feasibility of establishing a women's health center at Webster Hospital. His office conducts annual marketing and patient satisfaction studies and publishes the hospital's Community Benefit Statement. When asked to comment on the impact of recent physician losses and the increasing number of physicians having staff privileges at both Webster and MIDCARE, Schmidt replied, "I am confident that we are adjusting well to these and past dynamics!"

MANAGEMENT INTERN

This advisory staff position is currently held by Ms. Holly Perkins, who recently earned a master of business and hospital administration from an eastern university and is completing a 24-month postgraduate fellowship program recognized by ACHE. Under the terms of this fellowship, the hospital has made no long-term employment commitment to her. The daughter of an osteopathic physician, Perkins was a unit manager at a large medical center before entering graduate school. Currently, she provides staff support to the president as well as to several board and hospital committees and has been managing Webster Hospital's Employee of the Month/Year program. She is a member of ACHE.

INTERNAL REVENUE SERVICE FORM 990 DISCLOSURE

According to Webster Hospital's recent IRS Form 990, the following are the ten highest-paid hospital employees. Current salary is the total earnings reflected on the W-2 withholding form.

Staff Name	Position	Current Salary ($)
Steve Swisher	President/CEO	530,812
June Taylor	CFO	373,450
Gregg Schmidt, RN	VP, Clinical Services	257,261
Jay Jill, RN	Associate VP, Clinical Services	166,431
Carla Fox	Associate VP, Administration	146,420
Ellen Wilgus	VP, Professional Services	146,028

Heidi Watkins	Associate VP, Finance	105,230
David Story	VP, Marketing	104,220
David Crow	Laboratory Director	102,312
Marvin Gardens	Pharmacy Director	98,350

Total compensation also includes benefits, which are 36 percent above salary. The hospital does not directly employ any physicians in these specialties: emergency, radiology, pathology, and anesthesiology. These services are provided by contracted professional associations.

MEDICAL STAFF AND MEDICAL RESOURCES

Over the last five years, the Webster Hospital medical staff has experienced numerous resignations. Of the 28 physicians who resigned, 14 elected to remain in Hillsboro County, 6 retired, and the other 8 relocated outside the county and/or state. All indicated that the turmoil and uncertainty associated with the collapse of OHA was their deciding factor.

All currently affiliated physicians are board certified. See table 5.2 for a full list of Webster Hospital's medical staff. All consulting physicians are required to maintain active status on the medical staff at another accredited hospital. At Webster Hospital, the majority of the active medical staff provides primary care. Patients who need higher-level procedures, tests, and medical interventions are referred or transferred to another hospital. Webster Hospital also maintains a helicopter landing pad on its roof to allow the rapid transfer of emergency patients to Capital City Medical Center. Air travel time is approximately 26 minutes. When weather conditions do not permit air transfer, patients are moved in an ambulance to Capital City General or MIDCARE.

CLINICAL SERVICES CONTRACTS

Webster Hospital has a contractual relationship with the each of following Capital City–based provider groups or professional associations (PAs) for the following services.

- *Anesthesiology.* Capital City Anesthesiology Associates PA assigns four anesthesiologists and four nurse anesthetists as well as other staff as needed.

- *Emergency medicine.* Capital City Emergency and Occupational Health Associates PA assigns emergency physicians on a permanent basis along with other physicians as needed. Webster Hospital augments the emergency medicine staff with employed physician assistants.

- ◆ *Pathology.* Capital City Pathology Services PA assigns physicians who perform pathology services. As needed, additional pathologists are brought in or the procedure is done at Capital City General.

- ◆ *Radiology.* Capital City Radiology Services PA assigns radiologists and provides other clinical services. This group's main office and primary service locations are electronically linked so that its radiologists—wherever they may be working—can access Webster Hospital patient data, read and interpret scans and images, and dictate reports.

DEPARTMENT OF MEDICINE

This department comprises physicians in private practice whose specialties include general and family practice, internal medicine, pediatrics, cardiology, and ENT (ear, nose, throat). Dr. George Taff is the elected chair of the Department of Medicine.

DEPARTMENT OF SURGERY

This department comprises physicians in private practice whose specialties include general surgery, OB/GYN (obstetrics and gynecology), and orthopedic surgery. Dr. Doris Felix is the elected chair of the Department of Surgery.

SUBSIDIARY ORGANIZATIONS

Webster Affiliate, Inc.

This tax-paying physician hospital organization (PHO) engages in projects of mutual interest to both Webster Hospital and members of its medical staff who are in private practice. Webster Hospital owns 70 percent of the Webster Affiliate stock and thus appoints two of the PHO's three board members. Currently, Webster Affiliate owns a number of medical offices and leases the facilities to the physicians for a fee.

Webster Physicians, Inc.

Owned solely by Webster Hospital, Webster Physicians, Inc., is a tax-paying corporation that owns or operates medical practices for physicians affiliated with Webster Hospital. It has also been used to acquire the practice of a retiring physician and then sell the practice to a newly recruited replacement. In addition, it also provides contractual management services—such as information technology, maintenance, and billing—to other medical practices.

MEDICAL STAFF ORGANIZATION

Dr. George Taff (Department of Medicine) has been president of the medical staff for the past three years. The president is elected every two years and provided with a small stipend by Webster Hospital. Dr. Meagan Lincoln (Department of Pathology) is the vice president, and Dr. Charles Stein (Department of Surgery) is the secretary. The standing committees of the medical staff are utilization review and quality assurance, medical records, credentials, tissue, pharmacy and therapeutics, and executive. Composed of the chairs of each standing committee and each department, the medical staff's executive committee meets monthly or as needed. The other committees also meet monthly. The entire medical staff meets quarterly. At its annual meeting, the medical staff votes on recredentialing. In an interview with select members of the medical staff, Dr. Taff called the relationship among members of the medical staff "very professional" and noted that some of the older physicians seem uncomfortable with the speed of many of the changes the medical staff and the hospital have rolled out over the years. Asked about the relationship between Webster Hospital and the physicians, he stated, "Collaboratively, the hospital has assisted us with expanding our reach to young, well-trained primary care doctors. The demise of OHA and OMC, however, is very regrettable as it changed the relationship between our hospital and its affiliated physicians. This change, coupled with the impact of the pandemic, led to a number of physicians retiring, leaving the area, and/or developing medical staff privileges at MIDCARE. Our medical staff feels that it has faced and will continue to face many transitions and challenges." He also noted that "recent market dynamics also continue to destabilize our future."

Dr. Taff shared that being president of the medical staff feels like a full-time job and that without the stipend he would be unable to meet many of its expectations. Still, he is on board to help Webster Hospital achieve its priorities. "The hospital has to continue to rebuild its primary care network, even if this means building offices and directly hiring more doctors. That should be a priority," he said. "The immediate priority of the PHO should be medical practice management. The previous priority of installing an information system that supports both the clinical and administrative sides is now a reality. I'm very impressed with how the hospital implemented the EHR and ensured its meaningful use. We were a model within the OHA system. Medically, the hospital needs to establish a much stronger presence outside the greater Middleboro area."

Other physicians interviewed agreed with Dr. Taff. For example, Dr. Lasker, a member of the medical staff for 32 years, said, "Reducing inpatient beds after years of expansion felt strange but clearly was the right thing to do." He admitted that the relationship he has with many nurses really helps him practice high-quality, cost-effective medicine. "The ongoing studies for appropriate ways to shorten lengths of stay are one example of how this hospital has faced up to the challenges and responded appropriately," he said. Dr. Kelly, another longtime member of the medical staff, indicated that the hospital needs to continue to expand outpatient services and provide community outreach to high-risk individuals, especially in the rural area to the north of the city. According to her, the medical staff fully supports Webster Hospital's acquisition of select medical practices. "For those physicians, this model removes the burden of managing a practice and gives them direct access to the hospital's EHR," she explained.

Dr. Able, a new member, shared that she sees great possibilities with the PHO, strongly supports the recruitment of family practice physicians from Capital City (like herself), and appreciates the support Webster Hospital gives to those who want to start a thriving practice. "Although my practice is located in a rural area, I do not feel isolated because of all the support I get. I still have a good relationship with many of the faculty who trained me at medical school." She added, "A number of physicians indicated that the hospital was very supportive in helping them establish telehealth capabilities during the pandemic."

Dr. Pelopolis, a veteran at the hospital, was the only physician who offered any critical comments. He explained, "I am most concerned that some contracted physicians—such as Dr. Lincoln—hold leadership positions on our medical staff. Our medical staff has lost the ability to chart its own course. As our hospital's financial position improves, I have no doubt of its ability to attract new physicians and would recommend we recruit both allopathic and osteopathic physicians. I believe the era of an all-osteopathic medical staff is over, and like MIDCARE, we should solicit and grant medical staff privileges to allopathic physicians." He indicated that this perspective regarding medical staff membership at Webster Hospital is shared by several other Webster Hospital physicians, especially those who joined the medical staff in the last ten years.

Currently, Webster Hospital does not employ hospitalists. Dr. Taff said, "This may be one of the reasons some of our medical staff have secured admitting privileges at MIDCARE or left the area. Webster needs to move in this direction."

At a recent meeting, board chair Daniel Will stated that the recent article in the *Middleboro Sentinel* was relatively correct. Prior to the dissolution of the OHA network, OMC had requested that Webster Hospital provide OMC with a short-term bridge loan. When OMC subsequently filed for Chapter 11 bankruptcy protection, Webster was informed that the loan would eventually be repaid. However, when OMC changed its filing to a Chapter 7 bankruptcy, Webster Hospital lost all standing regarding this specific debt. "It was the decision of our board to write off the total loan in 2020," Will said.

"Obviously, our due diligence did not adequately present OMC's weakened fiscal condition. The board took total responsibility for this matter. We tried to help." At this same meeting, he also indicated that the board would receive "briefing papers" on the following issues. He asked all members to review these materials for the next meeting's discussion:

Additional information on Webster Hospital is provided in tables 5.1–5.8. Hospital performance based on Centers for Medicare & Medicaid Services (CMS) Core Measures is located in table A.5 in the appendixes.

Table 5.1
Webster
Hospital Facility
Codes

Adult Cardiology Services	Obstetrics
Adult Diagnostic Catheterization	Occupational Health Services
Airborne-Infection Isolation Room	Oncology Services
Auxiliary Organization	Optical Colonoscopy
Birthing Room–LDR Room–LDRP Room	Orthopedic Services
Cardiac Intensive Care	Outpatient Surgery
Cardiac Rehabilitation	Pain Management Program
Case Management	Patient Education Center
Chemotherapy	Patient Representative Services
Children's Wellness Program	Pediatric Diagnostic Catheterization
Community Health Education	Pediatric Intensive Care Services
Community Outreach	Physical Rehabilitation Outpatient Services
Emergency Department	Positron Emissions Tomography/CT
Endoscopic Intrasound	Primary Care Department
Endoscopic Retrograde	Psychiatric Care
Enrollment Assistance Services	Psychiatric Outpatient Services
Health Fair	Single Photon Emission CT (SPECT)
Health Screening	Sleep Center
Hospital-Based Outpatient Care Center Services	Social Work Services
	Support Groups
Inpatient Palliative Care Unit	Tobacco Treatment/Cessation Program
Linguistic/Translation Services	Trauma Center Certified
Magnetic Resonance Imaging (MRI)	Ultrasound
Medical-Surgical Intensive Care Services	Volunteer Services Department
Multislice Spiral CT (64 + Slice CT)	Women's Health Center/Services
Nutritional Programs	

Notes: (1) Facility codes as reported to and defined by the American Hospital Association. (2) CT: computed tomography; LDR: labor-delivery-recovery; LDRP: labor-delivery-recovery-postpartum.

Name	Off	Age	Specialty	Patient Days	Discharges
Department of Medicine, Active Staff					
Able	1	39	Family Practice	604	115
Adelson	1	51	Family Practice	601	120
Dows	1	54	Family Practice	578	121
Dawes	1	44	Family Practice	590	120
Standish	1	49	Family Practice	593	119
Newton	1	44	Family Practice	456	86
Best	1	35	Family Practice	340	54
Devishson	2	31	Family Practice	186	43
Doogle	2	36	Family Practice	397	88
Baker	2	38	Family Practice	200	44
Evans	2	39	Family Practice	197	45
Charles	2	29	Family Practice	187	40
Child	3	49	Family Practice	184	35
Kidd	3	47	Family Practice	256	61
Pelopolis	4	43	Family Practice	363	75
Easter	4	58	Family Practice	375	80
Kelly	5	51	Family Practice	28	6
Hamilton	6	60	Family Practice	165	34
Lasker	7	57	Family Practice	129	25
Masterson	8	59	Family Practice	102	18
Morgan	1	35	Internal Medicine	625	121
Lieu	1	54	Internal Medicine	498	86
White	1	34	Pediatrics	177	49
Vicenezio	1	35	Pediatrics	96	24
Hogan	1	50	ENT	165	31
Taff	1	40	ENT	156	29
Department of Surgery, Active Staff					
Sawyer	1		General	659	155
Colon	1		General	621	142
Team	1		General	241	53
Stem	1		General	426	85

Table 5.2
Webster Hospital Current Medical Staff as of December 31, 2024

continued

Table 5.2
Webster
Hospital Current
Medical Staff as
of December 31,
2024
(continued)

Name	Off	Age	Specialty	Patient Days	Discharges
Huan	1		Orthopedic	560	105
Dolittle	1		Orthopedic	562	124
Hernandez	1		Orthopedic	426	91
Felix	1		Oncology	303	70
Shaw	1		OB/GYN	315	70
Kirby	1		OB/GYN	44	10
Munsen	1		OB/GYN	325	79
Kim	1		OB/GYN	336	74
Munson	1		OB/GYN	341	90
Lewis	1		OB/GYN	408	101
Department of Medicine, Consulting Staff					
Lady	2	40	Family Practice	278	62
Dudoveci	1	50	Family Practice	287	50
Winslow	1	62	Endocrinology	129	24
Isaacson	9	50	Cardiology	293	41
Chokie	9	43	Rheumatology	134	42
Johnson	9	47	Cardiology	206	32
Gregson	9	54	Internal Medicine	175	32
Werner	9	53	Pulmonary Medicine	123	21
Department of Surgery, Consulting Staff					
Miller	3		General	45	7
McKinley	3		General	38	5
Merrill	9		General	48	8
Pierce	9		General	62	10
Skierski	8		Orthopedic	120	18
Nguyen	9		Orthopedic	83	12
Fremont	9		Orthopedic	30	4
Fremont	9		Orthopedic	160	25
Davids	9		Orthopedic	75	10
Nioxon	9		Orthopedic	18	3

continued

Name	Off	Age	Specialty	Patient Days	Discharges
Grant	9		Orthopedic	32	4
McGovern	9		Thoracic	103	14
Gruen	10		Thoracic	140	20
Daves	10		General	106	20
Steimpf	10		General	124	18
Other Physicians				78	21
			Total	16,702	3,421
Pathology and Radiology, Active Staff					
Lincoln			Pathology		
Erickson			Radiology		
Holland			Radiology		
Jipped			Radiology		
Yip			Pathology		
Stern			Pathology		
Roassi			Pathology		
Pathology and Radiology, Consulting Staff					
Currie			Radiology		
Douglas			Radiology		
San Remo			Radiology		
Sanchez			Pathology		
Fillerantz			Pathology		
Gathews			Pathology		
Anesthesiology, Active Staff					
Villanneva			Anesthesiology		
Westerman			Anesthesiology		
Chamberlin			Anesthesiology		
Wilson			Anesthesiology		
Emergency Medicine, Active Staff					
Abelson			Emergency		
Ferreira			Emergency		
Schlossman			Emergency		

Table 5.2
Webster Hospital Current Medical Staff as of December 31, 2024 *(continued)*

continued

Name	Off	Age	Specialty	Patient Days	Discharges
Lyons			Emergency		
Calson			Emergency		
Hiller			Emergency		
Sams			Emergency		
Sanus			Emergency		
Bodensky			Emergency		
Emergency Medicine, Consulting Staff					
Majors			Emergency		
Sallowash			Emergency		
Ritco			Emergency		
Fisher			Emergency		

Notes:

Code	Location
1	Middleboro
2	Mifflenville
3	Jasper
4	Harris City
5	Statesville
6	Carterville
7	Boalsburg
8	Minortown
9	Capital City
10	Other

ENT: ear, nose, throat; OB/GYN: obstetrics/gynecology; OFF: location.

Hospital Service	2024	2023	2022	2021
Pediatrics				
Beds	2	2	2	3
Patient Days	403	285	230	312
Occupancy	55.21%	39.04%	31.51%	28.49%
Maternity				
Beds	8	8	10	10
Patient Days	2,144	1,735	1,430	1,520
Occupancy	73%	59%	39%	42%
Medical-Surgical I				
Beds	16	16	18	18
Patient Days	4,075	3,567	3,256	4,008
Occupancy	69.78%	61.08%	49.56%	61.00%
Medical-Surgical II				
Beds	16	20	22	22
Patient Days	3,725	3,342	3,023	5,003
Occupancy	63.78%	45.78%	37.65%	62.30%
Medical-Surgical III				
Beds	16	18	22	22
Patient Days	2,899	2,445	2,845	3,830
Occupancy	49.64%	37.21%	35.43%	47.70%
Intensive Care Unit				
Beds	12	12	11	10
Patient Days	3,456	3,646	3,546	2,867
Occupancy	78.90%	83.24%	88.32%	78.55%
Total Hospital				
Beds	**70**	**76**	**85**	**85**
Patient Days	**16,702**	**15,020**	**14,330**	**17,540**
Occupancy	**65.37%**	**54.15%**	**46.19%**	**56.54%**

Table 5.3
Webster
Hospital
Inpatient
Occupancy by
Service

Table 5.4
Webster
Hospital
Detailed
Utilization
Statistics

Month	Dis	Patient Days	IP Surgery	OP Surgery	Births	ED Visits	ED Admits	OP Visits
2024								
January	290	1,532	40	152	41	1,034	31	2,085
February	301	1,453	31	140	33	1,008	27	2,549
March	312	1,545	178	172	34	1,357	34	2,467
April	301	1,642	44	154	42	1,174	42	2,349
May	263	1,289	40	156	44	1,104	37	2,438
June	270	1,292	51	157	46	1,056	39	2,156
July	245	1,215	54	154	45	1,156	37	2,845
August	270	1,266	48	142	40	977	37	2,436
September	310	1,614	51	163	45	1,035	32	2,134
October	306	1,429	42	188	47	1,195	30	2,056
November	250	1,420	51	162	48	1,044	38	2,745
December	303	1,005	28	137	36	1,009	39	2,178
Total	**3,421**	**16,702**	**658**	**1,877**	**501**	**13,149**	**423**	**28,438**
2023								
January	288	1,256	48	143	32	1,094	31	2,241
February	280	1,167	46	142	30	956	26	2,078
March	300	1,401	52	147	38	1,102	34	2,033
April	290	1,267	48	159	38	1,097	30	2,672
May	276	1,223	47	156	40	1,090	28	2,534
June	295	1,283	51	148	30	1,145	31	2,549
July	289	1,248	50	151	25	1,014	34	2,937
August	302	1,240	53	161	40	1,003	30	2,654
September	289	1,263	55	156	36	1,002	27	2,854
October	345	1,276	57	151	31	1,108	31	2,634
November	387	1,231	59	158	37	1,184	33	2,703
December	279	1,165	48	172	39	1,127	31	2,766
Total	**3,620**	**15,020**	**614**	**1,844**	**416**	**12,922**	**366**	**30,655**

Notes: (1) Dis: discharges; ED: emergency department; IP: inpatient; OP: outpatient. (2) ED Visits are total ED visits. (3) ED Admits are ED visits that led to an inpatient admission. (4) OP Visits are outpatient visits that exclude ED visits.

Assets	2024	2023	2022
Current Assets			
Cash	10,548,737	8,846,082	5,823,616
Short-Term Investments	181,223	176,383	167,220
Accounts Receivable—Gross	22,867,078	23,574,991	25,991,012
Allowances for Uncollectibles	4,356,127	4,145,612	4,067,220
Accounts Receivable—Net	18,510,951	19,429,379	21,923,792
Due from Third-Party Payers	867,131	803,578	891,450
Inventories	2,433,410	2,678,912	2,936,412
Prepaid Expenses	87,353	93,220	82,560
Total Current Assets	**59,852,010**	**59,748,157**	**61,883,282**
Noncurrent Assets			
Property, Plant, and Equipment—Gross	102,445,383	102,334,929	102,868,431
Less Accumulated Depreciation	81,885,440	76,287,093	70,763,235
Property, Plant, and Equipment—Net	20,559,943	26,047,836	32,105,196
Other Investments	14,628,836	19,023,365	22,654,921
Total Assets	**95,040,789**	**104,819,358**	**116,643,399**
Liabilities			
Current Liabilities			
Accounts Payable	9,452,737	8,923,441	8,723,468
Accrued Salaries and Wages	655,129	672,367	692,345
Accrued Interest	93,294	91,535	90,220
Other Accrued Expenses	564,998	534,111	512,771
Due to Third-Party Vendors	923,447	748,239	8,204,657
Long-Term Debt Due Within One Year	7,353,282	8,002,171	8,230,772
Total Current Liabilities	19,042,887	18,971,864	26,454,233
Long-Term Debt	36,014,037	41,370,734	41,293,476
Total Liabilities	**55,056,924**	**60,342,598**	**67,747,709**
Net Assets			
Restricted	11,957,299	12,648,410	10,512,578
Unrestricted	31,604,359	28,562,788	38,383,112
Total Net Assets	39,983,865	44,476,760	48,895,690
Net Assets + Liabilities	**95,040,789**	**104,819,358**	**116,643,399**

Table 5.5
Webster Hospital Balance Sheet as of December 31

Notes: (1) For fiscal years ending December 31. (2) Numbers are in US dollars.

	2024	2023	2022
Revenues			
Patient Services Revenue			
Inpatient Net of Allowances and Uncollectibles	112,546,030	110,334,232	108,858,334
Outpatient Net of Allowances and Uncollectibles	40,233,469	40,223,121	46,343,112
Total	**152,779,499**	**150,557,353**	**155,201,446**
Expenses			
Salaries and Wages	70,363,229	69,353,220	68,546,223
Fringe Benefits	17,334,282	18,003,282	17,956,273
Supplies	49,364,003	47,242,993	46,453,124
Professional Fees	90,252	99,343	98,901
Interest	712,575	800,334	870,334
Depreciation	5,598,347	5,523,858	5,423,404
Amortization	1,003,267	1,324,303	1,534,220
Other	13,880,344	13,675,293	12,565,223
Total	**158,346,299**	**156,022,626**	**153,447,702**
Net Income from Operations	**−5,566,800**	**−5,465,273**	**1,753,744**
Other Revenues			
Unrestricted Gifts and Bequests	43,450	49,254	98,243
Income from Investments	893,202	854,202	834,229
Miscellaneous Non–Patient Services Revenue	138,253	142,887	154,383
Total	**1,074,905**	**1,046,343**	**1,086,855**
Profit or (Loss)	**−4,491,895**	**−4,418,930**	**2,840,599**

Notes: (1) Years ending December 31. (2) Numbers are in US dollars.

Diagnosis	2024	2023	2022	2021
Medical Back Problems	318	302	345	378
Chest Pain	298	287	301	325
Coronary Atherosclerosis	170	171	194	167
Normal Newborn*	144	165	254	303
Simple Pneumonia, Pleurisy	142	162	159	156
Vaginal Delivery, No Complication	124	131	201	256
Other Digestive System Disorders	110	103	96	89
Chest Pain	95	82	80	77
Major Joint Reattachment of Lower Extremity	81	75	73	67
Cholecystectomy	72	65	55	60
Cesarean Section	20	34	53	47
Total Top Ten Discharges (Excluding Births)	**1,574**	**1,577**	**1,811**	**1,925**
Total Hospital Discharges	**3,421**	**3,620**	**3,645**	**3,756**

Table 5.7
Webster Hospital Top Ten DRG Discharges

Note: *Counted as births, not discharges.

Table 5.8
Webster Hospital Patient Days by Type and by Payer

Type of PT Day	Total PT Days (%)	Medicare (%)	Medicaid (%)	BC HMO (%)	BC PPO (%)	BC Indem (%)	CS PPO (%)	Comm PPO (%)	Comm Indem (%)	VA + Mil (%)	Other (%)	Self-Pay (%)
Medical	24.5	11.3	3.9	0.0	2.0	1.9	0.5	0.0	2.2	1.4	0.2	1.1
Surgical												
Nonorthopedic	14.4	5.4	2.2	0.2	0.3	1.1	0.3	0.0	3.0	1.0	0.3	0.6
Orthopedic	8.0	2.3	1.1	0.2	0.1	1.3	0.0	0.0	1.1	1.3	0.1	0.5
Obstetric	19.9	0.0	2.7	1.1	6.7	0.0	0.8	0.0	4.2	0.1	0.5	3.8
Newborn	9.0	0.0	2.3	0.9	2.4	0.0	0.2	0.0	2.4	0.0	0.3	0.5
Other Pediatric	1.8	0.0	1.1	0.3	0.0	0.1	0.1	0.0	0.0	0.0	0.0	0.2
ICU/CCU	13.5	5.4	0.7	0.2	0.2	2.4	0.3	0.0	1.6	1.5	0.5	0.7
Psychological/ Psychiatric	5.5	2.0	0.2	0.0	0.0	0.0	0.0	0.0	0.0	1.3	0.0	2.0
Substance Abuse												
Detox	1.5	0.0	0.0	0.0	0.0	0.0	0.0	0.0	0.0	1.0	0.0	0.5
Rehab	1.9	0.5	0.0	0.0	0.0	0.3	0.0	0.0	0.2	0.4	0.0	0.5
Total	**100.0**	**26.9**	**14.2**	**2.9**	**11.7**	**7.1**	**2.2**	**0.0**	**14.7**	**8.0**	**1.9**	**10.4**

Note: BC: Blue Cross; Comm: Commercial; CS: Central States; HMO: health maintenance organization; ICU/CCU: intensive care unit/coronary care unit or cardiac ICU; Indem: indemnity; Mil: military; PPO: preferred provider organization; PT: patient; VA: Veterans Administration.

CASE 6

MIDCARE, INC.

Middleboro Medical Center (MIDCARE) was established on January 1, 2015, as "a health system designed to meet the needs of Hillsboro County." This 501(c)(3) nonprofit is composed of the hospital and Health Next, Inc. It is also an affiliate of Treeline Health System. The hospital provides diagnostic, outpatient, therapeutic, and emergency medical services and has its own regional cancer center.

MIDCARE—called Middleboro Community Hospital until 2014—is licensed by the state and approved to operate 240 acute care beds, of which 189 beds are currently staffed as the hospital maintains its significant commitment to ambulatory care. It accepts Medicaid patients, is approved for Blue Cross participation, and is certified for participation in the Medicare program. In addition, it is accredited by The Joint Commission (TJC), and its cancer center is accredited by the American College of Surgeons. Table 6.1 lists the hospital's current services, as reported to the American Hospital Association.

Health Next is a 501(c)(3) that MIDCARE launched in 2021. Its mission and vision statements prioritize improving community health and facilitating access to medical services using telehealth and telemedicine technologies. Recent efforts have been directed at helping MIDCARE-affiliated physicians use remote patient monitoring (RPM). MIDCARE envisions Health Next to be the primary way to coordinate the hospital's community-based services with the public health priorities established by the Hillsboro County Health Department. The importance of such institutions was especially apparent during the recent pandemic. Health Next's executive director is Ruth Martin, and its board comprises three current MIDCARE board members (Waters, Wilson, and Meadows) as well as two former board members (Grace Niebauer, a homemaker from Harris City, and Bret Crop, an agricultural business executive from Minortown). Each board member serves a five-year term and has no term limits, making the board self-perpetuating. MIDCARE provides all support services and office space to Health Next. In 2022, Health Next entered into a cooperative agreement with State University's Medical School to secure funds to evaluate the impact of telemedicine in rural areas, a particularly timely initiative during the pandemic. Health Next has recently learned that the R. W. Baxter Foundation has declared its recent grant application a finalist in a competition for a multiyear demonstration grant involving the northern rural communities in Hillsboro County.

MIDCARE joined Treeline Health System in 2015. Founded in 1992, Treeline is a cooperative system of 24 tax-exempt hospitals and regional medical centers located in the tri-state area. It has become one of the stronger regional systems in the United States. Shared services include group purchasing and inventory management, physician and nurse practitioner recruitment, long-term capital borrowing at prime rate plus 0.5 percent, a range of health insurance plans and re-insurance products, a state-of-the-art electronic medical record system, joint liability insurance coverage for physicians and hospitals, and a lease-holding company through which member hospitals can lease capital equipment.

Being a member of Treeline requires MIDCARE to pay annual dues for the services it selects and to appoint one member to the Treeline governing board. Treeline or MIDCARE can cancel this affiliation with 180 days' notice. To become a member, an accredited hospital or medical center must apply and furnish comprehensive financial, quality, and utilization information. Every year, Treeline reviews and comments on the revenues, expenses, and capital budgets of its members. When interviewed, MIDCARE president James Higgens said, "Treeline has helped us in several ways. One good example of this affiliation's value is the reduction of our supply expenses per case-mix-adjusted discharge. We hope to do even better using Treeline's group purchasing organization for even more of our supplies. Treeline's prices are currently approximately 15% less than regional averages based on case-mix-adjusted hospital discharge." He also indicated that Treeline's assistance with staff recruitment and capital costs and its electronic health record (EHR) has meant financial savings for MIDCARE.

HISTORY

PHYSICAL STRUCTURE

Since being erected, the MIDCARE building has been a model of hospital engineering and has garnered community interest. Construction involved demolishing obsolete facilities to make way for a five-story facility on a 68-acre campus. Ample parking surrounds the buildings. Over the years, increasing service demands have required physical additions to the original structure. Each time a wing or structure was added, the existing space was also modernized. Fundraising campaigns raised the majority of funds for the additions completed in 1924 and 1946. Federal Hill-Burton monies were used to partially finance the 1962 and 1966 additions. The 2002 construction relied on retained earnings, community philanthropy, and long-term borrowing. A facility-wide modernization program was completed in 2014. This modernization converted a significant number of semiprivate rooms into private rooms and updated the birthing facilities.

In 1970, with the cooperation of Middleboro Trust Company, the hospital established a medical office park on the hospital campus and then constructed a three-story building with adjacent parking on the land. In 2013, the hospital constructed a new medical office building to house ambulatory care clinics and services, physician practices, and high-rise parking. The new building accommodates all the medical practices from the former building and has ample space for additional occupants. All medical practices in the new building rent their office space.

MIDDLEBORO COMMUNITY HOSPITAL

MIDCARE was originally named Middleboro Community Hospital. The nonprofit hospital opened its doors in 1890 as a short-term, general acute care facility with a 40-bed capacity. Since then, it has slowly grown to its present bed size and has multiplied its offerings with a significant number of outpatient services.

In 1919, the hospital founded a school of nursing. This three-year diploma program was one of the largest in the state and trained many of the nurses who worked at the hospital. In 1985, however, the increasing costs to run the school, the declining interest of local residents, and the increasing popularity of university/college-based nursing programs led to the hospital's board of trustees to make the decision to close the school. In 1987, the school officially closed. In 1988, the hospital established a clinical affiliation with State University and area community colleges. Today, the hospital continues to provide clinical rotations for advanced student nurses. Note that due to the regional shortage of registered nurses (RNs), the hospital has recently formed a study group to reestablish its own RN diploma program.

Although basically tranquil in nature, the hospital has experienced volatile periods in its history. First, major disagreements—which started in the 1930s—between area physicians (MDs and DOs) have created two independent systems in Middleboro. For example, DOs—physicians trained in osteopathic medicine—refer patients to other osteopathic physicians (who are often located in Capital City) even though MDs or allopathic physicians who could manage these cases practice in the same city or town and the surrounding areas. More recently, the certificate-of-need application for the regional cancer center required the approval of Webster Hospital. After many rounds of negotiation, it was decided that Webster Hospital–affiliated physicians could direct the care of their patients in this facility.

Within the last two years, a number of osteopathic physicians previously affiliated with Webster Hospital applied for and were granted medical staff privileges at MIDCARE. Note that since 1990, application for medical staff privileges at MIDCARE required being board certified. Recently, a small group of MIDCARE physicians petitioned the board to accept only former Webster-affiliated physicians who would complement—not compete with—current MIDCARE–affiliated physicians and that all be qualified for "consulting" medical staff status at Capital City General Hospital in Capital City.

In 2014, the hospital changed its name to Middleboro Medical Center or MID-CARE to signify its transition to a full-service community hospital *and* regional medical center. Community philanthropy, retained earnings, and long-term borrowing funded the hospital's expansion and modernization. As MIDCARE, its "only goal is to better serve the people of Hillsboro County."

GOVERNANCE

MIDCARE's board of trustees is composed of ten members, each of whom is elected to a four-year term. Elections are held at the board's annual meeting, and nominees for trustee-at-large and trustee officers are presented by the board nominating committee to all hospital incorporators for consideration. Staggered terms of office ensure that no more than three new members are elected annually. Board members may succeed themselves, as there are no limitations on the number of terms an individual can serve on the board. Current board trustees of MIDCARE are as follows; the (number)* indicates the number of years remaining on the current board term:

MIDCARE Board of Trustees

Members	*Residence*
Michael Rich (2)*, *Chair* President, Middleboro Trust Company	Mifflenville

Peter Steel (1), *Vice Chair*
    President, River Industries   Middleboro

Leslie Drew (3), *Secretary*
    Attorney, Giles, Giles & Drew   Boalsburg

Winston Meadows, CPA (4), *Treasurer*
    Accountant, Meadows and Associates   Middleboro

Dean Cornwall (1), *At-Large*
    Farmer   Carterville

Elton Giles (2), *At-Large*
    Attorney, Giles, Giles & Drew   Middleboro

Jasmine Wilson, (4), *At-Large*
    Real estate agent, Land Sales, Inc.   Mifflenville

Melvin Seed (1), *At-Large*
    Owner, Mid-State Oil Company   Jasper

Harry Waters (3), *At-Large*
    Owner, Waters Hardware   Middleboro

Rosemary Wheat (2), *At-Large*
    Vice president, Wheat Farming Supplies   Statesville

Michael Rich has been chairperson for the past 12 years and has served this board for more than 16 years. He is stepping down as chair next year. Peter Steel has been vice chair for 11 years and has served for more than 20 years. His term as vice chair ends this year. All other members, except Elton Giles, have previously served at least one complete term. Melvin Seed has recently given notice that he is unable to serve another term. MIDCARE president Higgens and medical staff president Dr. Frederick Maxwell are ex-officio members.

The standing committees of the board are as follows:

◆ Executive (all board officers)

◆ Long-Range Planning (Steel, Wilson, Meadows)

◆ Finance (Meadows, Waters, Cornwall, Giles)

◆ Quality Assurance (Drew, Seed, Wheat)

◆ Nominating (Seed, Rich, Wilson)

The board meets quarterly, and committees meet monthly. Before its annual meeting in March, the board holds a two-day retreat to review the progress toward and to update corporate plans. Once every two years, MIDCARE sponsors each board member to participate in a continuing education program presented by either the American Hospital Association or the State Hospital Association. For the past ten years, the board has retained a consulting firm to assist with its annual self-study. At its next meeting, the board will consider a bylaw change to increase board service to six years.

MANAGEMENT TEAM AND ORGANIZATIONAL STRUCTURE

PRESIDENT

James Higgens holds a bachelor's in sociology and a master of hospital administration from a major midwestern university. Prior to becoming president, he completed a two-year postgraduate residency at Lake Shore Hospital in Chicago and was, for many years, the chief operating officer at Capital City General Hospital in Capital City. He served two years in the US Army Medical Service Corps in Europe.

He is a Fellow in the American College of Healthcare Executives (ACHE) and is currently vice chair of the board of directors of the State Hospital Association. He has authored several professional papers on hospital management and is noted for his ability to interact well with the medical staff and for his understanding of hospital operations. The senior vice presidents report directly to him.

SENIOR VICE PRESIDENT OF FINANCE/CHIEF FINANCIAL OFFICER

John O'Hara, CPA, has held this position for nine years. He is responsible for the Admitting Department and the Business Office, and he is CEO of the physician–hospital organization (PHO). In addition, he provides staff support to the board finance committee and regularly attends all board meetings. His education includes a bachelor's in accounting from State University and a master of business administration from an eastern university. A certified public accountant and an active member of the Healthcare Financial Management Association, he has more than 25 years of professional experience, including as vice president of Finance at Seneca Hospital and as assistant controller at two New England hospitals.

Since arriving at MIDCARE, O'Hara has revised and updated many financial practices. On six different occasions, he has received special commendations for excellence from the board, the most recent for upgrading telecommunication services in the hospital at a reduced cost.

When asked what the organization needs in the near future, he mentioned a financial information system that better links financial and patient care data (for which he is preparing an RFP—request for proposal—for review of the management team and the board). Also, he thinks "a budgetary process that is based on budgeted units of services instead of FTEs [full-time equivalent employees]" is also necessary.

He negotiates all of the hospital's contracts with physician groups (e.g., radiology professional associations) and, since 2012, has been leading efforts to employ hospitalists and to purchase select medical practices. "We have acquired a number of practices from physicians who are either retiring or leaving to be hospital employees," he said. "We have also expanded our medical staff with a number of physicians who were affiliated with Webster Hospital and have helped them transition to their new affiliations with MIDCARE."

O'Hara implements plans that are designed and approved by the president, the management team, and the board. Some of these plans are controversial, such as downsizing inpatient acute care capacity. Current and former employees have blamed him for this decision to terminate or reassign staff. In fact, nurses have signed a petition to hold a unionization election because they fear the implications of the downsizing plan. The nursing staff has voted on unionization before—in 2016—but it resulted in a no vote (57 percent no/43 percent yes). To some nurses, management's termination approach ignores staff seniority and emphasizes "competency and job performance." On at least three occasions, terminated employees had written negative social media posts or comments on the local newspaper's website, insisting that the hospital is looking to retain "only those workers who would work for less."

SENIOR VICE PRESIDENT OF PATIENT CARE SERVICES

This position is newly created but yet to be filled. It will oversee the following patient departments: Anesthesiology, Dietary, Health Education, Laboratory, Nursing, Pharmacy, Physical Therapy, Occupational Therapy, Radiology, Recreation Therapy, Speech Therapy, and Social Services as well as all outpatient departments (including the Emergency Department). "Our intent for this position is to allow greater coordination between and among our inpatient, outpatient, and community-based patient services," Higgens explained. "We expect it to enhance these programs' effectiveness and efficiency." The new senior vice president of Patient Care Services (SVPPCS) is responsible for hiring a direct report—the new vice president of Nursing or chief nursing officer (CNO). The recruitment and selection process for both positions is expected to take nine months. MIDCARE has retained a recruitment firm to identify qualified candidates.

VICE PRESIDENT OF NURSING/CHIEF NURSING OFFICER

The right person for this position, which is currently vacant, must have a high degree of nursing experience and demonstrated administrative and management talents. The following departments are under this position: Pediatrics, Maternity and Nursery, Medical-Surgical, Intensive Care Unit (ICU) and Coronary Care Unit, Nursing Education and

Staff Development, Nursing Quality Assurance, Case Management, Central Sterile Supply, and Operating Rooms.

During the past 15 years, no vice president of Patient Care Services or CNO has lasted for more than five years. Conflicts with the medical staff about patient care practices and with administration about nurse scheduling and staffing levels have led to the most recent resignation from this post. Administration accepted the resignation in stride, telling the board that the former VP could not effectively manage the Nursing Department or communicate administration's policies to the nursing staff. The former VP did not support the decision to reduce the staffing levels in nursing and to replace some registered nurses with licensed practical nurses. While she understood the need to lower hospital expenses, she recommended doing so by using smaller nursing units, each with its own manager and support team.

The director of Nursing Education and Staff Development, Gemma Guevara, RN, is currently the acting CNO. She plans to return to her regular duties as soon as the SVPPCS has permanently filled the position. She hopes it will be soon, as she has already expressed her plans to retire in 18 months.

DIRECTOR OF NURSING EDUCATION AND STAFF DEVELOPMENT

Gemma Guevara, RN, has held this position for 20 years. She earned a bachelor's in nursing and master's in nursing education from State University. Her combined 36 years of experience in nursing and nursing education includes serving in a variety of positions at MIDCARE, such as staff nurse, charge nurse, evening nursing supervisor, and night nursing supervisor. On three different occasions, she has been acting CNO. Well-liked and highly regarded by department heads, charge nurses, and head nurses, she knows and gets along well with every nurse at the hospital.

As a direct report of the CNO, Guevara is responsible for ensuring all nurses remain proficient and updated in nursing practice. Not only does she provide relevant in-hospital seminars and workshops, but she also serves as the liaison between the Nursing Department and the student nurses and administrators from State University School of Nursing.

VICE PRESIDENT OF MEDICINE/CHIEF MEDICAL OFFICER

Dr. Olivia Stickle was appointed to this position three years ago. She graduated from college and medical school and completed her residency training in internal medicine on the East Coast. After 15 years of clinical practice, she earned a master of health administration from a southern university and became the medical director in a community hospital in another state and then the deputy medical director for Treeline Health System. She joined MIDCARE to manage its hospitalist program. She serves on multiple committees of The

Joint Commission, the American Medical Association, and the State Medical Society. She indicated that "we are delighted that the recent affiliation of a number of highly qualified physicians previously affiliated with Webster Hospital has been seamless and very beneficial to all. We also look forward to the continued development of telemedicine and telehealth services. We learned how important this can be during the pandemic. We also learned the high value of Health Next. Our ability to provide the highest quality care to our patients throughout Hillsboro Country, especially in the rural areas to the north, depends on both telehealth and Health Next."

SENIOR VICE PRESIDENT OF OPERATIONS/CHIEF OPERATING OFFICER

Rob Stewart was appointed to this position when it was created several years ago. Prior to that, he was assistant administrator for seven years and then vice president for 15 years for the Professional Services Department, and he completed his graduate program's administrative residency at the hospital. He holds a bachelor and master of health administration from a southern university, is an active member of ACHE, was in the Medical Service Corps of the US Air Force Reserve for six years, and serves on committees of the State Hospital Association. At MIDCARE, he chairs the hospital disaster planning committee and is responsible for the vice president of Human Resources and the assistant vice president of Operations.

VICE PRESIDENT OF HUMAN RESOURCES

Prior to her position, Gloria Bunker was the director of Human Resources for a major bank in Capital City for three years and for a large community hospital in the Midwest for 15 years. Born and raised in Jasper, she has a bachelor's in psychology from State University and a master of business administration from a private West Coast university. She is a member of the American Society for Healthcare Human Resources Administration (ASHHRA) and is the former chair of the statewide chapter of ASHHRA in a midwestern state. Since being appointed, she has streamlined the employee evaluation system, retained the services of a national consulting firm to perform extensive wage and salary studies, reviewed and revised all job descriptions, and revised the employee recruitment and outplacement processes. Also, she supervises MIDCARE's volunteer program.

ASSISTANT VICE PRESIDENT OF OPERATIONS

Twenty-eight years ago, Ted Beck graduated from high school and was hired by the hospital as a billing clerk. Since then, he has been accounts receivable manager, director of purchasing, and director of the business office. He was promoted to his current position when the previous assistant vice president retired. Having completed a bachelor's degree in health administration at State University, he enrolled in the university's master of business administration program and became a member of ACHE. For the past three years, MIDCARE employees have voted him "Outstanding Supervisor." At his urging, the hospital sought an affiliation with a national voluntary chain of hospitals, which has enabled the hospital to access joint purchasing services. Currently, he is developing a plan for shared laundry services with area nursing homes.

He is in charge of the following departments: Patient Access, Parking/Security, Engineering and Maintenance, Patient Experience, Housekeeping, Laundry, and Purchasing/Materials Management/Supply Chain Management. He was also very involved with helping coordinate services with other healthcare providers during the pandemic.

SENIOR VICE PRESIDENT OF INFORMATION SYSTEMS/CHIEF INFORMATION OFFICER

Mabel Watkins was appointed to this position six years ago and was tasked with adopting Treeline's EHR system for use in MIDCARE and all of its owned medical practices. She also oversees all aspects of MIDCARE's information technology (IT) infrastructure, including security. Prior to joining the management team, she was deputy chief information officer for a major medical center in a midwestern city. She earned a bachelor's in computer science at State University and a master of business administration at a private eastern university. She has 15 years of experience in hospital IT and is a member of the College of Healthcare Information Management Executives.

According to Watkins, implementation of the Treeline EHR continues to involve all MIDCARE departments and all owned and affiliated medical practices. She also indicated that some of her most difficult challenges include managing the staggering number and types of vendor and service contracts, assessing the value of new technologies, and staying compliant with regulations and best practices for securing protected health information. She also serves as senior technical consultant for Health Next. Her direct reports include the offices of Medical Information and Services, Medical Records, IT Systems Services, IT Grants and Contracts, and IT Systems Security and Telecommunications.

VICE PRESIDENT OF MEDICAL INFORMATION AND SERVICES

Appointed to his position two years ago, Dr. Sindar Manhatten is responsible for MIDCARE's EHR and other information systems that capture, analyze, and report clinical information and data. Although trained in internal medicine, he holds a master of healthcare analytics degree. Prior to this job, he was chief medical information officer for a regional healthcare system in another state and served three years in Capital City as an

EHR consultant to area hospitals and medical centers. He is a recognized expert in CMS's Promoting Interoperability Programs and guided MIDCARE through the latest stages of this program. He helped establish the protocols so that all owned medical practices are linked to MIDCARE's master EHR and was instrumental in making sure the organization's enhanced telemedicine capabilities were effectively linked to the EHR. He publishes papers on electronic records regularly and is a noted speaker on system security. He also chairs the technical advisory committee for Health Next.

SPECIAL ASSISTANT OF MANAGEMENT

Six months ago, Marie Calley had just earned her master of health and hospital administration from a private eastern university when she was offered the position to work directly under the president. In graduate school, she studied with one of the leading experts in the area of hospital strategic planning, but her professional experience is limited to a two-year residency at Coastal Medical Center in a major city on the West Coast. At MIDCARE, she is assigned special projects, performs market and demographic analyses, writes public relations pieces and contributes to publications, assists the senior management team with strategy-related work, and provides administrative support to select committees of the medical staff. She and her husband just moved to Middleboro when he accepted a position with the law firm Giles, Giles & Drew.

INTERNAL REVENUE SERVICE FORM 990 DISCLOSURES

MIDCARE's recent IRS Form 990 indicates its ten highest-paid employees:

Staff Name	Position	Compensation ($)
James Higgens	President	830,667
John O'Hara	Senior VP, Finance/CFO	513,255
Mabel Watkins	Senior VP, Information Systems/CIO	443,458
Olivia Stickle, MD	VP Medicine/CMO	422,560
Rob Stewart	VP Operations/COO	406,312
Sindar Manhatten, MD	VP Medical Information Systems	401,452
William Lewis, MD	Hospitalist	398,934
Megan Gupta, MD	Hospitalist	354,378
Marc Shine, MD	Hospitalist	314,445
Gemma Guevara, RN	Acting VP Nursing/CNO	267,335

Total compensation includes benefits, which average 34 percent above salary, as well as performance bonus payments. Emergency, radiology, pathology, and anesthesiology services are provided by contract. Currently, the hospital does not directly employ any physicians in these specialties. Salary data for physicians employed by the PHO are not included here and are reported in the (confidential) annual reports of the PHO.

MEDICAL STAFF AND MEDICAL RESOURCES

In 1990, the hospital established a policy that physicians who have "consulting" status on the medical staff must maintain "active" status at Capital City General Hospital or at University Hospital in University Town. In addition, any appointment to the active or consulting medical staff requires the physician to be board certified and to meet any credentialing requirements.

See table 6.2 for a full list of MIDCARE's medical staff. The medical departments at MIDCARE are as follows:

◆ *Department of Anesthesiology.* The hospital maintains a contractual relationship with Anesthesiology Associates of Middleboro Professional Association (PA) to provide all anesthesiology services. Dr. Maxwell is the president of this PA and chair of this department.

◆ *Department of Emergency Medicine.* The hospital maintains a contractual relationship with Emergency Medical Associates of Middleboro PA to provide emergency services. Dr. Simi Hines is the president of this PA and chair of this department.

◆ *Department of Hospital Medicine.* The hospital employs nine physicians trained in internal medicine to provide in-house, 24/7 care and services as hospitalists. Hospitalists cannot admit nor vote on medical staff resolutions. Hospitalists are managed and supervised by Dr. Stickle, chief medical officer.

◆ *Department of Medicine.* This department includes private practice physicians in a variety of specialties, including family practice, general internal medicine, pediatrics, allergy and immunology, cardiology, gastroenterology, ENT (ear, nose, throat), psychiatry, and oncology and hematology. Dr. Godfrey Hunt is the chair of this department.

◆ *Department of Pathology.* The hospital maintains a contractual relationship with Pathology Associates of Middleboro Professional Association (PA) for all pathology services. Dr. Douglas Lafta is the president of this PA and chair of this department.

◆ *Department of Radiology.* The hospital maintains a contractual relationship with Radiology Associates of Middleboro PA for all radiology services. Dr. Adam Glorioso is the president of this PA and chair of this department.

◆ *Department of Surgery.* This department is made up of private practice physicians in a variety of specialties. Dr. Felix Limpey is the chair of this department.

MEDICAL STAFF ORGANIZATION

Dr. Maxwell (Department of Anesthesiology) has been president of the medical staff for 12 years. The president is elected every two years. No additional compensation is given to elected officers. Dr. Carlos Leatros (Department of Pathology) is vice president. Dr. Limpey (Department of Surgery) is employed part-time by the hospital as the medical staff coordinator. He provides staff support to all medical staff committees. For example, he cochairs the monthly meeting of the CMS Core Measures Working Group.

Standing committees of the medical staff include bylaws, cancer, credentials, critical care education, emergency services, executive, hospitalist practice, medical records, pharmacy and therapeutics, quality assurance, tissue/transfusion, and utilization review. The executive committee of the medical staff meets monthly or as needed, while other committees meet monthly. The entire medical staff meets annually, where the physicians address recredentialing.

Recently, Dr. Raymond Samuels (Department of Pediatrics) wrote to the medical staff officers to express his desire to be considered for president in the next election. Without criticizing the performance of the incumbent, he indicated that the interests of the medical staff are better represented by a physician in private practice than by a physician in a hospital-based practice. His letter suggests that the leadership positions of the medical staff be reserved for physicians with admitting privileges.

CHALLENGES AND OPPORTUNITIES

SPECIAL STUDY OF EMERGENCY DEPARTMENTS

The Department of Health Services Management at State University recently released a report about persons suffering from psychosis or nervous breakdown who are in need of acute mental health services. According to the report, these patients frequently must wait in the emergency department (ED) for extended periods before they can be transferred to appropriate service providers. The state mental hospital east of Capital City is the closest facility that accepts involuntary emergency admissions. Local mental health services only provide outpatient treatment. The report states that, in the past year, four such people waited more than three days in the ED before transfer and, for five days, mental health patients awaiting transfer occupied 12 of the 27 beds in the ED. The Department of Health Services Management collected these data as part of a pilot study to determine whether appropriate emergency services are available in communities served by two or more emergency departments (i.e., ED). The study suggests that operational costs in the ED are approximately 18 percent above the operational costs incurred in similar hospitals with similar utilization.

Note that the *Middleboro Sentinel* recently published a series of articles on Webster Hospital's current "change of mission" that questions the need for two EDs and ambulance services in the Middleboro area. The issue of ED use by behavioral health patients became much timelier with the recent ruling on this topic by the state Supreme Court.

Strategy Discussions at the Board Retreat

Six weeks ago, the board, president, and all senior vice presidents gathered for a two-day strategic review of MIDCARE. The retreat was organized and directed by Rich and Steel, chair and vice chair of the board, respectively. Both had attended an American Hospital Association seminar on strategic options for community hospitals, and both returned asking whether MIDCARE should develop additional off-campus services; acquire and operate additional medical practices; and affiliate with other service providers, including through an asset merger. Attendees of the retreat agreed to not publicly discuss these topics until everyone has had the opportunity "to study the strategic options presented and the most appropriate ways to address them." The retreat conveyed to the entire board the significance of their input into these and other issues. The retreat also included an in-depth presentation of Health Next and efforts to expand and become a national model for using telemedicine and telehealth. Also discussed at the retreat was the issue of collaboration and coordination of services with other healthcare organizations in the community, which came to light during the pandemic.

Expanded Maternity Services

In 2019, MIDCARE's maternity ward was renovated and its services were upgraded. Today, the hospital offers three types of maternity rooms that "exactly meet our needs and are one of the reasons we are increasing our services to the community," explained Higgens:

1. *Labor-delivery-recovery-postpartum (LDRP) room.* An LDRP room is equipped to accommodate the mother and baby throughout the birthing process and the days afterward, assuming a patient transfer to another unit is not

necessary. A designated nurse cares for both mother and baby. The planned length of stay in an LDRP room is 24 to 48 hours after delivery.

2. *Labor-delivery-recovery (LDR) room.* An LDR room is equipped to be used throughout the birthing process and the period of recovery after childbirth. Then, the new mother and baby are transferred to a room and the nursery, respectively. An LDR room may be used by a mother who does not desire LDRP or whose baby needs care in the newborn nursery.

3. *Labor room.* A labor room is equipped to handle an expectant mother in labor, before she is transferred to a delivery room or an operating room for a cesarean section.

This addition has expanded expectant or new mothers' choice of obstetricians, gynecologists, pediatricians, and other related providers. As stated by Higgens, "We want the birthing experience at MIDCARE to be excellent in all regards. It is one of our signature services!" In addition, the PHO continues to support new physicians and specialties.

Interview with the President

When asked to assess the current state of MIDCARE, Higgens said,

> The past five years have been filled with a great deal of turbulence and change. We continue to accomplish our core objectives even though the pandemic had a significant influence on all phases of our operation. Using expertise provided us by Treeline and others, we were able to secure all the necessary technology (e.g., ventilators) and prepare and support our staff for the specific challenges associated with this pandemic. During the height of the pandemic, only three employees tested positive, and all recovered. The pandemic also taught us to better serve our communities. We must become a leader in telehealth and telemedicine. During this era, we downsized our inpatient capacity and added many single-occupancy rooms. We also adjusted staffing to demand. No employees had to be furloughed during this time period. This year we expanded our inpatient bed capacity for the first time in seven years. By remodeling our physical facilities with expansions and contractions, we were able to maintain or even deepen our reach into our primary markets. Our supply chain worked especially well during this most difficult time. Plus, because of our PHO, we now have a much tighter and larger network of affiliated physicians. In some ways, our ability to navigate the pandemic may be based on the redefinition/downsizing of Webster Hospital and the recent affiliation of physicians previously affiliated with Webster Hospital with our medical staff. Although we encountered many financial challenges during this era, it

appears that our financial turbulence is almost behind us and we are optimistic about
the future.

Higgens named the medical staff and the board as MIDCARE's primary strengths.
In contrast, he cited the inadequate health insurance coverage of county residents and the
low reimbursement rates from state Medicaid and federal Medicare as MIDCARE's primary threats. To cope with these rates, he said, "We have to continue to strive for respect-
able inpatient occupancy by downsizing when necessary and lowering our operational
costs throughout the hospital." Although he is aware that a national for-profit firm has
recently purchased a hospital in Capital City, he sees no consequences for the local market.

Tables 6.1 through 6.8 describe MIDCARE's recent performance and the services
it has provided. A table detailing hospital performance based on CMS Core Measures is
located in the appendixes.

Table 6.1
MIDCARE
Hospital
Services

Adult Cardiac Electrophysiology	Enrollment Assistance Services
Adult Cardiac Surgery	Extracorporeal Shock Wave Lithotripter
Adult Cardiology Services	Fitness Center
Adult Interventional Cardiac	Freestanding Outpatient Center
Catheterization	Full-Field Digital Mammography (FFDM)
Airborne Infection Isolation Room	Genetic Testing/Counseling
Ambulatory Surgery Center	Geriatric Services
Bariatric/Weight Control Services	Health Fair
Birthing Room—LDR Room—LDRP Room	Health Research
Blood Donor Center	Health Screening
Breast Cancer Screening/Mammograms	HIV—AIDS Services
Cardiac Intensive Care	Hospital-Based Outpatient Care Center
Cardiac Rehabilitation	Image Guided Radiation Therapy (IGRT)
Case Management	Immunization Program
Chaplaincy/Pastoral Care	Indigent Care Clinic
Chemotherapy	Inpatient Palliative Care Unit
Chiropractic Services	Intensity-Modulated Radiation Therapy
Community Health Education	Magnetic Resonance Imaging (MRI)
Community Outreach	Meals on Wheels
Complementary and Alternative Medicine	Medical-Surgical Intensive Care Services
Computer-Assisted Orthopedic Surgery	Mobile Health Services
Crisis Prevention	Multiline Spiral CT
CT Scanner	Neurological Services
Dental Services	Nutritional Programs
Diagnostic Radioisotope Facility	Obstetrics
Emergency Department	Occupational Health Services
Enabling Services	Oncology Services
Endoscopic Infrasound	Orthopedic Services
Endoscopic Retrograde	Outpatient Surgery

continued

Table 6.1
MIDCARE
Hospital
Services

Palliative Care Program	Robotic Surgery
Patient Education Center	Single Photon Emission CT (SPECT)
Patient Representative Services	Sleep Center
Patient-Controlled Analgesia	Social Work Services
Pediatric Intensive Care Services	Sports Medicine
Physical Rehabilitation Inpatient Services	Support Groups
Physical Rehabilitation Outpatient Services	Teen Outreach Services
Primary Care Department	Tobacco Treatment/Cessation Program
Psychiatric Care	Trauma Center Certified
Psychiatric Child and Adolescent Services	Ultrasound
Psychiatric Consultation/Liaison Services	Urgent Care Center
Psychiatric Education Services	Virtual Colonoscopy
Psychiatric Emergency Services	Volunteer Services Department
Psychiatric Geriatric Services	Women's Health Center/Services
Psychiatric Outpatient Services	Wound Management Services
Psychiatric Partial Hospitalization	

Note: CT: computed tomography; LDR: labor-delivery-recovery; LDRP: labor-delivery-recovery-postpartum.

Table 6.2
MIDCARE
Medical Staff as
of December 31,
2024

	Name	Note	Off	Age	Specialty	P-Days	Dis
	ACTIVE MEDICAL STAFF						
	Family Practice: Active Staff						
1	Apple		6	50	Family Practice	174	44
2	Banero		8	52	Family Practice	119	31
3	Fistru		7	58	Family Practice	160	36
4	Mix		2	45	Family Practice	130	30
5	Player		5	60	Family Practice	85	21
	Internal Medicine: Active Staff						
6	Barton	MA	1	45	Internal Medicine	476	121
7	Beata		3	60	Internal Medicine	80	23
8	Crush		3	58	Internal Medicine	280	49
9	Cushing		3	62	Internal Medicine	87	14
10	Davis		3	58	Internal Medicine	203	43
11	Douglas	MA	1	41	Internal Medicine	467	143
12	Eason	MA	1	56	Internal Medicine	490	134
13	Figher		3	54	Internal Medicine	306	55
14	Filly		1	58	Internal Medicine	240	39
15	Grist		3	50	Internal Medicine	140	32
16	Hippster		1	56	Internal Medicine	250	58
17	Horse		1	68	Internal Medicine	344	83
18	Hunt		8	55	Internal Medicine	172	32
19	Jessey		7	60	Internal Medicine	177	36
20	Justin		1	67	Internal Medicine	210	48
21	Justin		4	59	Internal Medicine	84	14
22	Kessler	MA	1	34	Internal Medicine	458	149
23	King		3	63	Internal Medicine	64	10
24	Knach		8	67	Internal Medicine	63	10
25	Lesko	MA	1	38	Internal Medicine	560	112
26	Mast		2	41	Internal Medicine	877	144
27	Master	MA	1	40	Internal Medicine	402	101
28	Meow		1	60	Internal Medicine	280	49
29	Michael		4	45	Internal Medicine	250	43
30	Nask		5	56	Internal Medicine	203	43
31	Nostrom		2	57	Internal Medicine	112	24
32	Ogg		2	39	Internal Medicine	472	85

continued

Table 6.2
MIDCARE
Medical Staff as
of December 31,
2024
(continued)

	Name	Note	Off	Age	Specialty	P-Days	Dis
33	Panisi		2	50	Internal Medicine	126	30
34	Quinn		6	63	Internal Medicine	156	33
35	Steel		3	50	Internal Medicine	416	74
36	Stocapy		3	57	Internal Medicine	150	27
37	Trip		6	52	Internal Medicine	263	46
	Vogel		5	55	Internal Medicine	103	19
38	**Pediatrics: Active Staff**						
39	Bickford		1	50	Pediatrics	92	29
40	Bill		3	59	Pediatrics	52	19
41	Eason	MA	1	56	Pediatrics	71	30
42	Gavin		1	44	Pediatrics	54	14
43	Hirsh	MA	1	46	Pediatrics	64	20
44	Kettel		3	57	Pediatrics	70	17
45	Pushy		1	50	Pediatrics	70	17
46	Reaper	MA	1	52	Pediatrics	81	25
47	Samuels	MA	1	47	Pediatrics	114	29
48	Sloan		1	48	Pediatrics	94	17
49	St. James	MA	1	40	Pediatrics	120	45
50	Turtle		1	58	Pediatrics	68	34
51	Vesh		1	52	Pediatrics	42	9
52	Warren		1	56	Pediatrics	84	19
	Allergy and Immunology: Active Staff						
53	Gustave		1	53	Allergy/Immun.	207	34
54	Hampshire		3	58	Allergy/Immun.	204	44
55	Sleek		1	49	Allergy/Immun.	448	97
	Cardiology: Active Staff						
56	Eastman		1	39	Cardiology	384	56
57	Hurst		1	42	Cardiology	334	49
58	Rusty		1	55	Cardiology	180	26
59	Underwood	MA	1	46	Cardiology	652	145
60	Victem		1	41	Cardiology	471	87

continued

	Name	Note	Off	Age	Specialty	P-Days	Dis
	Gastroenterology: Active Staff						
61	Amas		1	60	Gastroenterology	120	22
62	Autumn	MA	1	44	Gastroenterology	448	105
63	Eisher		1	55	Gastroenterology	128	25
64	Tiger		2	59	Gastroenterology	58	19
65	Wingate		2	64	Gastroenterology	86	20
66	Zaller		1	49	Gastroenterology	365	89
	Psychiatry: Active Staff						
77	Actor		1	42	Psychiatry	208	39
78	Voltaire		1	37	Psychiatry	202	39
79	Banana		1	50	Psychiatry	152	27
80	Isher		2	61	Psychiatry	127	20
81	Freud		1	50	Psychiatry	127	30
82	Stephens		1	41	Psychiatry	154	34
83	Jilley		1	39	Psychiatry	160	44
84	Zeus		2	40	Psychiatry	242	35
	Other, Medicine: Active Staff						
85	Zook	MA	1	50	Endocrinology	205	42
86	Carp		3	54	ENT	300	71
87	Fish		3	49	ENT	280	64
88	Tunsteb		1	60	ENT	80	18
89	Weckenson	MA	1	44	ENT	470	110
90	Walberger	MA	1	42	ENT	205	67
91	White		1	63	ENT	68	22
92	Whittier		1	44	ENT	353	101
93	Xerox	MA	1	42	ENT	497	145
94	Yalper		1	57	ENT	170	75
95	Divan		1	44	Oncology/Hemo	340	66
96	Hatcher		1	53	Oncology/Hemo	359	72
97	Schoen		1	39	Oncology/Hemo	401	77
98	Smith		1	32	Oncology/Hemo	290	42

Table 6.2 MIDCARE Medical Staff as of December 31, 2024 *(continued)*

continued

Table 6.2
MIDCARE
Medical Staff as
of December 31,
2024
(continued)

	Name	Note	Off	Age	Specialty	P-Days	Dis
	Surgery, Orthopedic: Active Staff						
99	Amberson		1	61	Orthopedic	1,420	260
100	Hooper		1	50	Orthopedic	1,053	196
101	Matthews		1	45	Orthopedic	1,499	291
102	Questrom	MA	1	39	Orthopedic	1,601	322
103	Rex		1	57	Orthopedic	1,744	383
104	Stanley	MA	1	49	Orthopedic	1,520	314
	Surgery General: Active Staff						
105	Blood		3	56	General	415	85
106	Cutter		3	63	General	240	50
107	Flores	MA	1	45	General	612	108
108	Hersh	MA	1	40	General	745	167
109	Isherum		1	57	General	545	145
110	Jackson	MA	1	39	General	634	140
111	Limpey		1	58	General	745	157
112	Munson		1	50	Genera	586	185
113	Never	MA	1	45	General	770	275
114	O'Connell	MA	1	49	General	516	104
115	Putter	MA	1	52	General	501	126
116	Timas		1	64	General	657	138
117	Victor		1	57	General	680	156
	Surgery: OB/GYN: Active Staff						
118	Dustin	MA	1	33	OB/GYN	405	195
119	Eberle		1	51	OB/GYN	90	36
120	Fisher		3	60	OB/GYN	154	41
121	Fraser		1	65	OB/GYN	180	31
122	Goldstein		3	50	OB/GYN	220	48
123	Gost	MA	1	40	OB/GYN	320	96
124	Stein		3	56	OB/GYN	362	80
	Surgery: Other: Active Staff						
125	Bernal		1	45	Neurosurgery	314	49
126	Blue		1	46	Ophthalmology	101	47
127	Clock		1	47	Thoracic	340	82

continued

	Name	Note	Off	Age	Specialty	P-Days	Dis
128	Crow		1	50	Neurosurgery	334	50
129	David		1	51	Vascular	510	77
130	Fession		1	44	Bariatric	480	96
131	Fixer	MA	1	43	Urology	404	92
132	Frederick		1	47	Vascular	355	74
133	Mold		1	45	Urology	300	63
134	Niyani		1	51	Urology	320	75
135	Seimer		1	59	Ophthalmology	145	34
136	Tho		1	42	Plastic	634	127
137	Underside		1	55	Thoracic	634	147
138	Wall		1	58	Plastic	247	51
139	Yellow		1	44	Thoracic	440	95
	TOTAL ACTIVE STAFF					**43,952**	**9,755**

CONSULTING STAFF

Department of Medicine, Consulting Staff

	Name	Note	Off	Age	Specialty	P-Days	Dis
140	Ange		9	48	Endocrinology	14	8
141	Carles		9	60	Pulmonary Medicine	28	6
142	Feada		9	63	Hematology	50	11
143	Flint		9	56	Oncology	154	25
144	Kipstein	MA	3	50	Cardiology	101	30
145	Klock	MA	3	49	OB/GYN	130	28
146	Lott		9	50	Hematology	83	17
147	Maeer	MA	3	42	Cardiology	101	19
148	Snipes	MA	3	44	Cardiology	94	18
149	Coolidge	MA	3	44	ENT	56	12
150	Kronberger	MA	3	50	ENT	70	18
151	Frost	MA	3	41	Internal Medicine	101	24
152	Washington	MA	3	43	Internal Medicine	108	26
153	Malone		9	55	Allergy	31	6
154	McVoy		9	47	Psychiatry	32	8
155	Chan	MA	3	37	Pediatrics	63	18
156	Miller	MA	3	49	Pediatrics	34	9
157	Otter	MA	3	37	Pediatrics	19	4
158	Quester	MA	3	40	Pediatrics	23	6
159	Unvey	MA	3	56	Pediatrics	32	7
160	Klock	MA	3	49	OB/GYN	30	12

Table 6.2
MIDCARE Medical Staff as of December 31, 2024 *(continued)*

continued

Table 6.2
MIDCARE
Medical Staff as
of December 31,
2024
(continued)

	Name	Note	Off	Age	Specialty	P-Days	Dis
161	Mustard	MA	3	39	OB/GYN	93	20
162	Polk	MA	3	40	OB/GYN	71	20
163	Parish		9	48	Dermatology	16	3
164	Rubble		3	54	Oncology	182	32
165	Thomas		9	51	Psychiatry	74	15
166	Vitter		9	57	Hematology	32	9
	Department of Surgery, Consulting Staff						
167	Lee	MA	3	40	Orthopedic	234	58
168	Goldwater	MA	3	44	Orthopedic	65	14
169	Quin	MA	3	47	Orthopedic	40	9
170	Finn	MA	3	49	Thoracic	131	26
171	Mike		9	60	Ophthalmology	118	20
172	Picture	MA	3	47	Orthopedic	185	34
173	Steve	MA	3	47	Thoracic	180	32
174	Wingate		9	64	Ophthalmology	32	8
	TOTAL CONSULTING STAFF					2,807	612
	TOTAL ACTIVE AND CONSULTING MEDICAL STAFF					46,759	10,367
	OTHER MEDICAL STAFF ← CONTRACTED						
	Department of Pathology						
	Fisher		1	54	Pathology		
	Lafta		1	49	Pathology		
	Leatros		1	47	Pathology		
	Mautz		1	44	Pathology		
	Mixture		1	61	Pathology		
	Mushroom		1	42	Pathology		
	Nerverto		1	56	Pathology		
	Pathos		1	56	Pathology		
	Wingate		1	37	Pathology		
	Department of Radiology						
	Glorioso		1	52	Radiology		
	Picture		1	56	Radiology		

continued

Name	Note	Off	Age	Specialty	P-Days	Dis
Quadic		1	45	Radiology		
Roetgen		1	61	Radiology		
Sunshine		1	40	Radiology		
Ray		1	45	Radiology		
Hines		1	50	Radiology		
Gershler		1	39	Radiology		
Jinks		1	45	Radiology		
Gotlike		1	52	Radiology		
Ricker		1	34	Radiology		
Smith		1	44	Radiology		
Trippe		1	49	Radiology		
Tracer		1	49	Radiology		
Department of Anesthesiology						
Aaron		1	38	Anesthesiology		
Carter		1	62	Anesthesiology		
Dexter		1	66	Anesthesiology		
Harrington		1	63	Anesthesiology		
Maxwell		1	50	Anesthesiology		
Nelson		1	60	Anesthesiology		
Thomas		1	64	Anesthesiology		
Fisher		1	54	Anesthesiology		
Gass		1	48	Anesthesiology		
Lister		1	61	Anesthesiology		
Mask		1	59	Anesthesiology		
Department of Emergency Medicine						
Casey		1	44	Emergency		
Catle		1	39	Emergency		
Cytesmath		1	60	Emergency		
Goodspeed		1	65	Emergency		
Hijosz		1	52	Emergency		
Hines		1	60	Emergency		
Hotlick		1	58	Emergency		
Ishabi		1	43	Emergency		
Jinks		1	45	Emergency		
Smooth		1	54	Emergency		
Tobias		1	51	Emergency		
Welby		1	56	Emergency		

Table 6.2
MIDCARE
Medical Staff as
of December 31,
2024
(continued)

continued

Table 6.2
MIDCARE
Medical Staff as
of December 31,
2024
(continued)

Name	Note	Off	Age	Specialty	P-Days	Dis
Department of Hospital Medicine						
Carlos		1	40	Hospitalist		
Drudge		1	35	Hospitalist		
Frost		1	39	Hospitalist		
Gupta		1	40	Hospitalist		
Lewis		1	50	Hospitalist		
Palmer		1	32	Hospitalist		
Ruderbacker		1	56	Hospitalist		
Shine		1	43	Hospitalist		
Stickle		1	61	Hospitalist		
Vail		1	44	Hospitalist		

Notes:

Middleboro = 1; Miffleville = 2; Jasper = 3; Harris City = 4 ; Statesville = 5;

Carterville = 6; Boalsburg = 7; Minortown = 8;

Capital City = 9; Other = 10.

ENT: ear, nose, throat; MA: Medical Associates; OB/GYN: obstetrics/gynecology; Off: office location; P-Days: patient days, Dis: discharges.

Hospital Service	2024	2023	2022	2021
Pediatrics				
Beds	4	6	6	6
Patient Days	863	1,467	1,143	993
Occupancy	59.11%	66.99%	52.19%	45.34%
Maternity				
Beds	16	16	16	16
Patient Days	3,844	3,903	3,978	3,655
Occupancy	65.82%	66.83%	68.12%	62.59%
Medical-Surgical I				
Beds	35	35	35	35
Patient Days	8,745	7,893	6,946	6,650
Occupancy	68.45%	61.78%	54.37%	52.05%
Medical-Surgical II				
Beds	31	31	32	32
Patient Days	7,138	7,035	7,437	7,437
Occupancy	63.08%	62.17%	63.67%	63.67%
Medical-Surgical III				
Beds	35	35	40	40
Patient Days	7,426	7,235	7,034	7,756
Occupancy	58.13%	56.63%	48.18%	53.12%
Medical-Surgical IV				
Beds	37	37	37	37
Patient Days	8,356	8,245	8,745	8,134
Occupancy	61.87%	61.05%	64.75%	60.23%
ICU/CCU				
Beds	35	35	24	24
Patient Days	6,205	6,378	6,402	6,435
Occupancy	48.57%	49.93%	73.08%	73.46%
Total Hospital				
Beds	189	189	184	184
Patient Days	46,759	42,526	40,542	40,067
Occupancy	67.78%	61.65%	60.37%	59.66%

Table 6.3
MIDCARE
Hospital
Inpatient
Occupancy by
Service

Note: ICU/CCU: intensive care unit/coronary care unit.

Table 6.4
MIDCARE
Detailed
Utilization
Statistics

Month	Dis	Patient Days	IP Surgery	OP Surgery	Births	ED Visits	ED Admits	OP Visits
2024								
January	923	4,067	232	390	101	2,167	256	10,640
February	856	3,823	190	330	85	1,956	239	10,005
March	1,067	5,013	215	283	97	2,438	273	10,334
April	873	3,977	207	304	97	2,377	264	10,433
May	801	3,807	213	392	103	2,639	252	10,045
June	856	3,741	189	329	98	2,267	267	9,945
July	756	3,409	205	348	110	2,376	269	9,355
August	745	3,457	207	326	93	2,845	273	9,625
September	893	3,645	256	423	112	2,440	269	10,452
October	945	4,189	272	427	98	2,389	254	10,004
November	798	3,756	215	434	104	2,531	256	9,956
December	854	3,875	177	418	101	2,186	259	8,350
Total	**10,367**	**46,759**	**2,578**	**4,404**	**1,199**	**28,611**	**3,131**	**119,144**
2023								
January	856	3,844	250	416	104	2,245	278	8,950
February	845	3,507	211	303	99	2,567	276	8,245
March	934	4,137	234	389	105	2,365	258	8,327
April	856	3,856	219	352	108	2,015	301	9,356
May	821	3,966	240	376	89	2,430	345	9,445
June	803	3,761	249	301	97	2,745	256	9,535
July	790	3,266	212	413	104	2,365	256	9,773
August	630	2,955	211	193	94	2,845	279	9,461
September	863	4,002	234	312	90	2,289	301	9,429
October	854	3,745	251	378	93	2,045	249	9,967
November	902	4,110	214	390	98	2,377	257	9,853
December	803	3,285	193	327	90	2,478	289	9,478
Total	**9,957**	**44,434**	**2,718**	**4,150**	**1,171**	**28,766**	**3,345**	**111,819**

Notes: (1) Dis: discharges; ED: emergency department; IP: inpatient; OP: outpatient. (2) ED Visits are total ED visits. (3) ED Admits are ED visits that led to an inpatient admission. (4) OP Visits are outpatient visits that exclude ED visits.

	2024	2023	2022
Assets			
Current Assets			
Cash	15,043,414	17,459,863	16,003,261
Short-Term Investments	5,624,781	5,662,163	8,023,303
Accounts Receivable—Gross	139,345,929	103,585,882	82,434,002
Allowances for Uncollectibles	34,464,223	27,995,374	17,787,339
Accounts Receivable—Net	104,881,706	75,590,508	64,646,663
Due from Third-Party Payers	3,284,339	1,456,929	19,263,445
Inventories	28,573,443	21,677,303	20,171,332
Prepaid Expenses	6,235,383	5,259,120	4,236,461
Total Current Assets	**157,407,683**	**121,846,766**	**128,108,004**
Noncurrent Assets			
Property, Plant, and Equipment—Gross	881,223,474	901,452,883	845,554,912
Less Accumulated Depreciation	122,545,223	154,373,102	165,949,223
Property, Plant, and Equipment—Net	758,678,251	747,079,781	679,605,689
Other Investments	26,081,417	25,228,856	79,223,761
Total Assets	**928,423,177**	**894,155,403**	**886,937,454**
Liabilities			
Current Liabilities			
Accounts Payable	18,465,332	17,342,334	12,646,112
Accrued Salaries and Wages	2,883,451	2,673,452	2,003,561
Accrued Interest	9,452,339	6,025,334	6,345,112
Other Accrued Expenses	23,967,339	2,562,338	3,562,330
Due to Third-Party Vendors	13,254,367	10,937,220	10,782,574
Long-Term Debt Due Within One Year	22,475,919	22,452,004	21,574,990
Total Current Liabilities	**90,498,747**	**61,992,682**	**56,914,679**
Long-Term Debt	194,708,938	206,374,001	204,232,009
Total Liabilities	**285,207,685**	**268,366,683**	**261,146,688**
Net Assets			
Restricted	279,029,989	152,458,402	79,026,523
Unrestricted	364,185,503	473,330,318	546,764,243
Total Net Assets	**643,215,492**	**625,788,720**	**625,790,766**
Net Assets + Liabilities	**928,423,177**	**894,155,403**	**886,937,454**

Table 6.5
MIDCARE
Balance Sheet
as of December
31, USD $

Table 6.6
MIDCARE
Statement of
Revenues and
Expenses,
USD $

	2024	2023	2022
Revenues			
Patient Services Revenue			
Inpatient Net of Allowances and Uncollectibles	408,453,125	359,335,272	303,884,230
Outpatient Net of Allowances and Uncollectibles	276,126,778	145,383,220	107,346,291
Total	**684,579,903**	**504,718,492**	**411,230,521**
Expenses			
Salaries and Wages	290,304,808	210,446,101	178,352,991
Fringe Benefits	100,472,341	72,805,660	53,896,112
Supplies	196,957,066	134,979,445	127,453,991
Professional Fees	21,466,569	16,700,341	10,663,786
Interest	12,133,615	7,342,997	4,023,776
Depreciation	9,239,555	10,565,002	13,784,008
Amortization	32,185,459	33,895,663	34,896,009
Other	21,435,223	20,563,887	24,089,442
Total	**684,194,636**	**507,299,096**	**447,160,115**
Net Income from Operations	**385,267**	**−2,580,604**	**−35,929,594**
Other Revenues			
Unrestricted Gifts and Bequests	627,445	354,220	800,232
Income from Investments	1,702,554	1,672,335	1,724,449
Miscellaneous Non-Patient	967,332	552,003	845,221
Total	**3,297,331**	**2,578,558**	**3,369,902**
Profit or (Loss)	**3,682,598**	**−2,046**	**−32,559,692**

Diagnosis-Related Group (DRG) Name	2024	2022	2021
Normal Newborn*	1,295	1,296	1,268
Vaginal Delivery, No Complication	1,009	974	995
Medical Back Problems	790	764	655
Angina Pectoris	400	419	401
Cesarean Section	323	336	342
Other Gastrointestinal	356	354	330
Chest Pain	292	296	328
Septicemia, Sepsis	267	285	265
Pneumonia, Pleurisy	203	197	197
Major Joint Operation	200	180	175
Cholecystectomy	103	124	106
Total Top 10 Discharges (Excluding Births)	**3,943**	**3,929**	**3,794**
Total Hospital Discharges	**10,367**	**9,957**	**8,993**
% Top Ten Discharges (Excluding Births)	**38.0%**	**39.5%**	**42.2%**

Table 6.7
MIDCARE
Top Ten DRG
Discharges

Note: *Counted as births, not discharges.

Table 6.8
MIDCARE Patient Days by Type and by Payer (Percentages)

Type of PT Day	Total %	Medicare	Medicaid	BC HMO	BC PPO	CS HPO	CS PPO	Comm PPO	Comm Indem	VA + Mil	Other	Self-Pay
Medical	43.1	16.2	2.8	0.2	3.3	0.8	0.7	5.1	10	2	0.2	1.8
Surgical												
Nonorthopedic	22.1	12.1	2.8	0.1	1.2	0.2	0.1	0.9	1.6	2.1	0.2	0.8
Orthopedic	10.7	3	2.7	0.1	0.4	0.2	0.2	0.6	1.6	1.7	0	0.2
Obstetric	7.5	0	2	0.4	1.3	0.1	0.1	0.8	1.7	0	0.2	0.9
Newborn	4.3	0	1.1	0.2	0.9	0	0	0.4	1	0	0.1	0.6
Other Pediatric	3.8	0	0.6	0.3	0.7	0.1	0.1	0	1.1	0.7	0	0.2
ICU/CCU	7.9	5.8	0.2	0.4	0.3	0	0.1	0	0.7	0	0.2	0.2
Psychological/Psychiatric	0.2	0.1	0	0	0	0	0.1	0	0	0	0	0
Substance Abuse												
Detox	0.1	0	0	0	0	0	0	0	0	0	0	0.1
Rehab	0.3	0	0	0	0	0	0	0	0	0	0	0.3
	100	37.2	12.2	1.7	8.1	1.4	1.4	7.8	17.7	6.5	0.9	5.1

Note: BC: Blue Cross; Comm: Commercial; CS: Central States; HMO: health maintenance organization; ICU/CCU: intensive care unit/coronary care unit or cardiac ICU; Indem: indemnity; Mil: military; PPO: preferred provider organization; PT: patient; VA: Veterans Administration.

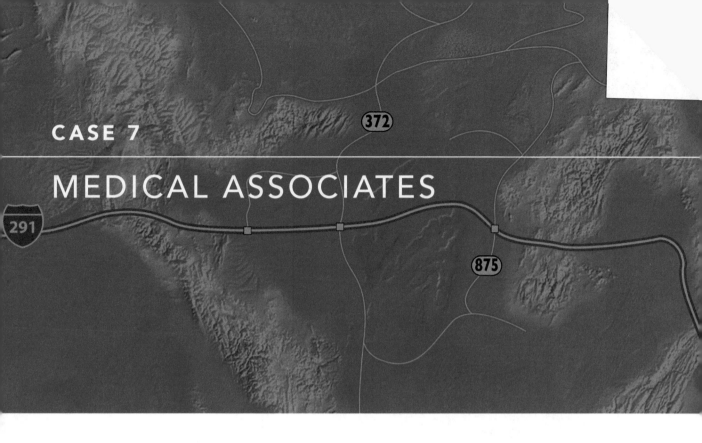

MEDICAL ASSOCIATES

Medical Associates is a for-profit multispecialty medical group. It operates two facilities—one is in Middleboro (which opened in 1995 and is approximately three miles from MIDCARE), and the other is in Jasper (which opened in 2002 on the eastern edge of town and is now adjacent to the new interstate). In 2017, Medical Associates added a 24/7 convenient care center—called Medical Associates Express—to its Jasper location.

All Medical Associates physicians maintain active staff privileges at an accredited hospital and consulting staff privileges at other hospitals. These physicians provide services in the following specialties: cardiology, ENT (ear, nose, throat), family medicine, gastroenterology, general surgery, internal medicine, obstetrics/gynecology, orthopedic surgery, pediatrics, urgent and convenient care, and urology. Currently, 28 physicians staff the facility in Middleboro and have active staff privileges at MIDCARE and consulting staff privileges at Capital City General Hospital. At the Jasper facility, 22 physicians provide medical services and maintain active staff privileges at hospitals in Capital City as well as consulting staff privileges at MIDCARE. Medical Associates physicians in Middleboro provide ambulatory surgery at MIDCARE.

Medical Associates is organized as a for-profit, professional corporation. Each of its shareholders has rights to distributed earnings based on a predetermined formula approved by the board of directors.

The total number of shares equals the number of shareholder physicians. For example, a new physician is recruited and hired on a three-year contract that provides a fixed salary and benefits. At the end of three years, the physician is either offered the opportunity to join Medical Associates as a shareholder or is terminated. If asked to join, the physician must purchase one share in the practice. If terminated, the physician leaves and the group repurchases the physician's share. According to the bylaws of Medical Associates, the buy-in and severance rate is "equal to the total equity of the corporation divided by the number of partner physicians." This formula can be changed by a two-thirds vote of the partner physicians.

All physicians affiliated with Medical Associates sign a contractual covenant that, should they or the group terminate the relationship, they cannot practice within a 30-mile radius of Middleboro and Jasper for two years without paying compensatory damages equal to the compensation they received from the group for the previous two years. In 1978, the covenant was tested in state court and found to be legal. Since that time, no former Medical Associates physician has disputed it.

HISTORY

Medical Associates was founded in 1951 as a single-specialty medical practice in Middleboro. Under the leadership of Dr. James R. Fairchild, a board-certified internist, it slowly expanded in size and, in 1963, added other specialties. It has provided specialty and subspecialty medical and surgical care since 1972.

Dr. Fairchild was an early proponent of multispecialty medical care. For almost 15 years, he chaired the committee on multispecialty medical practice of the State Medical Society. He received special awards from the American Medical Association for writing articles that examined the value of multispecialty medicine in rural areas. For many years, he personally recruited all new physicians. Trained in internal medicine at a midwestern medical school, he completed his residency training at a large midwestern medical center known for its innovative approaches to serving rural areas using a large multispecialty group. As he later expressed in his articles and many speeches, "multispecialty medical practices truly serve the patient's interests of high quality, convenience, and reasonable costs." In 1972, under his leadership, Medical Associates required all affiliated physicians to be board certified within three years, a decision that was controversial at the time. Throughout his career with Medical Associates, he served as its president and medical director. He also supervised all professional and administrative staff until 1972, when he hired a full-time executive manager.

On the occasion of his retirement in 1995, the Jasper facility was renamed Fairchild Medical Center. Although retired, Dr. Fairchild still attends the annual meetings of the board as an "interested observer." He has been a long-term critic of the two hospitals in Middleboro—namely, MIDCARE and Webster Hospital. When he retired, he blamed "the lack of innovation in medical care in our community on the self-interested behaviors and approaches each hospital has followed for decades. The problem is our hospitals do not listen to the practicing physician who knows best the needs of the patients."

In 1972, Medical Associates hired its first DO, a physician trained in osteopathic medicine. Dr. Maynard Kricnicki, who subsequently became a partner, practiced in Jasper but used the hospital resources in Capital City. According to Dr. Fairchild, the late Dr. Kricnicki was "one of our finest primary care physicians before primary care became the rage. He practiced successfully with the group for many years. Osteopathic Medical Center in Capital City even built and dedicated a memorial to him and his enormous contributions."

Over the past 15 years, all of the original Medical Associates physicians have either retired or left Hillsboro County. Many physicians have joined the group in the past ten years, most of whom did so immediately after completing a residency in their medical specialty. Recently, however, a number of osteopathic physicians previously affiliated with Webster Hospital have joined Medical Associates. Prior to joining Medical Associates, all had maintained active independent practices in Hillsboro Country and had medical staff privileges at Webster Hospital.

OPERATIONS AND SERVICES

THE FACILITIES

Each of the two Medical Associates facilities is a modern, one-story building with ample parking and room for expansion. The Middleboro facility is 48,500 square feet, T-shaped, and sits on a 9.75-acre campus. It opened in 1995 and was modernized and expanded in 2002 and 2012. It was featured in a 2013 article in the national trade publication *Medical Group News*. The Jasper facility is 48,590 square feet, H-shaped, and sits on a 25-acre campus. The building is divided into 35 medical suites and other services.

Both the Jasper and Middleboro facilities share a centralized appointment and patient registration system. Existing and new patients who prefer to use the Medical Associates website can register online, which generates a "medical portal" through which they can access their own health records and test results, schedule or change an appointment, contact their physician, and so on. Patients may also use the group's toll-free telephone number to conduct such business. Beginning in 2020, Medical Associates developed and expanded its ability to use telemedicine appointments and consultations and remote patient monitoring.

The Middleboro facility has a centralized waiting area and 25 medical suites. Physician suites (each with two to four examination rooms) are assigned by medical specialty. Family medicine and pediatrics are located in the east and west wings, and surgery is located in the south wing. The center of the facility houses the common waiting area and patient accounts. All other departments are located in the basement. The Jasper facility also has a centralized waiting area. Family medicine and pediatrics are located in the front wing, while surgery is located in the rear wing with medical records, imaging, and laboratory. All physician suites have three examination rooms. While both facilities have their own medical records, imaging, and laboratory, the Middleboro facility provides all other services (e.g., patient accounts) using telecommunications and computer systems.

Each facility is equipped with a comprehensive array of imaging technologies (such as ultrasound, X-ray, computed tomography [CT], and magnetic resonance imaging [MRI]) and drawing stations (leased from and calibrated by Wythe Laboratories in Capital City) for basic blood chemistries and urinalyses done in-house. Wythe Laboratories is under contract to administer and process medical tests for all patients at both facilities. Medical Associates also contracts with Radiology Partners in Capital City to read and interpret all diagnostic images. All X-ray, MRI, and CT images are transmitted electronically to Radiology Partners, which reads them and submits a report to the facility electronically. Under the existing agreement, Medical Associates owns and operates its own imaging equipment and employs the needed technicians. Other contracted services at both facilities include snow removal and grounds maintenance, janitorial, and laundry.

The operating hours at each facility are the same: open 8 a.m. to 6 p.m., Mondays through Saturdays; closed Sundays and on all federal holidays. All telephone inquiries before midnight are handled by a registered nurse; after midnight but before 7 a.m., inquiries are handled by an answering service, which contacts on-call physicians as needed. In 2015, Medical Associates extended its office hours to 9 p.m. on two evenings per week.

STAFF COMPENSATION AND BENEFITS

All full-time employees work a 40-hour week and qualify for a full benefits package, which includes two weeks' vacation and family coverage in a comprehensive health and dental insurance plan. Sick days are earned at the rate of one per month, with a maximum bank of 30 days. Medical Associates maintains a 401(k) retirement plan for all employees but does not contribute to any employee's plan. Part-time employees are hired at an hourly rate and receive no voluntary benefits or vacation days. Any part-time employee who is scheduled to work more than 948 hours in a calendar year may purchase the employee health insurance plan by paying the prorated difference between the percentage of time worked and the total annual premium.

All physicians are provided with comprehensive benefits, including fully paid medical liability insurance and five days of continuing medical education. Staff physicians are hired for a fixed two-year salary, negotiated at the time of hiring, and qualify for four weeks of paid vacation per year. Shareholding physicians are compensated using a predetermined formula based on the revenues they generate (the net revenue Medical Associates receives for the services provided by the physician) offset by their expenses (the physician's share of all direct and indirect costs associated with her practice). During the fiscal year, each physician is compensated monthly, according to an estimated difference between revenues and expenses. At the end of the fiscal year, the physician is given the difference between total funds previously drawn and his total share of corporate earnings as determined by the formula. To qualify for 100 percent of the share, the physician must work 230 days in a fiscal year. The total draw is reduced on a straight percentage basis for each day under the 230 days. Physicians who work more than 230 days share on a pro rata basis.

PATIENT INSURANCE AND THIRD-PARTY PAYER REIMBURSEMENT

Medical Associates provides services on a fee-for-service basis and has a long-standing policy of accepting "any insurance plan presented to us by patients." As such, it has a contractual relationship with area health maintenance organizations (HMOs) as well as preferred provider organizations (PPOs), including Statewide Blue Shield, Central State Good Health Plan, and two commercial HMOs/PPOs. Medical Associates also maintains a contractual relationship with managed care plans offered by Blue Shield and commercial insurers.

Prices charged at both facilities are exactly the same. All patients are provided a detailed bill or account statement. Patients covered by most insurance plans are billed only for any outstanding balances not paid by their insurer (which receives the bill first and directly from Medical Associates). Patients covered by indemnity or other forms of insurance are required to pay (by cash, check, or credit card) and are provided a bill to send to their insurance carrier for reimbursement. Wythe Laboratories, Radiology Partners, and other independent providers bill separately for services they rendered.

Medicare accounts for approximately 35 percent of Medical Associates' total gross revenue, while Medicaid accounts for approximately 15 percent. The other 50 percent of total gross revenue comes primarily from commercial/private insurance. During the recent pandemic, the percentage of patient revenue derived from commercial/private insurance decreased by approximately five percentage points, while Medicaid increased.

MEDICAL ASSOCIATES EXPRESS, INC.

On July 1, 2018, Medical Associates opened Medical Associates Express, housed in a 5,000-square-foot building across from the parking lot of the Jasper facility. Called Express for short, it is a convenient care or walk-in clinic that is open 24/7 per week, including on all holidays. It has four examination and treatment rooms, a basic X-ray service, and a reception area. It is a wholly owned subsidiary corporation, and its employees are not employees of Medical Associates. It pays a fee to Medical Associates to provide system support (for billing and reimbursement, use of the electronic health record [EHR], and information systems maintenance, among others) and services as the building's owner and landlord.

Medical Associates leases space in the building to other healthcare organizations, including Sockalexis Center, a behavioral health and counseling services provider. Adjacent to the Express suite is a regional drawing station owned and operated by Wythe Laboratories. The station is staffed by Wythe employees (e.g., phlebotomists) and is open for business from 7 a.m. to 11 p.m. on weekdays and from 7 a.m. to 7 p.m. on weekends. A med-evacuation helicopter pad is located on this side of the campus as well. Medical Associates donated the pad space to the Town of Jasper, whose emergency medical system is responsible for the pad's operation and upkeep. From this location, the average transfer time to Capital City General Hospital is 18 minutes.

Express has a three-member board of directors elected for a three-year term by Medical Associates' board of directors. Two of the three Express board members must be members of the Medical Associates board. Cynthia Worley, the executive manager of Medical Associates, also serves as the president of Express. Dr. Clyde Eason serves as Express's medical director and is responsible for all clinical appointments, clinical protocols, and case review.

Advanced registered nurse practitioners, physician assistants, and medical assistants provide the services. Generally, nurse practitioners are available from 7 a.m. to 11 p.m., and physician assistants cover the overnight shift from 11 p.m. to 7 a.m. Medical assistants work on all shifts, and receptionists are at the front desk from 7 a.m. to 11 p.m. The clinical staff can consult, as needed, with Medical Associates physicians, who are available on a rotating on-call basis. One innovative feature of the Medical Associates–Express linkage is that if an Express nurse practitioner, for example, referred a patient to Medical Associates, the patient is not charged for the Express visit.

Express does not treat broken bones; puncture wounds; injuries requiring sutures; injuries involving the eyes, face, or groin; back injuries; injuries from motor vehicle accidents; or workers' compensation injuries (or provide evaluations for such). It does offer care for minor illnesses (e.g., cold, flu, and allergy symptoms; sore and strep throat), minor injuries (e.g., mild burns, small cuts that need stitches, sprains and strains), joint pain, and temporary skin conditions (e.g., athlete's foot, shingles, rashes). It can perform suture and staple removal, screening and testing (e.g., for high cholesterol, diabetes, high blood pressure), and vaccinations (e.g., flu shot, pneumonia shot, children's immunization and booster shot, HPV [human papillomavirus] prevention injection). Birth control prescriptions are available for women. Every service has a specific price, and the Express website lists these prices as well as the current waiting times for procedures.

GOVERNANCE

For Medical Associates, a seven-member elected board of directors represents shareholder interests. Each director serves a three-year term, and the terms are staggered so that no more than three new members are elected annually. No term limits exist. The full board meets monthly and hosts its annual meeting in December, during which the members whose terms are not expiring elect new directors, with each shareholder having one vote. All shareholders are invited to the annual meeting. Continuing board members serve as a nominating committee and formally recommend a slate of candidates. New board members take office on January 1 of the following year. Once the new board members have been elected, the entire new board then elects its president, vice president, secretary, and treasurer. Following is a list of the board of directors (effective January 1, 2025):

Medical Associates Board of Directors

Members, Department	Term Expires
Raymond Samuels, Pediatrics, *President*	2025
Jules Putter, Surgery—General, *Vice President*	2026
Kevin Kipstein, Cardiology, *Secretary*	2027
Douglas Fixer, Urology, *Treasurer*	2027
Sarah Lee, Surgery—Orthopedic, *At-Large*	2025
Mark Stanley, Surgery—Orthopedic, *At-Large*	2026
Ursula Unvey, Pediatrics, *At-Large*	2027

Between the board's monthly meetings, the standing committees meet. Any five board members can request a special meeting of the board by providing written notice to the president.

The board has four standing committees and uses ad hoc committees as needed. Standing committees make recommendations to the full board. Standing committees include the audit, clinical standards and quality, finance, and management committees.

AUDIT COMMITTEE

This committee is chaired by the board's treasurer and is composed of two other board members. It oversees the preparation for Medical Associates' annual financial audit by an independent accounting firm. It is responsible for implementing all recommendations in the auditor's management letter. Every three years, the committee recommends to the board the individual or firm that should perform the audit. Current members of this committee are Dr. Fixer (chair), Dr. Stanley, and Worley (ex officio member).

CLINICAL STANDARDS AND QUALITY COMMITTEE

This committee is chaired by the board's vice president and includes one other board member and the medical director (ex officio, unless also an elected member of the board). It annually reviews Medical Associates' medical quality assurance plan and systems to monitor and manage quality. During the pandemic, this committee oversaw the expansion of the teleheath program, which expanded substantially. It also reviews the medical credentials of any new physician. Every third year, it recommends to the board who should be appointed (or reappointed) as medical director. This committee oversees Medical Associates' Meaningful Use program and medical information system. This committee also addresses all questions concerning the credentials and fitness of physicians. Current members of this committee are Dr. Putter (chair), Dr. Unvey, and Dr. Eason (ex officio member, medical director).

FINANCE COMMITTEE

This committee meets monthly to review Medical Associates' financial statements and to make recommendations to the full board. It also reviews the budget created by the executive manager and recommends this budget to the board for ratification. Medical Associates' fiscal year begins on January 1 and ends on December 31. In the December meeting, the board generally approves the budget for the upcoming fiscal year. Current members of this committee are Dr. Kipstein (chair), Dr. Lee, and Worley.

MANAGEMENT COMMITTEE

The board's president chairs this committee. Other members include the medical director, the chair of each medical department, one other board member, and the executive manager. This committee meets monthly to review Medical Associates' operations, including the budget performance, and to address management problems and issues. Current members of this committee are Dr. Samuels (board president and committee chair), Dr. Kipstein, Dr. Eason, Dr. Putter (chair of the Department of Surgery), Dr. Thomas Underwood (chair of the Department of Medicine), and Worley.

MEDICAL DEPARTMENTS AND ORGANIZATIONAL STRUCTURE

Medical Associates' medical director is appointed for a three-year term by the board. In accordance with the group's bylaws, "the medical director cannot be the board's president or vice president." The medical director oversees the development and implementation of the medical quality assurance plan, medical care protocols, and (with participating insurance plans) the formulary. The medical director must approve all new or revised contracts involving ancillary services, such as imaging and laboratory services, before the president can sign the contract. Increasingly, the medical director is responsible for all relations and contracts with managed care plans. As compensation, the medical director receives an extra 20 percent of his or her practice-based compensation.

Dr. Eason has been the medical director at Medical Associates for the past seven years. He is a graduate of an eastern medical school, completed advanced education in his medical specialty at a major midwestern medical center, and holds a master of public health in occupational medicine. He is board certified in his internal medicine subspecialty and in occupational health. Born in Middleboro, Dr. Eason returned to town after completing his medical education. He has been affiliated with Medical Associates for 15 years and is married to a member of the Fairchild family.

Medical Associates has two departments: medicine and surgery. Each department chair is elected annually in December by the physician shareholders assigned to the specific department. A chair receives a 12 percent stipend in addition to any practice-based compensation. A chair is responsible for convening monthly medical staff meetings and representing the medical department on the management committee. In addition, a chair serves as the supervisor for all clinical and administrative staff assigned to the medical department, such as registered nurses, medical assistants, and receptionists.

Dr. Putter is the chair of the Department of Surgery. He has held this position for the past seven years, but he has been affiliated with Medical Associates since the group recruited him 20 years ago. On three previous occasions, he served on the board of directors—and twice as board president. He is a graduate of a western medical school and completed a degree in advanced medical education in general surgery at a major midwestern teaching hospital.

Dr. Underwood has just been elected chair of the Department of Medicine. He is a graduate of a southern medical school and completed his advanced medical education at teaching hospitals in the Midwest and on the East Coast. Previously, he was chair of the board's ad hoc committee on long-range planning and medical recruitment.

The medical director resolves any disputes, while the chief of a medical department determines the work schedules of department physicians. All physicians rotate on-call duties and Saturdays. In the past, physicians typically worked one Saturday every six weeks.

ADMINISTRATION

Cynthia Worley is the executive manager at Medical Associates. She reports to the board president and is responsible for all nonmedical operations, including patient accounts, communications, building maintenance and grounds, materials management, medical records, information systems, imaging, laboratory services, and all nonclinical staff. She also serves as the controller for the corporation. A graduate from an eastern university and holder of a master of business administration and master of health services administration, she was appointed to her position when her predecessor retired in 2017. Prior to joining Medical Associates, she was the associate vice president of a midwestern medical center with responsibility for the acquisition and management of all medical practices and was the associate director of administration at a 65-physician group in a neighboring state. She is an active member of the Medical Group Management Association. Born and raised in Capital City, she still has family across Hillsboro County.

Worley maintains an office in the Middleboro facility and travels to the Jasper facility at least once a week. All employees not assigned to a specific physician or to Ambulatory Surgery (e.g., registered nurses, medical assistants) report directly to her. These employees include Ella Smythe (director of Patient Accounts and Business Operations), Christine Clark (director of Human Resources), Spencer Mangrove (bookkeeper), Hank Hammer (director of Maintenance), Shreya Batterjee (director of Medical Records), Alice Byte (director of Management Information Systems), Faith Kitchen (manager of Imaging Services, Middleboro), and Warren Kidder (manager of Imaging and Laboratory Services).

Successes, Challenges, and Plans

Compliance with Promoting Interoperability Programs

When asked to name her most significant accomplishment since joining Medical Associates, Worley cited Medical Associates' state-of-the-art electronic health record (EHR) that can—if desired—be linked to the EHR of any hospital in the area. She indicated that defining the system parameters, getting board approval for the most crucial elements, overseeing the installation, and then field-testing the finished system were some of the most complex tasks she has undertaken in her career. "I understand now why my predecessor decided to retire instead of roll out such a system" she joked. "Achieving initial and continued compliance with all criteria of CMS's Promoting Interoperability Programs was a lengthy, arduous process but a significant accomplishment." The EHR at Medical Associates is able to process all medication orders, generate and transmit prescriptions electronically, record demographics, record vital signs, record smoking status, report ambulatory clinical quality measures, incorporate clinical lab results, and provide immunization data. The system also provides clinical summaries and educational resources to patients and is the basis of Medical Associates' expanded website and patient information system. Worley also indicated that the current EHR has facilitated the development and expansion of telemedicine and remote access monitoring services, both critical during the pandemic.

Other Concerns and Plans

The clinical standards and quality committee recently recommended adding at least two primary care physicians to the Jasper facility. This recommendation has reopened the issue of whether Medical Associates should recruit physicians trained in family practice or physicians trained in general internal medicine, obstetrics/gynecology, or pediatrics. Dr. Putter, chair of the committee and the Department of Surgery, submitted a compelling argument in favor of family practice physicians, but he was directly challenged by Dr. Underwood, chair of the Department of Medicine. Dr. Putter has indicated that his committee remains gridlocked on this issue and cannot proceed with recruiting until it is resolved.

During the pandemic, Medical Associates implemented an aggressive program for staff and followed federal guidelines regarding social distancing and mask-wearing. Over the course of the pandemic, four staff members, including one physician, tested positive for the virus and were effectively quarantined, stemming the disease spread. The pandemic led to dramatic increases in telehealth services.

In addition, the committee informed the board that Medical Associates needs professional analysts on staff if it is to fulfill the expectations associated with population health and medical outcome studies requested by HMO clients and Blue Shield. Dr. Eason has reported that he devotes approximately 20 percent of his time to fulfilling requests for this type of information and that he needs professional assistance to relieve him of this burden. The board has yet to act on this information. The budget for 2024, however, was approved without the additional staff requested by Dr. Eason.

In 2017, Medical Associates agreed to participate in the second-opinion program of the Smith Brothers Clinic, a nationally recognized medical center known for its diagnostic expertise. Under this program, Medical Associates physicians and patients can visit a Smith Brothers Clinic or use telemedicine links to receive a second opinion. Medical Associates just began participating in a similar program for cardiology cases by the Cuyahoga Clinic, another highly regarded national healthcare organization. As a result of its participation in these relationships, Medical Associates is able to advertise that it is a clinical affiliate of both highly respected clinical networks. Worley explained that "these arrangements are part of Medical Associates' plan to brand its services and provide additional value to our patients. We plan to consider additional opportunities." The board has requested Worley to conduct an evaluation of these agreements and present her findings at the next annual meeting.

Additional information regarding Medical Associates' staffing, utilization, compensation, financial status, and operations can be found in tables 7.1 through 7.11.

Table 7.1
Medical
Associates
Affiliated
Physicians

Name	Specialty	Age	Facility	Gender
Kipstein	Cardiology	50	J	1
Maeer	Cardiology	42	J	2
Snipes*	Cardiology	44	J	1
Coolidge*	ENT	44	J	2
Kroneberger*	ENT	50	J	2
Finn	General Surgery	47	J	2
Goldberg	Internal Medicine	41	J	2
Washington	Internal Medicine	43	J	2
Klock, D	OB/GYN	39	J	1
Klock, M	OB/GYN	49	J	2
Mustard	OB/GYN	39	J	2
Polk*	OB/GYN	40	J	2
Goldwater	Orthopedic Surgery	44	J	1
Lee	Orthopedic Surgery	40	J	2
Picture	Orthopedic Surgery	47	J	1
Qin	Orthopedic Surgery	47	J	1
Chan	Pediatrics	37	J	2
Miller*	Pediatrics	49	J	1
Otter	Pediatrics	37	J	2
Quester	Pediatrics	40	J	2
Unvey	Pediatrics	56	J	2
Steve	Thoracic Surgery	47	J	1
Underwood	Cardiology	46	M	1
Zook*	Endocrinology	50	M	1
Walberger	ENT	42	M	1
Weckensen	ENT	44	M	1
Xerox	ENT	42	M	1
Autumn	Gastroenterology	44	M	1
Flores	General Surgery	45	M	1
Hersh	General Surgery	40	M	1
Jackson	General Surgery	39	M	2
Friedman	General Surgery	45	M	2
O'Connell	General Surgery	49	M	2
Putter	General Surgery	62	M	1
Barton	Internal Medicine	45	M	1
Douglas	Internal Medicine	41	M	1
Eason	Internal Medicine	56	M	1
Kessler	Internal Medicine	34	M	2

continued

Name	Specialty	Age	Facility	Gender
Lesko	Internal Medicine	38	M	1
Master	Internal Medicine	40	M	1
Dustin	OB/GYN	33	M	2
Gost	OB/GYN	45	M	1
Qestrom	Orthopedic Surgery	39	M	1
Stanley	Orthopedic Surgery	49	M	1
Hirsh*	Pediatrics	46	M	2
Reaper	Pediatrics	59	M	1
Samuels	Pediatrics	47	M	1
St. James	Pediatrics	40	M	2
Eason	Urology	56	M	1
Fixer	Urology	43	M	1

Table 7.1
Medical
Associates
Affiliated
Physicians
(continued)

Notes: (1) As of December 31, 2024. (2) Facility: J-Jasper, M-Middleboro. (3) Gender: 1-Male, 2-Female. (4) Unless otherwise noted, all physicians in the Middleboro office maintain active medical staff privileges at MIDCARE and consulting medical staff privileges at Capital City General. Physicians at the Jasper office maintain active medical staff privileges at Capital City General and consulting privileges at MIDCARE. (5) *: formerly affiliated with Webster Hospital; ENT: ear, nose, throat; OB/GYN: obstetrics/gynecology.

Table 7.2
Medical Associates Utilization Statistics for Middleboro Facility

Handwritten notes (left margin):
ENT
8635 >10.4%
7819 >19.4%
6549

7528 > -5.77%
7989 > 25.5%
6368

11,467 > 4.39
10,985 > -10.1
12,095

5944 > -16.4
7107 > 17.3
6058
3765 > 9.8
3428 > 10.7
3097

4906 > -11.6
11,054 > 32.3
8,353

Name	Specialty	2024			2023			2022		
		Appts	PT Days	Dis	Appts	PT Days	Dis	Appts	PT Days	Dis
Underwood	Cardiology	2,044	684	151 *8.8%*	1,878	506	125 *14.2%*	1,644	545	107
Zook	Endocrinology	1,735	238	488 *1.8%*	954	119	32	NA	NA	NA
Walberger	ENT	2,845	205	67	2,840	212	58	2,405	529	143
Weckensen	ENT	2,945	470	110	2,834	217	61	2,341	490	134
Xerox	ENT	2,845	497	145	2,145	301	87	1,803	312	102
Autumn	Gastroenterology	2,789	475	120 *3.1*	2,705	745	144 *1.8*	2,656	801	131
Flores	Gen Surgery	1,102	612	108	2,206	530	107	2,345	571	143
Putter	Gen Surgery	912	501	126	1,112	420	105	1,345	779	199
Friedman	Gen Surgery	970	770	175	903	290	88	744	256	65
O'Connell	Gen Surgery	1,456	572	114	1,045	418	91	867	436	109
Jackson	Gen Surgery	1,843	634	140	1,678	612	134	1,067	612	156
Hersh, M	Gen Surgery	1,245	745	167	1,045	633	145	NA	NA	NA
Master	Int Med	1,623	402	101	1,276	501	102	2,330	535	99
Lesko	Int Med	2,034	560	130	2,083	401	98	2,405	355	67
Kessler	Int Med	2,256	458	149	2,033	204	45	1656	206	61
Douglas	Int Med	2,003	467	143	2,867	434	102	2,456	402	65
Barton	Int Med	1,906	476	121	1,256	497	102	2,214	556	126
Eason, L	Int Med	1,645	557	146	1,470	459	101	1,034	403	190
Gost	OB/GYN	2,319	374	110	3,702	334	82	3,003	293	70
Dustin	OB/GYN	3,625	433	104	3,405	389	87	3,055	377	84
Stanley	Ortho	1,966	1,520	314	1,862	328	98	1,645	414	87
Qestrom	Ortho	1,799	1,601	322	1,566	953	208	1,452	1005	202
St. James	Pediatrics	2,231	134	34	3,302	105	24	2,269	108	32
Samuels	Pediatrics	2,167	114	34	3,254	123	30	2,987	106	32
Reaper	Pediatrics	1,234	81	25	1,846	102	24	1,745	98	32
Hersh, D	Pediatrics	2,439	78	23	1,006	60	12	NA	NA	NA
Eason, J	Pediatrics	1,835	71	30	1,646	53	12	1352	58	14
Fixer	Urology	2,403	460	101 *9.1*	2,202	480	142 *9.8*	2,005	538	109
Total		**56,216**	**14,189**	**3,358**	**56,121**	**10,426**	**2,446**	**48,825**	**10,785**	**2,559**

Notes: (1) Appts: appointments; Dis: discharges (all hospitals); PT Days: patient days (all hospitals).
(2) ENT: ear, nose, throat; Gen Surgery: general surgery; Int Med: internal medicine; NA: not applicable; OB/GYN: obstetrics/gynecology; Ortho: orthopedics.

Name	Specialty	2024			2023			2022		
		Appts	PT Days	Dis	Appts	PT Days	Dis	Appts	PT Days	Dis
Kipstein	Cardiology	3,544	617	140	3,682	506	125	3,933	612	150
Maeer	Cardiology	3,782	713	120	3,956	501	123	4,631	587	178
Snipes	Cardiology	3,155	549	94	2,657	423	101	NA	NA	NA
Coolidge	ENT	3,369	362	89	3,278	312	84	1,433	270	83
Kronberger	ENT	2,745	482	106	2,155	345	101	NA	NA	NA
Washington	Int Med	3,745	570	124	2,867	655	120	2,456	408	70
Goldberg	Int Med	3,850	402	100	3,156	412	84	2,077	508	87
Polk	OB/GYN	3,651	369	110	3,612	454	148	3,487	609	156
Klock, M	OB/GYN	3,749	349	87	3,256	356	80	3,356	402	90
Mustard	OB/GYN	3,317	460	114	3,450	406	82	4,245	314	90
Klock, D	OB/GYN	3,845	284	77	3,756	244	49	NA	NA	NA
Lee	Ortho	3,944	710	192	3,856	696	184	2,044	693	180
Quin	Ortho	2,156	574	165	1,935	590	193	1,689	556	178
Goldwater	Ortho	1,920	562	140	1,756	556	156	2,156	512	148
Picture	Ortho	2,877	677	137	2,645	607	136	2,034	405	85
Chan	Pediatrics	3,755	146	49	NA	NA	NA	NA	NA	NA
Unvey	Pediatrics	3,604	128	34	3,324	118	30	4,125	106	26
Otter	Pediatrics	3,745	95	25	3,654	88	19	4,209	60	14
Quester	Pediatrics	3,520	111	46	3,545	124	42	4,509	120	40
Miller	Pediatrics	3,689	105	30	3,978	104	24	3,956	90	23
Finn	Thoracic	1,034	274	56	990	202	44	832	212	49
Steve	Thoracic	1,255	368	71	1,178	305	60	700	301	60
Total		**70,251**	**8,907**	**2,106**	**62,686**	**8,004**	**1,985**	**51,872**	**6,765**	**1,707**

Table 7.3
Medical Associates Utilization Statistics for Jasper Facility

Notes: (1) Appts: appointments; Dis: discharges (all hospitals); PT Days: patient days (all hospitals).
(2) ENT: ear, nose, throat; Int Med: internal medicine; NA: not applicable; OB/GYN: obstetrics/gynecology; Ortho: orthopedics.

Table 7.4
Medical Associates Express Utilization (Visits)

Month	2024	2023	2022
January	2,750	2,985	2,976
February	2,189	2,245	2,890
March	3,004	3,056	3,348
April	2,861	2,971	2,880
May	2,893	2,912	2,901
June	2,990	2,654	2,736
July	2,045	2,481	2,381
August	2,456	2,655	2,827
September	2,203	2,435	2,304
October	2,585	2,406	2,456
November	2,877	2,745	2,880
December	3,044	2,878	3,124
Total	**31,897**	**32,423**	**33,703**
Weekdays			
7 a.m.–3 p.m.	23,803	23,472	23,885
3 p.m.–11 p.m.	5,270	5,588	5,971
11 p.m.–7 a.m.	2,344	2,866	3,317
Subtotal	**31,417**	**31,926**	**33,173**
Weekends			
7 a.m.–3 p.m.	264	294	313
3 p.m.–11 p.m.	113	107	111
11 p.m.–7 a.m.	103	96	106
Subtotal	**480**	**497**	**530**
Total	**31,897**	**32,423**	**33,703**

Note: Includes telehealth visits.

Department	Office	Patient Days		Discharges	
		All Hospitals	MIDCARE Only	All Hospitals	MIDCARE Only
Medicine	Middleboro	6,427	5,333	1,549	1,492
Surgery	Middleboro	7,762	8,475	1,677	1,970
Subtotal		**14,189**	**13,808**	**3,226**	**3,462**
Medicine	Jasper	4,627	1,000	1,140	290
Surgery	Jasper	4,280	961	928	203
Subtotal		**8,907**	**1,961**	**2,068**	**493**
Total		**23,096**	**15,769**	**5,294**	**3,955**

Table 7.5
Medical Associates Hospital Utilization by Office Location, 2024

Note: For 12-month period ending December 31, 2024.

Physician Name	Specialty	Facility	2024 Salary (US$)	Expiration Date
Otter	Pediatrics	Jasper	232,456	7/1/2025
Snipes	Cardiology	Jasper	438,254	12/31/2026
Kessler	Internal Medicine	Middleboro	251,650	12/31/2026
Polk	OB/GYN	Middleboro	308,359	7/1/2026

Table 7.6
Medical Associates Staff Physicians

Notes: (1) Expiration Date is the end of the physician's employment contract. At this date, the physician must be offered and accept a partnership or leave the practice. (2) OB/GYN: obstetrics/gynecology.

Table 7.7 Medical Associates Statement of Revenues and Expenses		2024	2023	2022
Revenues				
Patient Revenue—Gross		87,445,373	78,383,440	74,343,182
Allowance		13,674,978	11,783,563	11,357,223
Bad Debt		512,556	692,445	534,229
Net Patient Services Revenue		**73,257,839**	**65,907,432**	**62,451,730**
Other Revenue				
Management Fees		350,000	350,000	350,000
Real Estate Rentals		625,000	625,000	610,000
Other		12,738	10,563	11,472
Total Other		**987,738**	**985,563**	**971,472**
Total Revenue		**74,245,577**	**66,892,995**	**63,423,202**
Expenses				
Physician Compensation		33,783,223	30,762,939	29,828,556
Non-Physician Staff: Salary + Benefits		19,342,556	18,657,646	18,558,890
Consultants and Contractors		7,330,113	6,002,554	5,735,220
General Services		5,845,295	5,679,820	5,394,590
Fiscal Services		3,299,475	3,284,337	2,946,660
Interest		7,125	9,730	6,994
Depreciation		1,845,920	1,947,220	1,856,029
Total Operating Expenses		**71,453,707**	**66,344,246**	**64,326,939**
Pretax Income (Loss)		2,791,870	548,749	−903,737
Taxes		106,091	20,852	0
Profit or (Loss)		**2,685,779**	**527,897**	**−903,737**

Notes: (1) Years ending December 31. (2) Numbers are in US dollars.

	2024	2023	2022
Assets			
Current Assets			
Cash and Marketable Securities	9046455	4772872	896332
Accounts Receivable—Gross	4,342,567	4,034,282	5,562,939
Allowances for Uncollectibles	945,232	909,342	903,549
Accounts Receivable—Net	3,397,335	3,124,940	4,659,390
Due from Third-Party Payers	176,342	184,239	182,563
Inventory	402,331	404,293	415,330
Prepaid Expenses	58,520	55,320	61,970
Total Current Assets	13,080,983	8,541,664	6,215,585
Noncurrent Assets			
Property, Plant, and Equipment—Gross	73,518,976	74,635,569	70,334,020
Less Accumulated Depreciation	17,649,169	16,803,249	13,856,029
Property, Plant, and Equipment—Net	55,869,807	57,832,320	56,477,991
Other Investments	239,267	124,934	3,450,212
Total Assets	69,190,057	66,498,918	66,143,788
Liabilities			
Current Liabilities			
Accounts Payable	756,393	734,532	834,356
Accrued Salaries and Wages	1,610,463	1,607,834	1,666,547
Accrued Interest	170,234	173,235	154,330
Other Accrued Expenses	137,243	143,220	154,302
Accrued Vacation Days	91,670	92,992	90,256
Due to Third-Party Vendors	174,393	170,365	173,223
Long-Term Debt Due in 1 Year	45,230	46,992	47,890
Total Current Liabilities	2,985,626	2,969,170	3,120,904
Long-Term Debt	4,890,236	4,901,332	4,922,365
Total Liabilities	7,875,862	7,870,502	8,043,269
Net Assets	61,314,195	58,628,416	58,100,519
Net Assets + Total Liabilities	69,190,057	66,498,918	66,143,788

Table 7.8
Medical Associates Balance Sheet as of December 31

Notes: (1) For fiscal years ending December 31. (2) Numbers are in US dollars.

Table 7.9
Medical
Associates
Express
Statement of
Revenues and
Expenses

	2024	2023	2022
Revenues			
Patient Services — Gross	3,387,334	3,356,221	3,194,996
Allowances and Discounts	−7,327	−6,854	−4268
Deductions for Bad Debt	−1,307	−1,274	−1055
Patient Services — Net	3,378,700	3,348,093	3,189,673
Expenses			
Salaries and Wages	2,019,772	2,009,342	1,970,920
Benefits	509,262	501,033	512,439
Management Fee	350,000	350,000	250,000
Advertising	34,778	32,567	56,300
Computer Support	12,300	12,300	12,000
Insurance	20,563	19,045	18,850
Laundry and Housekeeping	6,869	6,244	6,390
Legal/Audit	1,405	1,803	1,850
Medical Supplies	22,451	18,337	14,923
Office Supplies	11,650	11,342	10,449
Printing and Postage	5,705	5,300	5,400
Facility and Equipment Rent	300,000	300,000	250,000
Repairs and Maintenance	1,980	1,045	1,267
Internet and Telephone	5,308	6,045	6,320
Interest	3,020	3,867	3,222
Depreciation	7,000	6,500	5,800
Total Expenses	3,312,063	3,284,770	3,126,130
Income (Loss) Before Taxes	66,637	63,323	63,543
Federal and State Taxes*	5,997	5,699	5,719
Income (Loss) After Taxes	60,640	57,624	57,824

Notes: (1) Years ending December 31. (2) Numbers are in US dollars. (3) *Includes carryforward tax credits.

	2024	2023	2022
Assets			
Current Assets			
Cash	85,295	108,426	68,352
Cash Equivalents	216,480	266,650	273,508
Accounts Receivable	63,464	58,398	51,254
Inventory	29,552	37,254	30,552
Prepaid Expenses	453	478	430
Total Current Assets	**395,244**	**471,206**	**424,096**
Investments	129,563	88,251	105,422
Property and Equipment			
Equipment and Leasehold Improvements—Gross	155,920	152,404	146,223
Less Accumulated Depreciation	27,803	20,803	14,303
Equipment and Leasehold Improvements—Net	128,117	131,601	131,920
Total Assets	**652,924**	**691,058**	**661,438**
Liabilities			
Current Liabilities			
Accounts Payable	83,226	90,363	97,364
Accrued Expenses	65,943	60,595	60,625
Total Current Liabilities	**149,169**	**150,958**	**157,989**
Notes Payable	53,140	150,125	162,098
Total Liabilities	**202,309**	**301,083**	**320,087**
Net Assets			
Common Stock Authorized and Issued*	900,000	900,000	900,000
Cumulative Operating Gain/Loss After Taxes	−449,385	−510,025	−558,649
Total Net Assets	450,615	389,975	341,351
Total Net Assets + Liabilities	**652,924**	**691,058**	**661,438**

Table 7.10
Medical Associates Express Balance Sheet

Notes: (1) *Common stock at $10,000 par value per share, 90 shares authorized. (2) For fiscal years ending December 31. (3) Numbers are in US dollars.

Table 7.11
Medical
Associates
Ambulatory
Surgical
Procedures at
MIDCARE

	2024				2023			
	ENT	**Ortho**	**Other**	**Total**	**ENT**	**Ortho**	**Other**	**Total**
January	53	102	103	258	43	99	91	233
February	52	67	88	207	50	60	80	190
March	77	70	70	217	79	60	54	193
April	80	55	78	213	76	55	78	209
May	76	58	64	198	72	58	64	194
June	66	67	56	189	69	67	56	192
July	49	58	90	197	50	58	90	198
August	35	70	79	184	43	70	79	192
September	40	79	88	207	35	79	88	202
October	59	80	69	208	60	80	69	209
November	36	91	81	208	45	91	81	217
December	71	98	70	239	68	98	70	236
Total	**694**	**895**	**936**	**2,525**	**690**	**875**	**900**	**2,465**

Notes: (1) ENT: ear, nose, throat; Ortho: orthopedic.

ENT- 0.58%
ORTHO- 2.3%
OTHER- 4%

JASPER GARDENS

Jasper Gardens is a tax-paying, Medicare- and Medicaid-certified nursing home with a license to operate 125 beds in both private and semiprivate rooms. It is approved to provide skilled nursing and rehabilitation services covered by Medicare, and a significant number of its residents and patients are covered by Medicaid. Physical, occupational, recreational, and speech therapy are offered on-site. Respiratory therapy is also available from a contracted provider. Jasper Gardens accepts all forms of payment.

Situated on 100 acres of land adjacent to the to-be-completed new highway—approximately five miles from the planned Jasper–East exit and eight miles east of the center of Jasper—the facility is a one-story modern building with ample parking and significant room for expansion. It is owned and operated by Jefferson Partners.

JEFFERSON PARTNERS, LLC

Jefferson Partners owns and operates nursing homes, assisted living facilities, retirement living communities, and adult day care centers in the greater Capital City area and other communities throughout the state. It is a private-equity partnership of investors, none of whom is involved in the day-to-day management of the corporation. It holds quarterly board meetings, and the board's executive committee meets monthly with the senior management team to review operations and issues.

Jefferson Partners has two operating divisions: Management and Property. The Management division provides centralized administrative services—such as payroll, legal, financial management, and group purchasing—to its facilities for a management fee. The Property division buys buildings and land and then leases them to wholly owned subsidiary corporations, which actually run and manage the individual operations such as Jasper Gardens. Jasper Gardens owns its current site and some physical assets and leases most of its current buildings from Jefferson Partners.

The senior management team of Jefferson Partners includes Ralph Jefferson, President and CEO; Wanda Charles, RN, vice president of Operations; Norman Fellows, director of Corporate Development and Acquisitions; and Gayle Wyman, chief financial officer. This team approves the annual budget for each facility. Charles meets monthly with facility administrators to monitor operations and to address problems and issues. Jefferson Partners maintains a central office with a small staff in Capital City. In 2019, Jefferson Partners sold a 38-acre parcel of land adjacent to its current campus to The Oaks, a nonprofit Continuing Care Retirement Facility (CCRC). The Oaks began construction in 2019 and formal operations in 2020. Jasper Gardens has a cooperative agreement with The Oaks involving skilled care.

History

Mary and John Decker founded Jasper Gardens Nursing Home in 1960. It was housed in a former resort that accommodated 45 residents in semiprivate rooms. In the 1970s, the facility was expanded to accommodate 77 residents and was licensed by Medicaid and Medicare. In 1980, the Deckers sold the facility to the Armstrong family, who built four new wings of patient rooms, each with 12 semiprivate rooms. On each expansion, the state awarded a certificate of need (CON). Between 1990 and 1995, Jasper Gardens was modified into its current configuration of five wings and a central building for administrative services. The resort house was demolished and replaced with a new structure, and a new wing was added to the existing four. Jefferson Partners acquired the facility in 1995 and has continually invested in updating it. Today, the facility is modern, spacious, and tastefully decorated to emphasize a warm, comfortable environment for its residents.

When it was originally founded, Jasper Gardens was in a relatively rural environment. Today, the area has become suburban, marked by a number of new housing subdivisions, chain stores and restaurants, and a shopping mall about a quarter of a mile away. The area is expected to grow and develop even more when the new interstate highway is completed between Jasper and Capital City.

In 2007, Resident Community Councils were introduced in Jasper Gardens. These councils enable residents to express their wishes and preferences, big and small. Jasper Garden's brochure and website stress this and other resident-centered features. It states:

> Jasper Gardens residents have a choice regarding how they want to live. We promise to listen to and strive to accommodate wishes and preferences so that we can fulfill them every day. They may wish to experience our Fine Dining program, which creates an inviting, restaurant-like atmosphere with fine china, polished silverware, tablecloths and cloth napkins, personal assistance from our attentive staff, and—of course—fresh and well-balanced meals. They may opt to dine at local restaurants occasionally or regularly by themselves or with a group of friends. Or they may prefer to bring food back to their rooms to enjoy in private. We honor residents' requests regarding bathing or showering times, days, and frequency. Our staff—each of whom is assigned to a resident—are happy to accommodate such requests and incorporate them, when possible, into the resident's daily care and routine. We open our doors to social functions, meetings, celebrations, and other events hosted and organized by community members. We encourage our residents to partake in activities that are open to everyone, but only if they choose to do so.

These efforts have resulted in Jasper Gardens being recognized as a regional leader in empowering residents and creating a home-like atmosphere. For the past four years, it has been a semifinalist for the statewide Quality-of-Life Award bestowed by the governor to a nursing home that consistently demonstrates its commitment to resident independence, choice, and well-being.

SERVICES AND OPERATIONS

Jasper Gardens classifies its patients and residents as follows: The term *resident* is used when the individual's average length of stay (ALOS) is 90 days or more, whereas the term *patient* is used when the individual's ALOS is less than 90 days. Similarly, it classifies its services as either *intermediate care* or *skilled care*. Intermediate care services emphasize long-term residential services. The ALOS for intermediate care is approximately 2.8 years and has been increasing. The average age of residents is approximately 87 years and has slowly been increasing. Most residents in the intermediate care category have the ability to pay for care when they are initially admitted. However, after "spending down" their available personal resources, these residents have to rely on Medicaid to finance their care. Over the past five years, the average spend-down period for residents has dropped from 26 months to 19 months. A few patients in this category are covered by private nursing home insurance or insurance provided by the Veterans Administration.

Skilled care services emphasize short-term treatment. These patients are in the nursing home for post-hospital rehabilitation, for example. Those older than 65 years rely on Medicare as their primary insurance and thus make use of physical, occupational, and speech therapy services. Those not eligible for Medicare typically rely on a private health insurance plan. The ALOS for Medicare patients has been decreasing over the past five years. Based on a contractual agreement with The Oaks, a neighboring Type A CCRC, skilled care nursing services are provided as needed to its residents. The Oaks is responsible for all associated expenses.

At Jasper Gardens, registered nurses (RNs), licensed practical nurses (LPNs), licensed nursing assistants (LNAs), and medication nursing assistants (MNAs) provide services. A part-time registered dietitian supervises all matters related to food and nutrition. Social work services are offered during the admissions process and on an inpatient basis. Pharmacy services are coordinated with DRUGCO, Inc., a pharmacy under contract with Jefferson Partners.

The medical director is James A. Child, DO, who is board certified in family practice and gerontology and operates a practice in Jasper with Drs. Freda Evans and David Contreras, who provide backup, on-call services as needed. All three physicians have active and consulting staff privileges at Valley Medical Center in Capital City. Dr. Child devotes approximately a half day per week to his patients in Jasper Gardens.

Four of the five wings in the building have nine semiprivate rooms and two private rooms, for a total of eight private rooms. The fifth wing has 13 semiprivate rooms and houses the Rehabilitation Services department. Each wing has a nursing station, a shower room, and a small library. Wireless Internet connection (Wi-Fi) is available throughout the facility. The beauty salon, library, music room, and barbershop are located in the central commons area.

Many patients enter Jasper Gardens after discharge from area hospitals. Primary referral sources include the hospitals located in Middleboro and Capital City. Upon completion of the new highway, the number of residents and patients from Capital City is expected to increase.

MANAGEMENT TEAM AND ORGANIZATIONAL STRUCTURE

Jasper Gardens has a flat management structure. Members of its senior management team report to the administrator, who in turn reports to the vice president of Operations for Jefferson Partners. The senior management team meets to review the budget reports furnished by Jefferson Partners. Each of the senior managers supervises and directs multiple departments and staff.

ADMINISTRATOR

Jayne Winters, NHA, is the licensed administrator of Jasper Gardens. Upon graduating with a bachelor's degree in health services management from an eastern university in 2006, she entered an Administrator in Training (AIT) program at a Jefferson Partners facility in Capital City. Upon completion of the AIT program, she earned her state license and was appointed as assistant administrator at Jefferson Partners' largest nursing home/assisted living and congregate living (apartment) facility in Capital City. She was appointed administrator of Jasper Gardens in 2010. She is active in the State Association of Long Term Care Administrators and lives in Jasper.

With the help of her administrative assistant Chloe Hyde, Winters handles all aspects of personnel and human resources functions, including advertising job vacancies, screening applicants (e.g., background checks), and administering compensation and benefit policies. Wage and salary rates are set during the annual budgeting process, and changes to the rates require the approval of Jefferson Partners. She is also responsible for all marketing activities, including producing advertisements, brochures, and in-person or online/social media promotions. Her employment contract includes certain incentives and penalties that are tied to quality of care and financial performance.

Winters relies on a "dashboard report" to stay abreast of the management issues in the facility. This weekly report includes the following information for the latest week, month, and quarter as well as year to date:

◆ Revenue and expense budget performance

◆ Payroll information (budgeted versus actual hours, dollars, and overtime)

◆ Patient census by payer

◆ Admissions and discharges

◆ Therapy revenue, expenses, and hours

◆ Employee health insurance claims submitted

In addition, she monitors the following primary quality indicators:

◆ Facility-acquired pressure ulcers

◆ Falls

◆ Injuries

- ◆ Weight loss

- ◆ Reportable events

- ◆ Acute discharges

Challenges and Successes

Over the past 18 months, three employees have filed formal grievances related to "unfair interpretations" of sick leave policies, merit pay adjustments, and rates paid to part-time workers who work on national holidays. During this same period, three employees were discharged for failure to perform stated duties. One of Winters's first actions as administrator was the dismissal of three employees for nepotism, a dismissal still remembered by many staff members who deemed it inappropriate because the employees were hired before a formal policy on nepotism was instituted. Recently, she dismissed two more employees for poor attendance and work performance.

When interviewed, Winters admitted that Medicaid pricing has continued to force the facility to reconsider its staffing levels and, in some instances, reduce staff. Like other nursing homes, Jasper Gardens works within very modest annual financial margins, so even small staffing increases could easily evaporate its modest profits. However, "patient acuity and levels of need have increased significantly," she said. "More and more of our older residents are exhibiting behavioral problems and seem to need more and more care. Our staffing level, though, has remained about the same."

A certified bargaining unit has never represented the hourly staff. Winters and her management team have heard rumors that a local union in Capital City was sending out cards to the hourly staff to determine their interest in being represented by a union. If a sufficient number of cards are returned to the union, then the union will petition the state labor board for permission to hold an election and form a certified bargaining unit at the facility.

Some residents use electric wheelchairs and mobility carts to get around inside the nursing home and to frequent the small park on campus. Medicare purchases these carts for any mobility-impaired individual who is aged 65 years or older. In the past 18 months, two crashes occurred inside the facility that injured three residents. Because the sidewalks outside Jasper Gardens are wide, a few residents use their wheelchairs and carts to go to the nearby shopping mall. To leave the campus, a resident must secure permission from the supervising nurse and take a cell phone furnished by the nursing home. Legal counsel is reviewing this practice to ensure that it is compliant with current laws and regulations. Two different families have requested that the residents be prohibited from using the carts outside the property. Current policies do not allow for such restrictions unless they are based on appropriate legal (e.g., power of attorney) or medical orders. Recently, one resident started walking to the mall, became disoriented on the way there, got lost, and had to be brought back to the facility by the police. This is the fifth such incident within the past two years.

In the past two years, Jasper Gardens has received a deficiency-free survey—Level B—from the state survey team. This score, Winters explained, is a notable improvement over the conditions at the facility when she arrived. Prior to 2010, the facility was consistently found to operate at Level E or Level F, which indicated widespread potential to cause more than minimal harm to patients and residents. She credited these positive surveys to her dedicated staff, changes in some job responsibilities, and a solid team effort.

Four years ago, the facility hired a certified therapeutic recreation specialist to staff its Recreation Services department. The first specialist was so well received that more specialists were hired. Today, Jasper Gardens' Recreation Services department is known as one of the best in the state.

Three years ago, workers' compensation rates at the facility soared, doubling the number of workplace injury claims from years past. The most common injury reported was lower back strain as a result of assisting or lifting residents and patients from their beds. In response, Jefferson Partners instituted a new policy and ordered new equipment designed to minimize injury and help staff protect themselves while assisting residents. Since then, no employee has reported back injuries.

Asked to comment on this assortment of issues, Winters said,

> I am very pleased with the progress we have made. The facility looks good, the staff is very dedicated, and the owners are comfortable with our profit margins. We have been challenged to get our personnel system in better shape, but we continue to work on improvements and have always been responsive to the needs of our workers. I sincerely hope that we do not unionize, although we fully support our employees' rights in this area. Jefferson Partners wants us to keep developing this facility, especially with the opening of the interstate highway.

DIRECTOR OF PATIENT SERVICES

Michele Regan, RN, was appointed director of Patient Services in 2009. She holds a bachelor's in nursing and a master's in geriatric nursing from State University and has more than 20 years of professional experience in long-term care nursing. In 2004, she joined the nursing staff at Jasper Gardens as the day-shift charge nurse. Her responsibilities as director include managing the day-shift (7 a.m.–3 p.m.) charge nurses—each of whom leads the caregivers for approximately half of the patients and residents—as well as the evening (3 p.m.–11 p.m.) and night (11 p.m.–7 a.m.) nursing supervisors. In addition, she oversees the Rehabilitation (physical therapy [PT], occupational therapy [OT], and speech therapy [ST]), Dietary, and Recreation Services departments as well as coordinates all pharmaceutical services.

When interviewed, Regan indicated that Jasper Gardens rarely has significant problems with hiring qualified RNs and LPNs, although it experiences the expected workforce turnover; she added that she would like to hire more MNAs. One problem with staffing has always been scheduling, as she explained:

> We seem to be in a catch-22. In the past, we relied on floating full-time staff to cover shifts as needed, but we recently started hiring part-time workers. Scheduling them to work a few extra hours to cover a shift occasionally has been very difficult. The critical complaint from part-timers has been not having sick leave, something that is very important to those who have to tend to their sick children.

Regan manages the facility's drug formulary, with guidance from Dr. Child, and ensures that adequate pharmacy stock is maintained and that effective inventory safeguards are in place. She is also responsible for ordering and inventorying all medical supplies. Medical supplies are purchased using contracts negotiated and administrated by Jefferson Partners.

When asked what changes she would like to see implemented, she offered this:

> Our current policy concerning residents being hospitalized and then returning may need to be reconsidered. The policy is that we will not keep a bed open for a resident who is admitted to a hospital unless the resident pays for the bed during the hospitalization or absence. Unless paid, we will refill the bed after 24 hours. We also have a 10-day limit on how long any bed may be unoccupied even if the per diem charges are being paid. This policy can cause problems for our residents, even though it might be a required business practice. We really try to accommodate our residents.

DIRECTOR OF ADMISSIONS AND SOCIAL SERVICES

Betsy Hemp has been the director of Admissions and Social Services since 1999. She holds a bachelor's and a master's in social work from a West Coast university and has more than 25 years of experience. Prior to this job, she held a similar position at a nursing home in Capital City. Hemp meets with all prospective residents and their families, assists potential and current residents in applying and qualifying for Medicaid, periodically leads the team that reviews the medical and social needs of all residents, and files reports as needed. Each resident maintains a modest cash account to support certain expenses or purchases (e.g., beauty shop). She manages this account, in keeping with federal and state regulations, and periodically files the needed reports. Aside from working with the discharge teams at MIDCARE, Webster Hospital, and Capital City hospitals, she also has regular contact with Hillsboro Health and other home health agencies in Capital City. When interviewed, she offered the following general comments:

> Overall, I enjoy working here. Jasper Gardens is not unique, but we have a dedicated staff that makes us special. Our resident population is getting older, and our recent admissions have required significantly more therapy and services than what I've seen in the past. Changes in Medicaid eligibility make aspects of my job demanding. For example, I spend a great deal of time completing the Minimum Data Set on residents to be admitted, and I spend a great deal of time filing reports on our current residents. This place really does reflect the community we serve. Most of our residents come from Jasper, although we're hoping the new interstate brings us some "out of towners" from Capital City. We are fortunate that a significant number of our residents have family and friends who still come to visit them. We seem to have more visitors than other nursing homes do.

Director of Plant Operations

As the director of Plant Operations, Connor Doyle is responsible for all aspects of the building and grounds, including maintenance, laundry, and housekeeping services. His staff maintains and operates the van that transports residents to appointments, shopping trips, and other outings. A military veteran, he has served in this role since 2010 and, before that, was the associate director of facilities at another nursing home in Capital City. Under his leadership, Jasper Gardens has received no negative reports or citations and has passed all inspections, including fire safety. In 2012, he led the installation of new on-site generators, enabling the facility to function "off the electric grid" for a minimum of 12 days. This installation completed a plan to make the nursing home energy independent to ensure the safety of all residents. Based on Doyle's recommendation, Jasper Gardens established a new policy that all residents who want to use motorized wheelchairs and carts must complete driving lessons from a trained instructor and earn an operator's license issued by the facility. Doyle offered insights into his responsibilities:

> As far as this facility is concerned, I am very proud of how the Plant Operations team has made and continues to make this old facility clean, well-lit, and look attractive. And safe—let's not forget safe! Now that we are energy independent, I sleep better at night. All of the employees understand and comply with our need to periodically have fire and

emergency drills. This has helped a great deal, as we don't hear any grumblings when we have to move a lot of people in and out of the wings in an orderly fashion. One of my many duties is security. We wear badges. We are trained to question any visitors, vendors, or strangers on the property. We have alarm systems and multiple security checks in place. I do question whether we can and should remain as open as we are now. Residents can potentially leave any time they want, and outsiders can enter multiple doors from 7 a.m. to 8 p.m., before the building is "locked" for the night. This may be an issue that needs attention.

SENIOR ADMINISTRATIVE ASSISTANT AND BOOKKEEPER

Bonnie Keana is responsible for preparing the payroll and supervising the posting of the financial journal and the general ledger. Jefferson Partners provides budget status reports every week and interim financial statements monthly based on information she prepares. She is also in charge of local purchasing, and she supervises the reception staff.

MANAGEMENT MEETINGS

Every Tuesday morning, Winters, Regan, and Hemp meet and review the status of all patients. Data include quality measures used by Medicare as well as other data reported to Jefferson Partners. Once a month, this trio invites others (including the medical director and members of Jasper Gardens' continuous quality improvement committee) to review all data to determine which patients/CMS (Centers for Medicare & Medicaid Services) items need attention, why, and the treatment and prevention approaches being used. Every Friday morning, this same group—along with Doyle and Keana—meets as the management team and reviews the most recent dashboard report and budget status report as well as discusses other issues that need management's attention.

CONCERNS AND OPPORTUNITIES

Winters and Regan indicated that access to qualified professional staff has not been a major problem. In fact, they have been able to hire highly qualified professionals who have generally stayed with the facility for a long time. Over the years, however, wages for some jobs have not kept pace with wages in the regional market. This trend is directly traceable to the Medicaid rates paid by the state. Over the past ten years, state Medicaid rates have fallen from being the tenth highest to the eighth lowest in the country.

Rehabilitation services (e.g., PT, OT, ST) are available to both Jasper Gardens residents and members of the community. Most users of these services have Medicare Part B or private insurance. Outpatient utilization continues to be modest. Currently, individuals in need of ambulatory rehabilitation services typically visit a local solo provider or travel to a group practice in Capital City, Jasper, or Middleboro.

During the pandemic, Jasper Gardens instituted a quarantine system to protect residents and staff from spread of the virus. Although the program was challenging for everyone, it was successful in limiting the direct impact of the pandemic. Four cases of the virus were diagnosed among Jasper Gardens staff and only one case among residents. No pandemic-related deaths occurred. That said, the quarantine program created painful separation between residents and families who were unable to visit their loved ones face-to-face in the facility. In addition, at the direction of Jefferson Partners, Jasper Gardens implemented a mandatory testing program for employees and strongly encouraged but did not require vaccination. These programs led to negative reaction from a vocal minority of staff who felt their personal rights were violated by imposing such requirements. Ultimately, no employees refused to be tested according to the established protocols, and none left Jasper Gardens' employ. The pandemic also led Jasper Gardens to implement new policies and procedures regarding infection control and prevention. Jefferson Partners was instrumental in creating these guidelines.

Jefferson Partners requires everyone who applies to be a patient or resident at Jasper Gardens to undergo a background check as a condition of admission. Compliance with this requirement ensures that no individual with a felony conviction as a sexual predator or offender will be admitted. The admission staff explains this policy to all applicants and inquirers. Jefferson Partners has implemented this policy at all of its facilities; however, it is under legal review at two of the corporation's nursing homes.

Within the last three years, Jasper Gardens has executed a cooperative agreement with Hillsboro Health for inpatient hospice services. Under this agreement, when a resident needs these services, Jasper Gardens provides a private room and other needed services to support the hospice care team provided by Hillsboro Health. Two years ago, Jasper Gardens opened a four-bed dedicated unit exclusively for memory care. This unit accepts only private-pay residents able to self-support their care for a minimum of 36 months. If residents in this unit need care for a longer period, Jasper Gardens accepts Medicaid reimbursement rates.

INFORMATION SYSTEMS DEVELOPMENT

Jefferson Partners has recently signed a continuing contract with Nursing Home Systems to install the latest version of a comprehensive electronic health record (EHR). Like other EHRs, this system is an integrated medical record with order-entry capabilities for supplies, tests, and all other clinical activities. Jefferson Partners requires each of its facilities that accepts Medicare or Medicaid to adopt this EHR. This installation takes advantage of the Wi-Fi already running throughout Jasper Gardens.

Valley Medical Center in Capital City invited Jasper Gardens to participate in its telehealth program. In this program, a Jasper Gardens patient or resident is evaluated, diagnosed, educated, treated, and monitored by an attending physician at Valley Medical Center using telecommunications means and self-taken health data. The system enables the patient or resident to consult with or "see" a physician without having to travel to that physician (unless necessary). Valley Medical Center directly bills a patient's health insurance for its services but did not indicate the cost of this telehealth program.

Additional information regarding Jasper Gardens' resident and patient population, staffing, financial status, and operations can be found in tables 8.1 through 8.7.

	2024	2023	2022	2021
Skilled Care/Insurance				
Medicare	33	30	28	21
Commercial	4	2	3	1
Other	3	1	0	0
Subtotal	**40**	**33**	**31**	**22**
Intermediate Care/Insurance				
Medicaid	35	38	44	44
Veterans Administration	2	2	4	6
Private Insurance	2	2	2	2
Self-Pay	15	22	18	8
Subtotal	**54**	**64**	**68**	**60**
Memory Care				
Self-Pay	2	0	0	0
Total Census	**96**	**97**	**99**	**82**

Table 8.1
Jasper Gardens
Patient Census
by Type of
Insurance, as of
December 31

Table 8.2
Jasper Gardens
Resident
Information as
of December 31,
2024

Number	Age	Gender	Months	Comm	Ins	Ref	S or I
1	99	2	81	9	2	4	I
2	99	2	88	5	2	2	I
3	98	2	32	9	2	3	I
4	97	2	75	9	2	2	I
5	96	1	41	1	2	3	I
6	96	2	30	3	2	4	I
7	94	2	21	1	2	2	I
8	94	2	27	3	2	2	I
9	93	2	76	5	2	5	I
10	93	2	17	3	2	1	I
11	93	2	34	2	2	1	I
12	93	1	25	3	2	2	I
13	58	2	31	1	2	2	I
14	92	2	20	3	2	1	I
15	92	2	73	9	2	3	I
16	91	2	84	5	2	1	I
17	90	2	72	5	2	2	I
18	56	2	56	5	2	6	I
19	90	2	24	5	2	1	I
20	70	2	30	9	2	1	I
21	89	1	23	1	2	4	I
22	47	2	19	3	2	2	I
23	77	2	19	3	2	2	I
24	90	2	39	3	2	6	I
25	73	1	48	3	2	1	I
26	83	2	23	9	2	5	I
27	89	2	24	3	2	3	I
28	62	1	38	3	2	2	I
29	89	2	22	3	2	2	I
30	69	1	60	3	2	5	I
31	89	2	4	2	2	6	I
32	78	2	30	9	2	5	I
33	88	2	38	3	2	2	I
34	89	1	30	3	2	2	I
35	80	2	5	3	2	5	I
36	72	2	24	9	6	6	I
37	58	2	26	9	6	5	I
38	48	1	35	3	6	1	I

continued

Number	Age	Gender	Months	Comm	Ins	Ref	S or I
39	57	2	30	5	6	1	I
40	53	2	21	9	6	6	I
41	27	2	30	3	6	2	I
42	87	2	8	10	6	6	I
43	87	2	9	1	6	5	I
44	86	2	30	3	6	3	I
45	86	2	35	3	6	1	I
46	34	1	34	3	6	6	I
47	66	2	26	3	6	3	I
48	67	1	23	3	6	3	I
49	85	2	33	2	6	6	I
50	52	1	7	4	6	6	I
51	84	1	20	6	6	5	I
52	84	2	37	3	6	1	I
53	84	1	32	3	3	5	I
54	84	2	31	3	3	1	I
55	83	1	8	3	5	5	I
56	44	1	13	3	5	5	I
57	72	2	2.7	9	1	4	S
58	66	1	2.7	9	1	5	S
59	68	1	2.5	9	1	2	S
60	89	2	2.5	3	1	2	S
61	71	2	2.5	3	1	1	S
62	68	2	2.3	3	1	2	S
63	66	1	2.2	3	1	5	S
64	70	1	1.9	3	1	2	S
65	68	1	1.7	3	1	2	S
66	67	2	1.6	3	1	1	S
67	65	2	1.4	3	1	5	S
68	70	1	1.4	3	1	3	S
69	59	1	1.4	1	1	2	S
70	79	2	1.3	3	1	1	S
71	78	2	1.3	1	1	1	S
72	75	1	1.2	3	1	1	S
73	65	2	1.1	3	1	2	S
74	66	2	1.0	2	1	1	S
75	90	2	1.0	5	1	4	S
76	89	1	1.0	5	1	6	S

Table 8.2
Jasper Gardens
Resident
Information as
of December 31,
2024
(continued)

continued

Table 8.2
Jasper Gardens
Resident
Information as
of December 31,
2024
(continued)

Number	Age	Gender	Months	Comm	Ins	Ref	S or I
77	88	2	1.0	3	1	1	S
78	88	2	1.0	5	1	2	S
79	85	2	0.9	3	1	2	S
80	82	1	0.9	2	1	2	S
81	82	2	0.8	9	1	5	S
82	80	2	0.8	5	1	2	S
83	80	2	0.8	5	1	4	S
84	80	1	0.8	3	1	1	S
85	80	1	0.7	5	1	4	S
86	78	2	0.6	1	1	4	S
87	78	1	0.6	3	1	4	S
88	77	2	0.5	3	1	1	S
89	73	2	0.5	3	1	2	S
90	71	2	0.5	3	1	3	S
91	70	1	0.5	5	1	2	S
92	70	2	0.5	3	4	4	S
93	69	2	0.5	3	4	1	S
94	68	2	0.3	3	4	2	S
95	68	1	0.2	3	4	3	S
96	67	1	0.1	3	5	2	S

Notes: (1) Number: Patient ID number. (2) Gender: 1—Male; 2—Female. (3) Comm: community of origin. (4) Ins: insurance. (5) Ref: referred from. (6) S: skilled care; I: intermediate care.

Code	Community	Insurance	Referral from:
1	Middleboro	Medicare	MIDCARE
2	Mifflenville	Medicaid	Webster Health System
3	Jasper	Veterans Administration	Valley Medical Center
4	Harris City	Commercial	Other Hospital
5	Statesville	Other Private	From Home
6	Carterville	Self-Pay	Other
7	Boalsburg		
8	Minortown		
9	Capital City		
10	Other		

	2024	2023	2022	2021
Administration				
Administrator	1.0	1.0	1.0	1.0
Director of Admissions	1.0	1.0	1.0	1.0
Nurses with Administrative Duties	1.5	1.0	1.5	2.0
Admin Assistant/Bookkeeper	0.8	0.8	0.8	0.8
Receptionist	2.0	2.2	2.3	2.0
Admin Clerks	1.0	1.5	1.5	1.5
Medical Records Tech	0.5	0.5	0.5	0.5
Other	4.0	3.0	4.0	4.0
Subtotal	**11.8**	**11.0**	**12.6**	**12.8**
Patient Services				
Director	1.0	1.0	1.0	1.0
Medical Director	0.2	0.2	0.1	0.1
Dentist	0.1	0.1	0.1	0.1
Registered Nurses	15.8	14.4	13.8	13.4
Licensed Nursing Assistants	26.3	27.3	30.1	32.1
Licensed Practical Nurses	10.3	9.3	9.0	8.9
Medication Nursing Assistants	3.0	4.0	4.3	4.0
Assistant Director, Rehab	0.9	0.5	0.7	0.7
Physical Therapists	2.5	2.5	2.3	2.3
Physical Therapy Assistant	0.7	0.5	0.5	0.3
Occupational Therapist	1.0	1.0	1.0	1.5
COTA	1.0	0.8	0.8	0.5
Speech Therapist	0.4	0.4	0.4	0.3
Mental Health Aide	0.0	0.3	0.3	0.4
Assistant Director, Dietary	1.0	1.0	1.2	1.2
Dietitian	0.7	0.7	0.7	0.6
Food Services Personnel	17.5	16.5	16.3	15.9
Assistant Director, Recreation	0.2	0.2	0.3	0.3
CTRS	0.8	1.3	1.2	1.5
Subtotal	**83.4**	**82.0**	**84.1**	**85.1**
Plant Operations				
Director	0.4	0.4	0.4	0.4
Housekeeping Personnel	7.5	7.0	7.5	7.4
Maintenance Staff	0.6	0.6	0.6	0.6
Subtotal	**8.5**	**8.0**	**8.5**	**8.4**
Total Staff	**103.7**	**101.0**	**105.2**	**106.3**

Table 8.3
Jasper Gardens Full-Time Equivalent (FTE) Staffing

Notes: (1) One FTE worker is paid for 2,080 hours per year. (2) For benefits, full-time is defined as 80 percent time or higher. (3) 100 percent time salaried workers work 1,896 hours per year. (4) COTA: certified occupational therapy assistant; CTRS: certified therapeutic recreation specialist.

Table 8.4
Jasper Gardens
Operational
Statistics by
Year

	2024	2023	2022	2021
Patient Days				
Skilled: Medicare	11,050	8,933	7,769	6,391
Skilled: Other	1,355	547	504	226
Skilled: Total	**12,405**	**9,480**	**8,273**	**6,617**
ICF: Medicaid	11,857	11,548	12,451	14,662
ICF: Self-Pay	5,522	4,653	6,044	2,628
ICF: VA	602	705	1,401	2,037
ICF: Private Insurance	730	712	738	525
ICF: Total	**18,711**	**17,618**	**20,634**	**19,852**
Total Patient Days	**31,116**	**27,098**	**28,907**	**26,469**
Total Operational Beds				
Skilled Beds	45	42	39	26
ICF Beds	64	67	70	68
Total Beds	109	109	109	94
Occupancy	78.2%	68.1%	72.7%	77.1%

Notes: (1) ICF: intermediate care facility; VA: Veterans Administration

Table 8.5
Jasper Gardens Statement of Operations, USD $

	2024	2023	2022	2021
Revenue				
Room and Board				
Skilled Care				
Medicare—A	5,267,202	4,779,155	4,063,187	3,521,441
Commercial and Other	954,667	419,650	203,760	202,722
Subtotal	**6,221,869**	**5,198,805**	**4,266,947**	**3,724,163**
Intermediate Care				
Medicaid	2,679,682	2,609,848	2,726,769	2,753,455
Self-Pay	2,261,000	1,868,069	1,598,920	1,953,283
Veterans Administration	237,790	257,325	511,365	743,505
Private Insurance	306,600	291,920	295,938	202,125
Subtotal	**5,485,072**	**5,027,162**	**5,132,992**	**5,652,368**
Ancillary Revenue				
Skilled Care				
Medicare—A and B	2,348,382	1,979,652	1,701,411	1,324,556
Commercial and Other	93,580	47,589	37,296	15,594
Subtotal	**2,441,962**	**2,027,241**	**1,738,707**	**1,340,150**
Intermediate Care				
Medicaid	19,732	17,429	14,327	13,659
Commercial and Other	15,147	10,429	9,935	9,243
Subtotal	**34,879**	**27,858**	**24,262**	**22,902**
Other Revenue				
Interest	10,414	14,334	9,322	7,833
Miscellaneous	4,328	3,723	3,422	2,367
Subtotal	**14,742**	**18,057**	**12,744**	**10,200**
Total Gross Revenue	**14,198,524**	**12,299,123**	**11,175,652**	**10,749,783**
Less Contractual Allowance and Fees	4,457,652	3,261,563	3,160,657	3,352,792
Total Net Revenue	**9,740,872**	**9,037,560**	**8,014,995**	**7,396,991**
Expenses				
Personnel				
Salaries and Wages	3,823,657	3,625,762	3,278,972	3,342,123
Benefits—All	1,097,390	1,040,594	941,065	956,838
Subtotal	**4,921,047**	**4,666,356**	**4,220,037**	**4,298,961**
Admin and General	**503,285**	**440,243**	**429,342**	**371,979**
Other Operating Expenses				
Maintenance	80,383	61,224	70,283	63,283
Utilities	315,334	312,554	310,335	305,227

continued

Table 8.5
Jasper Gardens
Statement of
Operations,
USD $
(continued)

	2024	2023	2022	2021
Oxygen Services	22,775	20,487	23,204	31,676
Food	504,339	429,385	425,394	405,239
General Supplies	298,384	260,485	267,403	215,254
Laboratory Services	36,293	33,294	32,504	30,668
Pharmacy Services	261,376	253,449	245,303	233,595
Imaging Services	17,392	16,451	14,395	12,006
Medical Equipment Rental	66,346	66,384	66,384	65,395
Capital Leases	800,000	650,000	650,000	650,000
Depreciation—All	325,304	243,033	233,450	219,563
Bad Debt	8,834	6,138	8,382	8,965
Subtotal	**2,736,760**	**2,352,884**	**2,347,037**	**2,240,871**
Other—Management Fee	**650,000**	**650,000**	**650,000**	**450,000**
Total Expenses	**8,811,092**	**8,109,483**	**7,646,416**	**7,361,811**
Pretax Profit (Loss)	929,780	928,077	368,579	35,180
All Taxes	260,339	259,862	103,202	9,850
Net Profit (Loss) After Taxes	**669,442**	**668,216**	**265,377**	**25,330**

Note: Admin and General includes: Equipment, Accounting Fees, Telephone Insurance, Payroll Services, Information System Management, Dues and Licenses, Office Supplies, Postage, Legal, Auto, Marketing and Advertising, Misc. Bank Charges, Admin Equipment Rental, Other Professional Fees, Printing and Publishing.

	2024	2023	2022	2021
Assets				
Current				
Cash + Marketable Securities*	5,467,798	4,387,139	3,513,931	3,167,228
Patient Trust Cash	34,670	32,887	29,335	26,487
Subtotal	**5,502,468**	**4,420,026**	**3,543,266**	**3,193,715**
Accounts Receivable—Net	1,433,628	1,600,373	1,692,373	1,643,393
Inventory	65,394	63,992	61,392	53,802
Prepaid Expenses	47,303	40,338	30,227	34,396
Subtotal	**1,546,325**	**1,704,703**	**1,783,992**	**1,731,591**
Property, Plant, and Equipment (PPE)				
Building and Land Improvements	1,802,343	1,790,925	1,735,220	1,814,900
Fixed and Leasehold Equipment	778,253	854,292	812,353	802,375
Furniture and Other Equipment	620,122	908,969	1,029,411	1,245,393
Vehicles	9,328	6,134	8,120	9,350
Gross PPE	**3,210,046**	**3,560,320**	**3,585,104**	**3,872,018**
Less Accumulated Depreciation	2,893,141	2,893,141	2,650,138	2,430,575
Subtotal Net PPE	**316,905**	**667,179**	**934,966**	**1,441,443**
Other Assets				
Investments/Deposits	58,863	56,240	59,336	56,230
Total Assets	**7,424,561**	**6,848,148**	**6,321,560**	**6,422,979**
Liabilities				
Current				
Accounts Payable	778,231	834,248	935,273	967,335
Accrued Expenses	278,334	290,345	302,662	354,220
Patient Trust Liability	34,670	32,887	29,335	26,487
Accrued Interest	2,035	2,749	3,349	4,578
Subtotal	**1,093,270**	**1,160,229**	**1,270,619**	**1,352,620**
Long Term				
Deferred Lease Obligations	33,440	43,782	50,227	52,694
Notes Payable	50,912	55,349	60,337	76,440
Line of Credit	40,239	51,530	71,335	98,560
Subtotal	**124,591**	**150,661**	**181,899**	**227,694**
Total Liabilities	**1,217,861**	**1,310,890**	**1,452,518**	**1,580,314**
Net Assets	**6,206,700**	**5,537,258**	**4,869,042**	**4,842,665**
Net Assets + Liabilities	**7,424,561**	**6,848,148**	**6,321,560**	**6,422,979**

Table 8.6
Jasper Gardens Balance Sheet as of December 31, USD $

Note: *On average, cash accounts for 31% of Cash + Marketable Securities.

Measure	Jasper Gardens	State Average
Health and Safety		
Number of health deficiencies	1	2
Number of complaints	1	>21
Fire Safety: Number of deficiencies	1	>10
Staffing		
Number of licensed staff hours per resident day	1 hr 41 min	1 hr 28 min
RN hours per resident per day	52 min	39 min
LPN/LVN hours per resident day	58 min	51 min
CNA hours per resident day	2 hr 20 min	2 hr 23 min
Quality: Short-Stay Residents		
Percentage of short-stay residents who were re-hospitalized after a nursing home admission	18.3%	20.8%
Percentage of short-stay residents who have had an outpatient emergency department visit	8.8%	10.3%
Percentage of short-stay residents who got antipsychotic medication for the first time	1.2%	1.8%
Percentage of residents with pressure ulcers/pressure injuries that are new or worsened	2.0%	2.5%
Percentage of short-stay residents who improved in their ability to move around on their own	72.0%	68.0%
Flu and Pneumonia Prevention Measure: Short-Stay Residents		
Percentage of short-stay residents who needed and got a flu shot for the current flu season	97.0%	82.9%
Percentage of short-stay residents who needed and got a vaccine to prevent pneumonia	96.0%	83.9%
Additional Quality Measures: Short-Stay Residents		
Percentage of residents whose medications were reviewed and who received follow-up care when medication issues were identified	93.5%	88.4%

continued

Measure	Jasper Gardens	State Average
Percentage of SNF residents who experienced one or more falls with major injury during their SNF stay	0.0%	0.0%
Percentage of SNF residents whose functional abilities were assessed and functional goals were included in their treatment plan	100.0%	99.1%
Percentage of residents who are at or above an expected ability to care for themselves at discharge	74.3%	52.8%
Percentage of residents who are at or above an expected ability to move around at discharge	53.7%	48.5%
Change in Residents' Ability to Care for Themselves		
Self-care score has improved, scores below 0 mean that the self-care score has worsened	54.0%	52.8%
Change in Residents' Ability to Move Around		
Rate of successful return to home and community from a SNF	49.2%	50.1%
Rate of potentially preventable hospital readmissions 30 days after discharge from a SNF	8.3%	7.7%
Medicare Spending Per Beneficiary (MSPB) for residents in SNFs	1.08	1.03
Long-Stay Residents: Quality of Resident Care Rating		
Number of hospitalizations per 1,000 long-stay resident days	182.0%	1.70
Number of outpatient emergency department visits per 1,000 long-stay resident days	130.0%	0.96
Percentage of long-stay residents who got an antipsychotic medication	10.4%	14.2%
Percentage of long-stay residents experiencing one or more falls with major injury	2.7%	3.4%
Percentage of long-stay high-risk residents with pressure ulcers	6.6%	7.3%
Percentage of long-stay residents with a urinary tract infection	3.0%	2.6%

Table 8.7
Jasper Gardens Performance Against CMS Quality Measures, January 1–December 31, 2024 *(continued)*

continued

Measure	Jasper Gardens	State Average
Percentage of long-stay residents who have or had a catheter inserted and left in their bladder	0.7%	1.8%
Percentage of long-stay residents whose ability to move independently worsened	11.3%	17.1%
Percentage of long-stay residents whose need for help with daily activities has increased	14.2%	14.5%
Flu and Pneumonia Prevention Measures: Long-Stay Residents		
Long-stay residents: Percentage of long-stay residents who needed and got a flu shot for the current flu season	98.3%	96.0%
Percentage of long-stay residents who needed and got a vaccine to prevent pneumonia	98.4%	93.9%
Additional Quality Measures: Long-Stay Residents		
Percentage of long-stay residents who were physically restrained	1.3%	0.2%
Percentage of long-stay low-risk residents who lose control of their bowels or bladder	39.50%	48.40%
Percentage of long-stay residents who lose too much weight	3.30%	5.50%
Percentage of long-stay residents who have symptoms of depression	3.60%	5.10%
Percentage of long-stay residents who got an antianxiety or hypnotic medication	12.60%	19.70%
Fire Safety		
Total number of fire safety citations	1	3

CASE 9

HILLSBORO COUNTY
HEALTH DEPARTMENT

Established in 1946, the Hillsboro County Health Department (HCHD) is a municipal department in the county's government that receives all of its funding from the county and from federal and state grants. HCHD is accountable to the Hillsboro County Commissioners. HCHD's mission and vision (revised and approved in 2022) are as follows:

Mission: To prevent disease, promote health, and work collaboratively and proactively with other community organizations to enhance the health of all Hillsboro County residents.

Vision: We want Hillsboro County to be as healthy as the other communities in our state and region. To accomplish this, we improve access to quality healthcare services and maintain an environment free of threats to the public's health. We will strive to move toward a healthcare environment within the county that minimizes healthcare disparities.

The following are HCHD's functional responsibilities:

◆ Collect, disseminate, and monitor health status information as part of its effort to identify physical and environmental health issues.

◆ Assess the accessibility, effectiveness, and quality of preventive, community health services.

◆ Serve as the county's public health advocate. As such, HCHD defines public health priorities and needs and relies on evidence-based practice to promote, prevent, and improve physical, mental, and environmental health and well-being. Services are provided directly to the public or, using grants, to area health agencies in an effort to carry out the core functions of public health and the essential public health services as defined by the state and the Centers for Disease Control and Prevention.

◆ Study and report health problems and hazards using epidemiology and standards and practices of population health.

◆ Enforce laws and regulations that protect physical, mental, and environmental health and that ensure safety.

◆ Oversee Manorhaven, a 110-bed long-term care facility. Located in Middleboro, Manorhaven is owned and operated by the county. Financially, it is independent of the HCHD, but it uses select administrative services (e.g., payroll, human resources) provided by the county. This facility is a distinct line item in the county budget because it is both a revenue and an expense. Its administrator is appointed by the Hillsboro County Commissioners, following the recommendation of the HCHD director, and reports directly to the HCHD director.

HILLSBORO COUNTY BOARD OF HEALTH

The Hillsboro County Board of Health—a member of the National Association of Local Boards of Health—is an independent board appointed by the Hillsboro County Commissioners. It was created by statute to identify public health issues and concerns as well as provide programmatic advice and policy guidance to HCHD. Its 12 members serve five-year terms each and can be reappointed; following is the current roster of members:

Hillsboro County Board of Health

Members	Term Expires
Doris Felix, DO, *Chair*	
Surgeon, Webster Hospital	2026
Micah Foxx, DO, *Vice Chair*	
Occupational Health Physician, Physician Care Services	2027
Grace Methuane	
School Nurse, Jasper	2025
Gemma Guevara, RN	
Director, Nursing Education, MIDCARE	2028
Edith Masterman	
Retired	2026
Catherine Newfields, RN	
Chief Operating Officer, Hillsboro Health	2027
Raymond Samuels, MD	
Pediatrician, Medical Associates	2027
Helen Vosper, RN	
Retired	2025
Afua Adjounabi	
Community Representative, Jasper	2028
Fran Cisneros	
Community Representative, Boalsburg	2026
John Snow, *Secretary, Ex Officio*	
Director, HCHD	
Paige Magnet, DO, *Ex Officio*	
Health Officer/Medical Examiner, HCHD	

The 2022 Annual Report published by the Board of Health includes revised state guidelines for physical activity in K–12 public schools. The board is considering using these recommendations to assist community leaders to establish locally supported "Action for Healthy Kids" programs. At least three members of the board advocate for these guidelines to be adopted as a public health priority for the next five years. In addition, a subcommittee of the board (Methuane, Vosper, Adjounabi, and Masterman) has been designated to review the objectives articulated in the recently updated Healthy People 2030 framework and to use this information in establishing pertinent goals for HCHD. A number of objectives contained in Healthy People 2030 are noted in table 9.14.

Driven to some extent by the recent pandemic experience, the annual reports for 2022–2024 focus attention on the importance of coordinating public health efforts and activities among local organizations. In particular, the report emphasizes the need for stronger coordination between the hospitals and the health department, as well as between the health department and health-related local businesses and providers, such as pharmacies. The *2024 Annual Report*, published during the pandemic, noted that HCHD stepped up to take key roles in many pandemic-related initiatives, such as vaccinating citizens. In this role, HCHD was aided in no small part by efforts of the National Guard and local fire and emergency squads. These additional functions placed substantial staffing and financial strains on HCHD resources.

MANAGEMENT TEAM AND ORGANIZATIONAL STRUCTURE

OFFICE OF THE DIRECTOR

Annually, the Hillsboro County Commissioners, on the basis of the Board of Health's recommendation, make a merit-based political appointment to fill the director of HCHD position. For the past 14 years, the commissioners have appointed John Snow, who has been employed by the department for 17 years. He holds a bachelor's in biology from State University and a master of public health from a leading midwestern university.

As director, Snow is responsible for safeguarding the health of the residents of Hillsboro County and for enforcing all state and local health regulations, including fining violators. He is on state and national task forces on developing a competent public health workforce for the next several decades, serves as the vice president of the State Public Health Association (and frequently attends the annual meeting of the American Public Health Association), is the leading spokesperson for public health in nonmetropolitan areas in the state, and has frequently testified before the Committee on Public Health sponsored by the governor and endorsed by the state legislature. In addition, he is responsible for executing Health Impact Assessments in accordance with the guidelines of the Centers for Disease Control and Prevention as well as the World Health Organization. Over the past three years, HCHD has conducted assessments of municipal transportation systems, land use, surge capacity and emergency services, and immunization planning. Many of these reviews were triggered by the worldwide pandemic experience.

When interviewed, Snow indicated that he is concerned that the public health challenges and agenda in Hillsboro County continue to grow but the funding sources continue to shrink. He noted that a perceived need among many, particularly politicians, to cut the county's appropriation for public health does not recognize the overall importance of public health in sustaining a high quality of life within the community, as well as failing to recognize the overwhelming challenges faced during the recent pandemic. He added that while increased attention to public health issues is warranted, he is concerned that rather than increasing overall funding for public health, decisions may be made to simply shift funding from long-standing programs, forcing the county to eliminate existing programs. He stated,

> I'm not sure we learned much of a lasting lesson from the pandemic—we seem to be headed back to the days of marginalizing public health rather than intensifying our efforts. Now that the peaks of the pandemic have thankfully passed, in no small part due to our efforts at collaboration and vaccination, people seem to have forgotten how we got ourselves in trouble in the first place. We are too reactive. We were not prepared for the pandemic and have not done nearly enough to develop sustainable, proactive efforts in such areas as disease tracing, immunization planning and implementation, supply chain coordination, etc. We forget all too soon.

In addition, six years ago, the State Department of Public Health employed a professional liaison in Washington, DC, to monitor and inform the state and its counties of available federal grants related to their public health missions. Counties will need to contribute funds to this effort when the liaison's contract is renewed after 2024. "This Washington liaison service has led to our public health needs being first in the nation when grant funding is made available," Snow said.

An ongoing area of concern is the drug addiction epidemic and lack of prevention and treatment programs in the county. He said, "The recent report by the Hillsboro County Police Chiefs Association documents our issue with drug abuse and opioid addiction, especially in the smaller communities. We need to act quickly. As many parts of our country and state have done, we may have overlooked a significant public health issue for far too many years. The pandemic made things even worse, as many substance use and overuse issues escalated during isolation and quarantine." Substance abuse issues were also a key focus of Healthy People 2030. Snow has included this topic in the agenda for the Board of Health's next meeting. More broadly, the issue of behavioral health is a major area of focus for the board. Informal surveys taken during and after the pandemic revealed increased levels of stress, feelings of isolation, and depression among area residents.

Yet another of Snow's concerns is the aging of his department personnel. "Within five years, more than one-third of our workers will be eligible for retirement," he stated. "It has always been difficult for government offices to attract qualified workers, especially in the area of environmental health services. We anticipate it will be just as hard to replace retiring employees with trained individuals just starting their career."

Other challenges stem from the department's unique relationship with Manorhaven. Manorhaven has a separate budget that is approved by the Hillsboro County Commissioners. By county regulation, however, HCHD is responsible for any financial losses the facility incurs. The regulation was established in 1999, following the recommendations of a blue-ribbon commission to increase the efficiency of local and county governments.

Seven years ago, for example, HCHD had to cover an $84,000 shortfall in the facility's budget. Today, state Medicaid reimbursement rates have become so low that Manorhaven faces an uncertain future. To maintain oversight, Snow meets quarterly with the facility's management team to review its finances. There has been speculation that he has met with the county's attorney to discuss the potential sale of Manorhaven.

When asked about plans for working with accountable care organizations (ACOs), Snow indicated that the department is fully prepared to work with one or more ACOs that share its mission to improve the health of the citizens of Hillsboro County. Swift Water ACO, based in Capital City, has recently been established. In addition, HCHD has been communicating with Webster Hospital and MIDCARE to collaborate on updating the community health needs assessment. He noted that "perhaps one of the advantages of the pandemic, if you want to call it that, is that organizations have begun to work together in some areas. Coordinating the vaccination response required all players in the healthcare arena to be at the table and to work together—at least more than in the past. It has been a major challenge getting the two hospitals to agree with each other on much of anything, but the challenge of the pandemic brought us somewhat closer together. However, keeping on top of the community assessment is something we all have to do." Healthy People 2030 has created a goal of 71.8 percent of local jurisdictions establishing a health improvement plan. The county has not yet fulfilled this objective.

Webster has participated in HCHD projects in the past. Five years ago, using Federal Demonstration Partnership grant money and space donated by the local towns involved, the department—along with Webster Hospital and other organizations—sponsored the opening of two rural health primary clinics in Carterville and Harris City. Each clinic is a 501(c)(3) facility with a local board of directors. Today, both Rural Clinics, Inc., locations serve patients from 10 a.m.–3 p.m., Monday through Saturday. Given stresses from the pandemic, as well as the deteriorating financial position of the now independent Webster Hospital, the sustainability of these programs is somewhat questionable.

Snow gives credit to HCHD's website and Twitter account for significantly extending the reach and enhancing the reputation of the department. He thinks the department's continued social media presence will eventually lessen—if not eliminate—the need for printed annual reports and consumer information sheets. He added, "Other health departments have had more success with social media, which is something we need to copy. We're a little behind the digital times, but we're quickly catching up."

HCHD's senior management team meets every two weeks to review plans and accomplishments. At this meeting, budget variances are discussed and plans are reviewed for the next 30 to 60 days. Before developing a budget request, which is submitted to and approved by the Hillsboro County Commissioners, team members meet with their counterparts in the State Department of Public Health to best estimate state support for county public health programs.

ADMINISTRATIVE SERVICES DIVISION

This division provides management, financial, and administrative support, including grant review and oversight, to the entire department. It is responsible for preparing and managing the budget and staffing plans. As director of the division, Jimmy Pagget retains the part-time services of Dr. Paige Magnet as Hillsboro County's health officer and medical examiner. Pagget has held this position for 18 years; prior to this appointment, he was a senior analyst for the State Department of Revenue Administration.

By statute, each incorporated city and town in Hillsboro County must designate a health officer to coordinate local services and needs with the HCHD. Every quarter, Dr. Magnet meets with each of the designated health officers. The current health officers are as follows (* indicates that the person receives from the city or town a stipend of $1,000 per year to cover his or her time and expenses):

City or Town	Name	Position
Boalsburg	Simon Fistru*	Physician, General Practice
Carterville	Gus Burns	Deputy Chief, Carterville Fire and EMS
Harris City	Audra Adams*	Physician, General Practice
Jasper	Nathan Spark	Chief, Jasper Volunteer Fire Department
Middleboro	Bruce Sullivan	Director, Public Works
Mifflenville	Josephine Fufe*	Deputy Mayor
Minortown	Ivan Kelly*	Physician, General Practice
Statesville	Gloria Silvo	Nurse, retired

In his interview, Pagget emphasized Snow's perspectives on the department's budget: "While I am grateful that a significant portion of our financial support comes from grants and contracts, they create a vulnerability and potential volatility. Without this support, we could not fulfill our mission." During the pandemic, funding from federal and state sources enabled the department to meet many of its increased obligations. Much of that funding was temporary, however, and ended or will end soon as the pandemic wanes.

In addition, he mentioned that the State Public Employees Union recently signed a five-year contract with salary increases of 2 to 3 percent per year but no increases in benefit coverage. Beginning next year, the state's contribution for health and dental insurance will be frozen at its current rate, and employees will be required to contribute to the cost of their own health insurance. Employees who opt out of the health insurance benefit will receive $4,000. An additional week of vacation will be granted to employees with more than 20 years of service. The state and union continue to discuss employee pensions. Currently, workers do not contribute to the state retirement plan, which is an unfunded liability. The county identifies this as a significant issue.

The Administrative Services division is responsible for distributing all grants and contracts. For grants that allow indirect cost recovery, HCHD has a 3 percent negotiated indirect cost rate with the Environmental Protection Agency (EPA) and the US Department of Health and Human Services. There are no indirect cost recoveries for other federal grants. HCHD receives no indirect reimbursement from state grants and private foundations. When the department awards grants and contracts, it makes no allowances for indirect costs; only direct costs are covered.

Currently, HCHD's budget allocates money for facility maintenance and utilities. When an HCHD division is located in a privately owned facility, the department is not responsible for building rental or lease expenses. These costs are covered directly in the facility budget of the county. Each HCHD division has an equipment budget that covers the acquisition and maintenance of all office equipment, including computer hardware and software. A departmentwide committee, chaired by Pagget, prioritizes and coordinates the acquisition of all equipment. The supplies budget covers office supplies and work-related travel.

ENVIRONMENTAL HEALTH DIVISION

Sally Brownell, the director of this division, holds a master of science in environmental health from State University and is a registered environmental health specialist. She joined the department 18 months ago, having served in a similar position in a western state. She is a member of Hillsboro County's HAZMAT (hazardous material) team.

The division is in charge of the following programs or services: arboviral program, campgrounds (licensure and inspection), emergency preparedness, food service sanitation (licensure and inspection), health facility inspection, lead paint abatement, mosquito and tick control, public swimming pools, rabies control, radon control, safe drinking water, and private sewage treatment. During the pandemic, the emergency preparedness function took on increased importance and required greater coordination with other HCHD divisions. In addition, the division maintains multiple contractual relationships with independent and state public health laboratories to provide public health laboratory services. The State Department of Environmental Services performs air-quality surveillance.

Brownell said, "Each year's budget requires us to adjust to our level of support. For example, the division has had to prioritize its inspections. Our current policy is that if an establishment that engages in food preparation has passed inspection without any conditions for four consecutive years, the department can (if needed) waive the fifth-year inspection."

She noted other environment-related areas of concerns. First, the lead paint abatement program did fewer home inspections this year because of a change in leadership that affected staff coverage, and a shift in staffing to support the pandemic programs. Old houses, especially in the northern part of the county, need increased attention given their age and the likelihood that they contain lead-based paint. The resettlement in the community of refugees and immigrants who have limited English proficiency also contributes to the issue, given the difficulty of communicating lead abatement strategies to this population. When secondary prevention measures are implemented, children regularly present with elevated blood lead levels. If not addressed, these elevated blood lead levels can eventually stunt children's cognitive development and school performance, leading to increased social costs. Unless the division can better demonstrate to the state the need for this program, it may be curtailed or eliminated.

Second, a bedbug infestation is menacing the lower-income districts of the county. This environmental issue may be attributed to absentee landlords, poor-quality living conditions, social determinants of health, and cultural and language differences that impede communication. This division educates the occupants of these infested units about preventive measures and connects them with social service agencies that can provide replacement furniture.

Third, since DDT spraying was banned many years ago, mosquito control has remained an issue. State funding has ceased for mosquito surveillance in the county. As a result, the division has resorted to enlisting community volunteers. It is a cost-effective approach to conducting surveillance for the presence of mosquito-borne diseases, such as West Nile virus and Eastern equine encephalitis.

Fourth, the EPA has identified one hazardous waste site in the county. In the 1950s and 1960s, the JM Asbestos Company inadvertently contaminated the soil, groundwater, and the Swift River that runs through the county. The extent of the environmental contamination and the resultant health effects on the employees and their families—as well as local residents who lived within a five-mile radius and those who fished downstream from the plant—qualified this site to be declared a Superfund site. This division is currently working with the EPA and the Agency for Toxic Substances and Disease Registry (ATSDR) to conduct a public health assessment. Recently, at HCHD's request, the ATSDR provided a health consultation to identify and assess the site owned by Carlstead Rayon. Preliminary studies indicate that Carlstead Rayon will be designated a hazardous waste site. Carlstead ceased operations in Middleboro recently, but the environmental issue remains unresolved.

Thus far in her tenure, Brownell has testified before the state legislature regarding the following bills:

◆ HB 2701 would eliminate water fluoridation. This bill is being amended to require a warning to property owners served by the municipal water system that their water supply is fluoridated. This warning would be included in the quarterly water bill. Maintenance and expansion of water fluoridation programs is a stated objective of Healthy People 2030.

◆ HB 2405 would allow communities to impose a moratorium on refugee resettlement in the county. Brownell testified against this bill.

Disease Prevention Division

For 27 years, Candice McCory, RN, has been the director of this division. She holds a bachelor's in nursing and an advanced certificate in epidemiology from State University. As needed, she fills in for Snow as the deputy director of HCHD.

The division provides direct services and contracts with healthcare agencies in the area to fulfill prevention-related services, such as breast and cervical cancer screening; communicable disease control, including case investigations; family planning education and services; healthy eating; HIV/AIDS counseling and testing; immunization planning and clinics; sexually transmitted disease (STD) diagnosis and treatment referral; and a women, infants, and children (WIC) program. The number of cases of community-acquired MRSA (methicillin-resistant Staphylococcus aureus) nationally has attracted local concern. Snow has asked the senior staff for policy recommendations on this issue.

In addition, this division was charged with coordinating and managing HCHD's response to the recent pandemic, responsibilities that greatly challenged the Disease Prevention staff. At times, responsibilities between the divisions became unclear.

Division responsibilities associated with the pandemic program included:

◆ Monitoring local health status and disease incidence

◆ Contact tracing

◆ Taking the lead on program activities involving coordination with other programs and organizations, including hospitals, physician groups, schools, libraries, etc.

◆ Surveillance, communication, risk assessment and mitigation

◆ Virus testing and eventually vaccination initiatives

When interviewed, McCory indicated her division "has the highest level of professionalism and productivity. I am especially proud of our workers and what we have accomplished with limited resources during these trying times." She noted that in addition to coordinating pandemic programs, her division continued to manage the ongoing program of "routine" countywide immunizations and the dental health program, saying, "We are especially fortunate that so many area dentists volunteer their time to provide indigent dental care, particularly in the rural parts of our county." Enhanced dental services for both rural and low-income populations are objectives of Healthy People 2030.

She expressed concern about the health of women in rural areas: "Women's health is a significant issue in this county, especially in our very rural communities. Needs and issues just aren't identified, or they are not addressed. In response to this concern, we now either hold or sponsor family planning clinics throughout the county frequently, in conjunction with programs and services provided under the WIC program. Our attempts to organize women's health outreach programs with hospitals and other providers have had limited success. Of all the area providers, Hillsboro Health has been the most responsive to our needs."

Recently, state funding for sexually transmitted disease (STD) screening, including HIV/AIDS counseling, was cut. As a result, the Public Health Specialist I position was eliminated. Prior to the termination of this position, the standardized mortality ratio for HIV/AIDS in the county was greater than 1.0, indicating more deaths than expected.

Last month, Snow asked McCory to develop recommendations and a budget for expanding the ongoing, non–pandemic-related, adult immunization services provided by HCHD. Given that flu shots are available in local pharmacies, HCHD may no longer have to provide this service and instead focus its resources on other immunizations, such as shots for pneumonia and shingles for senior citizens.

COMMUNITY HEALTH AND HEALTH PROMOTION DIVISION

Russell Martin has been the director of this division for nine years. His credentials include a master of public health from a leading midwestern university and more than ten years of experience in a similar position with the State Department of Public Health. He serves on the regional and state Emergency Preparedness Task Force. He is scheduled to retire in the next two years.

The division attempts to address the objectives of Healthy People 2030 in designating its priorities. It contracts with healthcare providers in the area to address a number of community health needs, such as vision screening, hearing screening, tobacco control, school health (including oral health), substance abuse prevention, and adult health promotion. In addition, it runs an adult health program as well as an osteoporosis prevention and screening program. It frequently cosponsors initiatives with the local chapter of AARP, Red Cross, and Rural Clinics, Inc. It holds clinics and screenings in facilities across the county, including at Manorhaven, as well as health promotion seminars, workshops, and fairs in every public school in the county. Three times a year, with funding from one or more corporate sponsors, it organizes a 5K road race to promote an active lifestyle and call attention to the dangers of obesity.

The tobacco control program includes enforcing the state and county regulation that prohibits smoking in public spaces and in any licensed establishments such as restaurants, bars, coffee shops, and stores. It offers smoking cessation classes quarterly and tobacco-free literature at numerous health fairs throughout the county.

The oral health program is run by two dental hygienists who travel by van to six elementary schools during the school year. The hygienists conduct oral screenings for dental caries, perform cleanings, and apply dental sealants. Once a week, they are joined by two volunteer dentists, who perform minor procedures such as extractions. The Kiwanis Club donated the dental van. The van is currently in need of major repairs, and a replacement van will cost approximately $300,000.

Six months ago, the Jasper Regional Educational Cooperative approached the HCHD to provide staffing and services to the Jasper school system. The school board would transfer all school health funding to HCHD for a five-year renewable contract. This plan is currently under review.

Martin indicated he is hopeful that grant funds might be available to expand health promotion, especially in the area of health behavior, such as a hand-washing campaign in schools and healthcare facilities.

Snow has recently asked Martin to draft a response to an open letter published in the *Middleboro Sentinel*. The letter called for school officials to ban sugary drinks and to adopt a "healthy vending" policy in all public schools. The leader of a county coalition of concerned parents and nurses signed the letter.

OTHER HCHD ISSUES

Just prior to the outbreak of the pandemic, the statewide Task Force on Public Health, comprised of business and civic leaders, was tasked by the governor to examine whether regional rather than county-specific health departments would be more economical. The preliminary recommendations, temporarily tabled during the height of the pandemic, supported a realignment by which regional health departments that cover between 1 and 1.5 million lives would be organized under the direct control of the State Department of Public Health. Individual counties would be billed for their share of the cost. The statewide chapter of Hillsboro County Commissioners has opposed this plan because it removes local control but requires local taxes to support statewide programs. This initiative is slated to be revisited now that the pandemic has waned.

The HCHD is responsible for implementing the statewide Home and Community-Based Services (HCBS) waiver under section 1915(c). The HCBS waiver allows Medicaid to cover the expenses of community-based homes for special populations (e.g., persons with mental health issues or developmental disabilities) and to screen all Medicaid-eligible patients before they are admitted to a residential long-term care facility. Under the current plan, any individual who is Medicaid eligible and can be cared for at home will be denied admission into a nursing home. In the past five years, the state has twice been found to be in violation of the 1999 US Supreme Court decision in the case *Olmstead v. L.C.*

More statistics about HCHD and its programs can be found in tables 9.1 through 9.14.

	2024	2023	2022	2019	2014
Annual Licensed Food Establishments					
Routine Inspections Conducted	669	377	301	956	1,320
Reinspections Conducted	55	51	22	177	237
Complaint Investigations Conducted	42	59	31	167	163
Temporary Food Stand Inspections	199	148	87	312	102
Food Certification Classes	7	5	0	23	9
Potable Water Supply					
Water Well Permits Issued	47	29	31	56	45
Water Wells Installed	19	17	15	32	15
New Water Wells Inspected	19	17	9	28	20
Complaint Investigations Conducted	5	7	3	18	12
Private On-Site Wastewater Disposal					
Systems Permits Issued	49	18	32	177	152
Systems Installed	29	19	17	101	98
Systems Inspected	68	62	75	130	164
Complaint Investigations Conducted	11	14	10	14	21
Lead Hazards Removal					
Environmental Assessments	33	31	29	77	60
Homes Mitigated	27	18	12	85	15
Other					
Indoor Tanning Establishment Inspections	4	3	5	24	15
Body Art Establishment Inspections	1	1	0	2	4
Camp (Summer) Inspections	5	1	0	58	59
Health Facility Inspections	8	4	7	18	12
Public Swimming Pool Inspections	2	6	3	11	10
Rabies Control Investigations	11	7	2	8	5
Radon Control Inspections	4	2	2	14	12
Vector Control Public Contacts	68	53	87	201	245
Vector Control Inspections	29	24	12	133	80

Table 9.1
HCHD
Environmental
Health Statistics

	2024	2023	2022	2019	2014
Adult Health Program					
Health Clinics Conducted	21	14	7	18	21
Clients Seen	1,398	1,174	489	1,466	1,405
Vision Screening Clients	119	43	15	689	459
Hearing Screening Clients	51	32	11	818	857
Substance Abuse Pamphlets Distributed	2,582	1,742	1,602	1,400	1,350
Health Promotion Presentations					
Community Programs Given	82	57	21	80	34
Community Program Attendees	1,477	1,365	643	1,326	978
School Health Program Presentations	20	18	5	156	159
School Health Program Attendees	569	401	68	3,648	3,948
Health Fairs	87	59	0	14	16
Health Fair Attendees	1,030	721	0	492	459
Osteoporosis Prevention/Screening					
Women Screened	81	49	23	203	224
Tobacco-Free Community Programs					
Smoking Cessation Program Enrollees	196	108	59	157	112
Program Classes	46	14	5	36	14
Smoke-Free Complaints	12	13	9	81	64
Smoke-Free Inspections	2	0	0	3	5
Smoke-Free Fines Assessed	0	0	0	3	8

Note: Data for 2022–2024 include virtual sessions.

	2024	2023	2022	2019	2014
Communicable Diseases Reported					
Giardiasis	6	4	2	9	5
Lyme Disease	21	19	13	9	22
Meningitis (Viral)	0	0	0	1	0
Salmonellosis	11	12	17	14	9
Shigellosis	7	4	2	11	5
Tuberculosis	1	3	2	3	0
Case Investigations (Includes STD)	7	3	4	6	9
Dental Health Program					
Examinations	1,018	584	432	2,503	3,277
Sealants	198	114	24	503	509
Other Dental Services	2,342	1,194	1,029	4,129	3,715
Family Planning					
Clinics Held	7	4	1	4	4
Immunizations (Non–Pandemic Related)					
Adult Immunization, Doses Administered	1,182	668	645	3,823	3,512
Adult Immunization, Clients Served	984	565	454	2,156	2,546
Childhood Immunization, Doses Administered	5,560	4,684	3,842	8,934	9,213
Childhood Immunization, Clients Served	2,758	2,042	1,053	3,925	4,098
H1N1 Vaccine, Doses Administered	58	79	48	1,201	823
Influenza Immunization, Adult Doses	497	204	158	623	434
Influenza Immunization, Infant/Child Doses	458	308	275	602	338
Sexually Transmitted Disease (STD)					
Clinic Patient Encounters	1,457	708	672	2,099	1,856
HIV Counseling and Testing at Clinics	587	520	483	757	892
Chlamydia Cases Reported	797	495	358	1,130	956
Gonorrhea Cases Reported	406	472	387	386	402
Syphilis Cases Reported	1	1	2	1	0
Women, Infants, and Children (WIC) Program					
Clients Certified	7,584	7,374	6,835	6,022	5,103
Clients Attending Nutrition Classes	3,821	2,972	1,746	3,156	3,046
Breastfeeding Peer-Counseling Contracts	203	187	201	187	N/A
High-Risk Infant Visits	103	79	67	134	87
Children with Elevated Blood Lead Levels	44	33	17	51	69
Women's Health					
Clients Seen	2,544	2,462	1,562	2,014	2,056

Table 9.3
HCHD Disease Prevention Statistics

Note: Data for 2022–2024 include virtual sessions.

Table 9.4
HCHD
Statement of
Revenues and
Expenses

	2024	2023	2022	2019	2014
Revenues					
Federal Grants					
CDC—Environmental Tracking	7,039	7,382	8,372	8,450	8,200
EPA—Asthma	33,763	33,876	34,827	35,688	33,903
CDC—Oral Health	21,705	22,283	22,049	24,340	27,393
Rural Health Development	194,204	200,859	183,509	212,440	118,209
Rural Poverty/Homeless	75,289	84,583	74,509	90,450	85,303
Pandemic Support	503,200	402,000	81,209	0	0
Subtotal	**835,200**	**750,983**	**404,475**	**371,368**	**273,008**
State Grants					
County Health Department Development	185,000	175,209	165,209	200,000	200,000
EMS Assistance	84,209	86,209	64,509	103,409	99,209
EMS Preparedness	80,375	79,029	64,309	50,000	43,509
HIV Control/Prevention	54,837	49,209	49,209	48,209	44,029
Immunization	68,029	54,290	55,209	52,309	51,309
Lead Control	8,092	6,304	5,209	12,409	15,209
Medicaid Oral Health	45,390	46,209	58,209	85,209	88,109
Primary Health Demo	120,309	98,435	104,309	145,209	139,029
STD Control/Prevention	70,109	65,209	62,309	74,592	71,209
Tobacco Use Control	24,509	28,409	35,408	56,309	73,498
WIC Administration	82,308	81,879	65,309	85,209	85,593
WIC Services	306,409	302,098	330,209	325,309	319,097
Pandemic Emergency	24,502	21,902	16,208	0	0
Subtotal	**1,154,078**	**1,094,391**	**1,075,615**	**1,238,173**	**1,229,800**
Private Foundations					
Breast Cancer	32,058	30,209	30,209	35,309	0
Obesity Control Prevention	0	0	1,403	5,309	10,309
Subtotal	**32,058**	**30,209**	**31,612**	**40,618**	**10,309**
Subtotal External Grants and Contracts	**2,021,336**	**1,875,583**	**1,511,702**	**1,650,159**	**1,513,117**
Licenses and Permits					
Food Services	5,290	4,683	3,940	5,470	6,208
Campgrounds	2,683	2,535	2,297	1,902	1,872

continued

	2024	2023	2022	2019	2014
Tanning Facilities	385	450	125	560	0
Special Fees/Fines	2,392	2,093	1,820	3,839	5,297
Subtotal	**10,750**	**9,761**	**8,182**	**11,771**	**13,377**
Overhead Recovery	**98,750**	**108,409**	**111,309**	**115,209**	**150,209**
County Appropriation/Tax Levy	**1,555,298**	**1,818,398**	**1,984,387**	**1,615,090**	**1,790,284**
Total Revenues	**3,686,134**	**3,812,151**	**3,615,580**	**3,392,229**	**3,466,987**
Expenses					
Office of the Director					
Personnel	331,741	327,698	326,593	335,711	324,550
Supplies	17,309	14,509	12,409	19,209	22,309
Equipment	8,209	10,309	9,209	16,274	18,373
Utilities	2,104	1,935	1,837	2,462	2,402
Marketing/Promotion	4,304	2,739	3,209	4,029	3,509
Miscellaneous	1,423	859	539	693	1,103
Staff Development	1,400	1,000	928	500	6,490
Grants to Local Agencies	0	2,405	194	2,109	1,902
Subtotal	**366,490**	**361,454**	**354,918**	**380,987**	**380,638**
Administrative Services Division					
Personnel	574,656	569,609	610,372	667,425	733,994
Supplies	15,209	20,095	18,386	28,394	25,309
Equipment	2,309	1,536	874	1,309	2,293
Utilities	30,354	28,354	28,383	27,059	25,209
Marketing/Promotion	0	0	450	576	499
Staff Development	1,500	1,250	1,298	894	1,109
Miscellaneous	302	154	202	146	167
Grants to Local Agencies	0	0	0	32,847	0
Subtotal	**624,330**	**620,998**	**659,965**	**758,650**	**788,580**
Environmental Health Division					
Personnel	549,727	540,448	535,348	593,678	580,977
Supplies	6,093	5,037	6,570	6,509	5,246
Equipment	2,109	1,092	1,057	2,643	2,984
Utilities	39,210	38,029	38,209	37,669	36,209
Marketing/Promotion	1,928	2,092	3,825	4,024	6,034

Table 9.4
HCHD
Statement of
Revenues and
Expenses
(continued)

continued

Table 9.4
HCHD
Statement of
Revenues and
Expenses
(continued)

	2024	2023	2022	2019	2014
Staff Development	1,000	500	500	4,000	3,575
Lab Contracts	1,972	2,438	3,562	13,209	3,790
Grants to Local Agencies	0	0	0	0	0
Subtotal	**602,039**	**589,636**	**589,071**	**661732**	**638,815**
Community Health and Health Promotion Division					
Personnel	887,532	1,044,941	1,014,559	991,862	956,701
Supplies	101,998	82,409	84,209	105,298	112,009
Equipment	40,290	36,882	30,938	23,450	25,309
Utilities	20,498	19,389	22,341	23,460	24,354
Marketing/Promotion	11,390	9,800	4,512	5,509	15,490
Staff Development	2,500	1,500	355	5,400	4,000
Miscellaneous	347	94	1,209	478	495
Grants to Local Agencies	185,093	143,827	124,565	172,398	174,509
Subtotal	**1,249,648**	**1,338,842**	**1,282,688**	**1,327,855**	**1,312,867**
Disease Prevention Division					
Personnel	1,460,701	1,558,292	1,391,729	1,014,203	1,101,403
Supplies	83,498	86,093	81,039	95,609	98,309
Equipment	24,509	23,609	21,481	17,093	12,046
Utilities	35,029	34,552	34,526	34,209	33,209
Marketing/Promotion	15,209	12,409	2,390	1,498	1,070
Staff Development	1,000	1,500	1,800	10,309	12,590
Miscellaneous	101	35	263	768	309
Other Pandemic Support	25,000	18,405	14,029	0	0
Grants to Local Agencies	167,089	117,368	125,668	132,184	106,534
Subtotal	**1,812,136**	**1,852,263**	**1,672,925**	**1,305,873**	**1,365,470**
Total Expenses	**3,686,114**	**3,812,103**	**3,615,578**	**3,392,378**	**3,466,917**
Excess Revenue	**20**	**48**	**2**	**−149**	**70**

Notes: (1) Total charges for utilities allocated on basis of square feet occupied. (2) Excess revenue is returned to general funds at end of fiscal year. (3) Years ending December 31. (4) Numbers are in US dollars. (5) CDC: Centers for Disease Control and Prevention; EMS: emergency medical services; EPA: Environmental Protection Agency; STD: sexually transmitted disease; WIC: women, infants, and children.

	Office of the Director	Administrative Services	Environmental Health	Community Health	Disease Prevention	Total
Federal Grants						
CDC Environmental			7,039			7,039
EPA Asthma			33,763			33,763
Oral Health					21,705	21,705
Rural Healthcare	21,000	50,000	80,060	43,144		194,204
Rural Poverty/ Homelessness	12,640			54,351	8,298	75,289
Pandemic Support	10,000	23,209	38,289	88,928	342,774	503,200
Subtotal	**43,640**	**73,209**	**159,151**	**186,423**	**372,777**	**835,200**
State Grants						
County General Grant	50,203	28,403	32,000	44,000	30,394	185,000
EMS—Total				164,584		164,584
HIV Control and Prevention				29,882	24,955	54,837
General Immunization					68,029	68,029
Lead Control			8,092			8,092
Medicaid—Oral					45,390	45,390
Primary Health Care			5,660	114,649		120,309
STD Control					70,109	70,109
Tobacco Cessation				24,509		24,509
WIC General Admin	25,109	14,389			42,810	82,308
WIC Services					306,409	306,409
Pandemic Emergency	24,502					24,502
Subtotal	**99,814**	**42,792**	**45,752**	**377,624**	**588,096**	**1,154,078**
Foundations						
Breast Cancer				32,058		32,058
Subtotal				**32,058**		**32,058**
Total Grants/ Contracts	143,454	116,001	204,903	596,105	960,873	2,021,336

Table 9.5
HCHD Budget by Source of Funds (USD $), 2024

continued

	Office of the Director	Administrative Services	Environmental Health	Community Health	Disease Prevention	Total
Licenses and Permits						
Food Services				5,290		5,290
Campgrounds				2,683		2,683
Tanning Facilities				385		385
Special Fees and Fines	2,392					2,392
Total	**2,392**			**8,358**		**10,750**
Overhead Recovery		98,750				98,750
Total Non-County Revenue	145,846	214,751	204,903	604,463	960,873	2,130,836
County Tax Appropriation	140,667	263,287	209,382	347,382	594,580	1,555,298
Total Budget by Division	286,513	478,038	414,285	951,845	1,555,453	3,686,134
County as % of Total Budget	49.10%	55.08%	50.54%	36.50%	38.23%	42.19%

Notes: (1) Numbers are in US dollars, except where indicated. (3) CDC: Centers for Disease Control and Prevention; EMS: emergency medical services; EPA: Environmental Protection Agency; STD: sexually transmitted disease; WIC: women, infants, and children.

Table 9.6
HCHD Staffing Budget (USD $)

Administrative Unit	2024 FTE	2024 Budget	2023 FTE	2023 Budget	2022 FTE	2022 Budget	2019 FTE	2019 Budget	2014 FTE	2014 Budget
Office of the Director										
Director	1.0	138,293	1.0	137,483	1.0	135,372	1.0	135,372	1.0	130,174
Administrative Assistant III	1.0	39,800	1.0	39,500	1.0	39,350	1.0	38,477	1.0	37,322
Administrative Assistant IV	0.0	0	0.0	0	0.5	32,500	0.5	30,721	0.5	29,799
Health Info Tech	1.0	77,092	1.0	75,092	0.5	44,003	0.5	43,669	0.5	42,359
Intern	0.0	0	0.0	0	0.0	0	0.5	10,000	0.5	10,000
Benefits		76,556		75,623		75,368		77,472		74,896
Subtotal	3.0	331,741	3.0	327,698	3.0	326,593	3.5	335,711	3.5	324,550
Administrative Services Division										
Director, Administration	1.0	92,330	1.0	92,200	1.0	92,000	1.0	90,483	1.0	88,674
Health Officer/Medical Examiner	0.5	99,500	0.5	99,211	0.5	98,517	0.5	98,517	0.5	98,517
Business Services Officer	1.0	77,000	1.0	76,000	1.0	75,000	1.0	73,787	1.0	72,340
Customer Services Rep II	1.0	53,315	1.0	53,000	1.0	52,500	1.0	52,249	1.0	51,204
Administrative Services Manager	1.0	51,550	1.0	51,500	1.0	51,000	2.0	63,409	2.0	60,325
Administrative Assistant II	1.0	31,348	1.0	31,250	1.0	31,000	1.0	30,721	1.0	30,107
Custodian	1.0	37,000	1.0	35,000	2.0	69,500	3.0	104,238	4.0	163,444
Benefits		132,613		131,448		140,855		154,021		169,383
Subtotal	6.5	574,656	6.5	569,609	7.5	610,372	9.5	667,425	10.5	733,994
Environmental Health Division										
Director, Environmental Health	1.0	103,233	1.0	102,000	1.0	101,168	1.0	101,168	1.0	101,168
Environ Health Specialist IV	1.0	54,223	1.0	54,200	1.0	54,139	1.0	53,139	1.0	53,139
Environ Health Specialist II	3.0	105,603	3.0	101,209	3.0	100,392	4.0	132,408	4.0	129,812
Public Health Specialist II	2.0	128,460	2.0	127,500	2.0	126,000	2.0	125,891	2.0	119,598
Administrative Assistant II	1.0	31,348	1.0	30,820	1.0	30,107	1.0	30,721	1.0	30,107
Administrative Assistant I	0.0	0	0.0	0	0.0	0	0.5	13,348	0.5	13,081
Benefits		126860		124,719		123,542		137,003		134,072
Subtotal	8.0	549,727	8.0	540,448	8.0	535,348	9.5	593,678	9.5	580,977

continued

Table 9.6
HCHD Staffing Budget (USD $) *(continued)*

Administrative Unit	2024 FTE	2024 Budget	2023 FTE	2023 Budget	2022 FTE	2022 Budget	2019 FTE	2019 Budget	2014 FTE	2014 Budget
Community Health and Health Promotion Division										
Director, Community Health	1.0	93,274	1.0	91,392	1.0	89,500	1.0	88,610	1.0	86,838
Community Health Nurse	5.0	310,283	5.0	308,000	5.0	304,000	6.0	367,882	6.0	360,525
Public Health Specialist II	3.0	192,960	4.0	248,000	4.0	246,289	3.0	183,312	3.0	179,646
Public Health Preparedness	1.0	86,200	2.0	156,409	1.5	127,092	1.3	109,819	1.0	82,752
Administrative Assistant I Admin	0.0	0	0.0	0	0.5	13,549	0.5	13,348	1.0	26,163
Benefits		204,815		241,140		234,129		228,891		220,777
Subtotal	10.0	887532	12.0	1044941	12.0	1,014,559	11.8	991,862	12.0	956,701
Disease Prevention Division										
Director, Personal Health	1.0	104,330	1.0	102,000	1.0	100,000	1.0	99,114	1.0	97,131
Public Health Specialist III	2.0	120,068	3.0	166,309	3.0	164,509	2.0	114,065	3.0	111,783
Program Director, Women's Health	1.0	84,670	1.0	82,089	1.0	81,050	1.0	80,437	1.0	78,828
Public Health Nurse	5.0	332,115	4.0	328,828	5.0	320,000	5.0	315,509	5.0	247,360
Case Control Investigators	3.0	245,093	3.0	243,829	3.0	234,000	1.4	86,173	2.0	162,336
Community Services Assistant	1.0	49,837	2.0	96,500	2.0	95,000	1.5	69,968	2.0	91,425
Administrative Assistant II	0.5	15,674	0.5	14,749	1.0	20,000	1.0	14,890	2.0	58,370
Pandemic Specialist	3.0	171,829	3.0	164,382	1.0	56,002	0.0	0	0.0	0
Benefits		337,085		359,606		321,168		234,047		254,170
Subtotal	16.5	1,460,701	17.5	1,558,292	17.0	1,391,729	12.9	1,014,203	16.0	1,101,403
Total	44.0	3,804,357	47.0	4,040,988	47.5	3,878,601	47.2	3,602,879	51.5	3,697,625

Note: FTE: Full-time equivalent.

City/Town	Percentage of Households in Hillsboro County Served by Municipal Water System		
	2024	2019	2014
Boalsburg	0	0	0
Carterville	12	12	10
Harris City	8	4	5
Jasper	54	50	44
Middleboro	74	73	70
Mifflenville	22	24	30
Minortown	5	10	12
Statesville	18	20	9

City/Town	Percentage of Households in Hillsboro County Served by Fluoridated Water System		
	2024	2019	2014
Boalsburg	0	0	0
Carterville	4	4	4
Harris City	0	0	0
Jasper	54	50	44
Middleboro	54	58	56
Mifflenville	22	24	0
Minortown	0	0	0
Statesville	0	10	12

City/Town	Percentage of 3rd-Grade Students with (2024)	
	Tooth Decay	Untreated Tooth Decay
Boalsburg	43.6	12.9
Carterville	19.3	14.3
Harris City	28.2	13.2
Jasper	23.5	8.1
Middleboro	24.9	10.7
Mifflenville	32.9	15.2
Minortown	31.4	23.7
Statesville	29.7	11.4

Table 9.7
HCHD Special Study: Oral Health and Fluoridation

continued

Table 9.7
HCHD Special
Study: Oral
Health and
Fluoridation
(continued)

City/Town	Time Since Last Cleaning by Dentist/Hygienist (2024)		
	2 Years	5 Years	6 Years or More*
Boalsburg	60	15	25
Carterville	56	10	34
Harris City	62	17	21
Jasper	79	10	11
Middleboro	70	14	16
Mifflenville	64	14	22
Minortown	77	10	13
Statesville	56	12	32

Note: * "Never" or "Did not know" included.

| AIDS Cases per 100,000 Population, All Ages | | | |
Location	2024	2019	2014	2009
Hillsboro County	3.1	3.4	3.6	3.9
Capital City	4.1	4.2	4.7	5.6
Statewide	5.3	6.2	6.7	7.2

| AIDS Cases per 100,000 Population, Adults and Adolescents | | | |
Location	2024	2019	2014	2009
Hillsboro County	3.5	3.5	3.7	4.1
Capital City	4.3	4.3	4.8	5.7
Statewide	8.2	7.6	8	9.3
By Sex, Hillsboro County				
Male	10.7	10.4	12.7	8.6
Female	3	3.2	4	2.7
By Sex, Capital City				
Male	12.3	11.5	12	10.6
Female	3.8	3.8	3.8	3.9
By Sex, Statewide				
Male	10.2	11.5	23.2	15.1
Female	3.5	3.7	3.5	3.7

| HIV Infections per 100,000 Population | | | |
Location	2024	2019	2014	2009
Hillsboro County	10.1	11.4	10.7	12.2
Capital City	17.5	17.3	18.4	19.8
Statewide	23.8	25.8	24.2	25.6

Table 9.8
HCHD Special Study: HIV and AIDS Prevalence

Table 9.9
HCHD Special
Study: Asthma
Prevalence

	2024	2019
Total Population with Asthma		
Hillsboro County	12.4	10
Statewide	11.8	10.5
Males with Asthma		
Hillsboro County	13.2	10.1
Statewide	12.4	10.3
Females with Asthma		
Hillsboro County	14	13.5
Statewide	17.5	14.3
By Age, Hillsboro County		
18–34	12.4	11.7
35–64	10.9	10.8
65+	7	7.6
By Household Income, Hillsboro County		
<$25,000	16.3	15.8
$25,000+	8.5	9.3
By Education, Hillsboro County		
Less Than High School	19.4	18.3
At Least High School/GED	10.3	10
By Employment Status, Hillsboro County		
Employed	9	9.4
Unemployed	14.5	12.7
Unable to Work	28.7	27.5
Homemaker/Student	12.3	14
Retired	7.4	7.9
Statewide	23.8	25.8

Notes: (1) All data, except total population, are percentage of population aged 18 years or older. (2) GED: general educational development.

	2024	2019
Percentage of Low Birthweight Births		
Hillsboro County—All	8	7.5
White	7	5.9
Black	9.3	9.4
Hispanic	7	7.4
Capital City—All	9	8.8
White	6	6.1
Black	12	13
Hispanic	8	9
Percentage of Preterm Births		
Hillsboro County—All	11	13
White	10.4	11.2
Black	15	14.6
Hispanic	11.2	11.4
Capital City—All	13.3	15.3
White	8	8.2
Black	17	17.4
Hispanic	12.9	9.3
Percentage of Overweight or Obese Children (Aged 10–17 Years)		
Hillsboro County—All	31.5	33
White	24.5	28.2
Black	36.3	38.4
Hispanic	33.5	31.2
Capital City—All	35	36.1
White	29	30.1
Black	37.2	34.8
Hispanic	32.4	33.8
Percentage of Children (Aged 0–17 Years) Who Had Medical and Dental Visits in Past 12 Months		
Hillsboro County—All	69.3	62.4
White	74	68.2
Black	61	58.9
Hispanic	60.1	52.3
Capital City—All	76.8	62.3
White	77.9	70.2
Black	65.9	60.3
Hispanic	70.2	63.2

Table 9.10
HCHD Special Study: Child Health

continued

Table 9.10
HCHD Special
Study: Child
Health
(continued)

	2024	2019
Percentage of Children (Aged 1–17 Years) with Oral Health Problems		
Hillsboro County—All	17.3	17
White	16.2	15.3
Black	18.9	18.3
Hispanic	17.4	17
Capital City—All	18.6	19.4
White	16	15.9
Black	17.5	17.5
Hispanic	17.1	16.8
Percentage of Children (Aged 2–17 Years) with Emotional, Developmental, or Behavioral Problems Who Received Mental Health Care		
Hillsboro County—All	58.2	53.5
White	63.4	62.5
Black	45.2	40.3
Hispanic	49.2	49.3
Capital City—All	58.9	52.5
White	66.2	60.2
Black	43.4	40.8
Hispanic	45.3	40.2
Percentage of Children (Aged 19–35 Months) Who Are Immunized*		
Hillsboro County—All	68.5	63.2
White	74.9	72.4
Black	66.5	60.2
Hispanic	74.6	70.4
Capital City—All	65.5	64.9
White	72	71.4
Black	60.7	59.4
Hispanic	70.3	70.9

Note: * Includes DTaP1, poliovirus, measles, Hib.

	2022
Chlamydia	
Reported Cases in Hillsboro County	690
Percentage, Male	28.1
Percentage, Female	71.9
Reported Cases in Capital City	828
Percentage, Male	25
Percentage, Female	75
Gonorrhea	
Reported Cases in Hillsboro County	184
Percentage, Male	47.5
Percentage, Female	52.5
Reported Cases in Capital City	267
Percentage, Male	46.2
Percentage, Female	53.8
Syphilis	
Reported Cases in Hillsboro County	10
Percentage, Male	94.1
Percentage, Female	5.9
Reported Cases in Capital City	34
Percentage, Male	95.3
Percentage, Female	4.7

Table 9.11
HCHD Special Study: Sexually Transmitted Diseases

Table 9.12
HCHD Special
Study: Women's
Health

	2024	2019
Cervical Cancer Deaths in Hillsboro County		
Rate per 100,000 Women		
All Hillsboro County	2.7	2.6
White	7.4	7.8
Black	7.7	8.1
Hispanic	6.5	6.9
Incidence Rate per 100,000		
All Hillsboro County	7.5	7.4
White	7.4	7.1
Black	7.7	8.3
Hispanic	N/A	N/A
Breast Cancer Prevalence in Hillsboro County		
Rate per 100,000 Women		
All Hillsboro County	21.7	23.1
White	20.9	20.1
Black	33.8	34.6
Hispanic	N/A	N/A
Incidence Rate per 100,000		
All Hillsboro County	118.6	115.4
White	113.6	113.7
Black	126.2	125.2
Hispanic	88.8	93.6
Legal Abortions in Hillsboro County		
Rate per 1,000 Women (Aged 15–44)		
All Hillsboro County	5.1	6.8
Percentage by Age		
Up to 19	14	16
20–29	58	545
30–39	25	26
40+	3	4
Percentage by Race		
White	80	83
Black	16	14
Other	4	3

Factor	Hillsboro County %	Capital City %
Adults told they have arthritis	29.3	24.0
Adults told they currently have asthma	11.1	9.0
Adults ever told they have asthma	12.8	9.8
Adults told they have had skin cancer	7.9	7.5
Adults ever told they have any other cancer except skin	8.2	7.9
Adults told they had a stroke	3.3	2.9
Adults ever told they had coronary heart disease, heart attack, or stroke	10.3	9.6
Adults told they had angina or coronary heart disease	5.9	4.7
Adults ever told they had a heart attack	4.9	4.5
Adults ever told they have high blood cholesterol	31.1	28.5
Adults with cholesterol checked in last 5 years	84.6	90.3
Adults told they have high blood cholesterol		
Adults who have had blood cholesterol checked in last five years	34.2	35.8
Adults with cholesterol checked in last 2 years	84.2	87.4
Adults ever told they have COPD, emphysema, or chronic bronchitis	8.4	8.6
Adults ever told they have depressive disorder	17.7	17.2
Adults ever told they have diabetes	12.4	12.1
Adults with glucose or diabetes test last 3 years	56.3	57.4
Average age diabetes diagnosed	48.6	50.3
Adults with serious difficulty remembering or making decisions	14.2	12.8
Adults with serious difficulty walking or climbing stairs	16.4	15.9
Adults ever told they have seizure disorder/epilepsy	2.0	1.9
Adults with seizure disorder seen by neurologist last year	40.3	44.6
Adults ever told they have hypertension	36.3	32.8
Adults ever told they have kidney disease	4.3	4.2
Adults who are overweight	39.2	36.4
Adults who are overweight or obese	66.2	63.8
Adults with mammogram in past year	56.7	58.2
Adults younger than 65 ever tested for HIV	54.7	60.2
Adults with flu shot in past year	33.6	34.8
Adults who ever received pneumonia vaccination	35.8	34.9
Adults who engage in heavy/binge drinking	19.5	19.5
Adults who are sedentary	28.3	26.5
Adults who are current smokers	16.4	14.2
Adults who are former smokers	27.8	25.2
Adults who have never smoked	55.6	59.2
Adult who are current smokers who tried to quit in past year	61.2	59.3

Table 9.13
Behavioral Risk Factor Surveillance System Data: Hillsboro County vs. Capital City, 2024

continued

Table 9.13
Behavioral
Risk Factor
Surveillance
System Data:
Hillsboro
County vs.
Capital City,
2024
(continued)

Factor	Hillsboro County %	Capital City %
Adults who currently use e-cigarettes	7.4	8.4
Adult former e-cigarette users	16.5	18.3
Adults who use chewing tobacco, snuff, or snus	1.8	2.1
Adults saying overall health good/excellent	76.4	80.2
Adults saying overall health fair/poor	23.6	19.8
Adults with good mental health past 30 days	84.9	88.3
Adults whose poor health kept them from usual activities in 14+ of past 30 days	20.4	18.1
Adults with healthcare insurance coverage	80.2	86.4
Adults with a personal doctor	74.5	82.1
Adults who could not see doctor past year due to cost	18.3	14.9
Adults who had medical checkup last year	76.4	76.8
Demographics Age (Years)		
18–24	9	12.5
25–34	19.5	16.5
35–44	20.4	21.5
45–54	18.8	19.5
55–64	23.5	14
65+	8.8	16
Demographics: Race/Ethnicity		
White	82.9	78
Black	9.5	12.5
Hispanic	3.6	5.5
Other	3	2
Multiracial	1	2
Demographics: Marital Status		
Married	73	65
Divorced	6	10.3
Widowed	9.2	7.3
Separated	1.3	1
Never Married	10.1	14.2
Partnered	0.4	2.2
Demographics: Children in Household		
None	50.1	63.2
One	16.9	17.2
Two	22.5	15.2
Three	5.5	3.1
Four	3.2	1
Five or More	1.8	0.3

continued

Factor	Hillsboro County %	Capital City %
Demographics: Highest Grade in School		
< High School	10.2	11.3
High School or GED	44.5	34.5
Some College	18.2	28.3
College+	27.1	25.9
Demographics: Employment		
Employed	54.3	48.2
Self-Employed	11.7	10.4
No Work > year	0.4	2.3
Homemaker	9.3	6.9
Student	4	4.8
Retired	17.3	22.2
Unable to Work	3	5.2
Demographics: Household Income (USD)		
< $15,000	12.4	14.8
$15,000–$24,999	18.3	11.3
$25,000–$34,999	10.2	10.8
$35,000–$49,999	18.9	11.8
$50,000+	40.2	51.3
Demographics: Gender		
Male	46.4	45.3
Female	48.5	47.4
Other or Not Disclosed	5.1	7.3
Sample Size	860	1245

Table 9.13
Behavioral Risk Factor Surveillance System Data: Hillsboro County vs. Capital City, 2024 *(continued)*

Note: Sample study conducted in 2021.

Table 9.14
Healthy People
2030 National
Objectives and
Recent State
Data

Objective	Healthy People 2030 Preliminary Objective (as of June 2021)	State Preliminary Objective (as of 2022)
People with substance abuse disorder who got treatment in the past year	14%	9%
People who had alcohol use disorder in the past year	3.90%	3.30%
People who had marijuana use disorder in past year	1.60%	3.70%
People who had drug use disorder in past year	2.70%	3.20%
People who had opioid use disorder in past year	0.50%	1.90%
Overall cancer death rate	122.7 per 100,000	134.8 per 100,000
Female breast cancer death rate	15.3 per 100,000	19.5 per 100,000
Colorectal cancer death rate	8.9 per 100,000	10.4 per 100,000
Prostate cancer death rate	16.9 per 100,000	17.3 per 100,000
Rate of new cases of end-stage kidney disease	268.6 per million	275.3 per million
Cardiovascular health in adults	3.5 mean score	3.2 mean score
Coronary heart disease deaths	71 per 100,000	86.3 per 100,000
Stroke deaths	33.4 per 100,000	41.9 per 100,000
Tuberculosis cases	1.4 per 100,000	0.9 per 100,000
Rate of hepatitis A	0.4 per 100,000	0.6 per 100,000
Rate of hepatitis B	0.9 per 100,000	1.0 per 100,000
Children with autism spectrum disorder who received special services by age 48 months	53.50%	49.70%
Adults with serious mental illness who got treatment	68.40%	64.30%
Adults with major depressive episodes who got treatment	69.50%	65.10%
Suicide rate	12.8 per 100,000	13.9 per 100,000
Suicidal thoughts in LGBTQ students	52.10%	54.20%
Adults with active or untreated tooth decay	17.30%	24.50%
Persons with dental insurance	59.80%	55.70%
Water systems with recommended amount of fluoride	64.60%	73.80%
Low-income youth who have had a preventive dental visit	82.70%	80.20%
Adults with osteoporosis	5.50%	5.70%
Adults with obesity	36.00%	39.50%
Pregnant women who receive early and adequate prenatal care	80.50%	76.90%
Pregnancies in adolescents	31.4 per 1000 females	38.2 per 1000 females
Maternal deaths	15.7 per 100,000 live births	14.8 per 100,000 live births
Deaths from COPD in adults	107.2 per 100,000	110.4 per 100,000
Lung cancer death rate	25.1 per 100,000	31.2 per 100,000

continued

Objective	Healthy People 2030 Preliminary Objective (as of June 2021)	State Preliminary Objective (as of 2022)
Adolescents aged 13–15 who get recommended HPV vaccine	74%	49%
Infants who are breastfed at 1 year old	54.10%	38.50%
Cirrhosis deaths	10.9 per 100,000	11.1 per 100,000
Fatal injuries	63.1 deaths per 100,000	70.1 deaths per 100,000
Persons who use the oral health care system	45%	43.30%
Females aged 50–74 who get screened for breast cancer	77.10%	72.80%
Adults aged 50–74 who get screened for colorectal cancer	74.4%%	65.20%
Females aged 21–65 who get screened for cervical cancer	84.30%	80.50%
Infections caused by Campylobacteria	10.6 per 100,000	14.5 per 100,000
Infections caused by Shiga toxin producing E.coli	3.2 per 100,000	3.5 per 100,000
Infections caused by Listeria	0.21 per 100,000	0.20 per 100,000
Infections caused by Salmonella	11.1 per 100,000	13.5 per 100,000
Current tobacco use by adults 18 and over	16.20%	20.10%
Current cigarette smoking in adults 18 and over	5.00%	5.80%
Tobacco use in adolescents grades 6–12	11.30%	17.40%
E-cigarette use in adolescents grades 6–12	10.40%	12.50%
Cigarette use among adolescents grades 6–12	3.40%	5.10%
Cigar smoking among adolescents grades 6–12	3%	5%
Use of smokeless tobacco among adolescents grades 6–12	2.30%	2.80%
Use of flavored tobacco products in adolescents grades 6–12 who use tobacco	59.20%	63.20%
Average tax on cigarettes	$2.60 per pack	$2.02 per pack
People 6 months + who get flu vaccine yearly	70%	49.20%
Children with no vaccine by age 2	1.30%	1.50%
Maintain vaccination for MMR by age 2	90.80%	88.40%
Maintain vaccination for MMR by kindergarten	95.00%	93.60%
Dtap vaccination coverage by age 2	90%	80.70%
Homicides	5.5 per 100,000	5.9 per 100,000
Local public health jurisdictions with community health improvement plan	71.80%	55.00%
Trips to work by mass transit	3.70%	5.10%
Persons with prescription drug insurance	61.40%	61.10%
People 18+ with broadband access	60.80%	55.90%
People who can't get medical care when they need it	3.30%	4.10%

Table 9.14
Healthy People 2030 National Objectives and Recent State Data *(continued)*

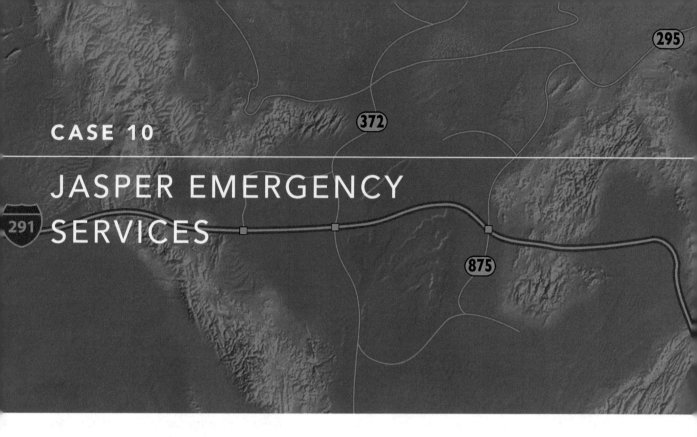

CASE 10

JASPER EMERGENCY SERVICES

Jasper Emergency Services (JES), a freestanding emergency room, was opened as a wholly owned subsidiary of Capital City General Hospital (CCGH) in April 2020. JES is located approximately five miles east of downtown Jasper, adjacent to the new highway connecting Jasper with Capital City and close to the Physician Care Services Jasper office. Highway on/off access is easy and convenient. CCGH's stated goals in developing the facility were to provide access to emergency services in eastern Hillsboro County and to increase CCGH's market presence in this growing location. The facility is open 24/7. JES is the only freestanding emergency room in Hillsboro County and the second opened by CCGH; the first CCGH facility is in Capital City. JES operates as a for-profit corporation. Based on state regulations, construction of the facility did not require a certificate of need. The facility is accredited by The Joint Commission.

GOVERNANCE

As an organization owned and operated by CCGH, JES does not have a distinct governing body; governing authority for the facility rests with the CCGH Governing Board. An Advisory Committee was created by CCGH to provide general guidance to the facility. The committee is composed of nine individuals, each of whom serves for a three-year term. Individuals are limited to three consecutive terms.

The Advisory Committee meets quarterly and is charged with reviewing the operations of JES. Findings and recommendations from the group are sent to the vice president, Operations, at CCGH for review and possible action. Since its inception, CCGH has found input from the Advisory Committee to be extremely valuable, especially in terms of obtaining feedback from the Jasper market regarding JES's image and reputation. Committee members have also been helpful in "spreading the word" about JES in the Jasper community. Members of the Advisory Committee are shown in table 10.1.

MANAGEMENT

On-site management of the facility is under the direction of a nurse manager, with backup assistance provided, as needed, by individuals in the CCGH Operations Division. The manager of JES is Ms. Beatrice Fowler, RN, MBA, who assumed her role following ten years of service as a floor nurse, emergency room (ER) nurse, and ER nurse manager at CCGH. Ms. Fowler is viewed as a skilled manager and excellent nurse and has the respect of JES staff. Ms. Fowler reports to the vice president, Operations, at CCGH and meets with the CCGH management team at least biweekly, often via teleconferencing. She receives a financial bonus for taking on her management role.

Bertram Collacio, MD, a board-certified emergency medicine physician, serves as JES's medical director. In addition to his standing responsibilities as an emergency physician, Dr. Collacio is responsible for providing clinical oversight and guidance, conducting reviews of medical charts, creating and ensuring compliance with infection control protocols, and providing overall direction to the on-site JES laboratory. Dr. Collacio received his MD degree from a midwestern university and is board certified in emergency medicine. He meets the Clinical Laboratory Improvement Amendments (CLIA) requirements for a medical director of a laboratory of moderate complexity. He assumed responsibilities at JES upon its opening, following a number of years of emergency medicine practice in University Town. Dr. Collacio is proficient in his duties and gets along well with facility staff.

JES has implemented an operations plan and manual based on best practices from CCGH, which has served the facility well to date. JES staff are responsible for implementation and have considerable input into the development of all policies and practices. JES personnel are recruited and evaluated by the JES management team, and all Human Resources policies and practices are consistent with CCGH. A personnel manual spelling out job descriptions, responsibilities, reporting relationships, and the like exists for JES. Decisions on employee retention are made at the "local" level.

STAFFING

JES staff work three 12-hour shifts weekly, beginning at 7:00 a.m. or 7:00 p.m. The facility is staffed at all times with a minimum of one board-certified emergency physician, two RNs with training and experience in emergency medicine and certified in both advanced cardiac life support and advanced pediatric life support, one radiologic technician, one office/administrative staff, one patient transport/health aide, and one housekeeping assistant. JES has a staff of 51 individuals, including both full-time and part-time staff. Table 10.2 details the staffing at JES.

SERVICES

JES is housed in a 6,500-square-foot facility located just off the interstate highway between Jasper and Capital City and has ample parking and easy access for ambulances. The facility is leased from the Jasper Industrial Development Authority.

The facility has a total of four examination rooms, which include two rooms designated as high-acuity suites that meet specifications for resuscitation rooms. In addition, one room is specially outfitted to handle pediatric emergency cases, and another is used to handle obstetrics/maternity patients.

Radiology and computed tomography (CT) scan are provided in a dedicated imaging suite staffed by an on-site radiological technician. Capabilities include basic X-rays, digital X-rays, CT scanning, and ultrasound. Direct links are provided between JES and CCGH imaging services to support interpretation and diagnosis as needed.

Point-of-care laboratory services are provided in an on-site CLIA-certified laboratory offering a variety of services, including cardiac enzyme testing, complete blood counts, kidney function testing, liver function testing, rapid strep testing, urinalysis, pregnancy testing, flu or respiratory syncytial virus testing, pandemic testing, venous blood gas testing, and mononucleosis testing. Arrangements with laboratory services at CCGH give JES access to more sophisticated testing in a timely manner.

An on-site pharmacy at JES makes available a formulary of medications approved by the state for such facilities, and a pharmacy technician is on-site at all times. A consulting pharmacist from CCGH provides assistance as needed. JES is equipped with a blood bank, enabling immediate transfusion services.

In 2022, during the pandemic, JES initiated a telehealth program that allows patients to contact the facility and receive a rapid review regarding whether a visit to the ER was warranted. Public reception to the service was very positive, although both CCGH and JES staff are concerned about potential liability regarding advice given without physically seeing the patient. The policy is under review.

Operations

The vast majority of JES's patients (approximately 94 percent) are treated at the facility and released. The remaining are either transferred to the CCGH ER for further care, admitted to CCGH, or die. Agreements are in place with CCGH that make patient transfer a relatively seamless process. Transfer agreements with other hospitals, including MIDCARE and Webster, do not exist. Consequently, if a patient requests a transfer to these facilities, delays and administrative issues can occur. Fortunately, such events have been rare. Patients and/or their representatives are informed both verbally and in writing (and must sign an authorization) that JES is affiliated with CCGH, and that if care is required beyond what is available at the facility, the patient may be transferred to CCGH. In addition, pursuant to state regulations, there is a posted sign as well as paperwork notifying the patient and/or their representative that they are seeking or receiving care in an emergency facility—not an urgent care center, clinic, or physician's office—and that hospital ER rates will apply.

A focus of ongoing operations at JES has been waiting time. Through effective triage and careful patient flow and throughput management, JES has been very successful at minimizing patient waits. For the last 12 months, the average waiting time between entering JES and being seen by a care team member has been seven minutes, and for 41 percent of patients there was no wait. The average length of treatment time for a discharged patient in the last 12 months was 125 minutes. Surveys reflect high levels of satisfaction among patients regarding waiting times. Occasionally, problems have arisen when transferring patients for admission to CCGH due to a bed shortage at the hospital. This problem is particularly common in behavioral health cases. In addition, the recent pandemic stressed the system and caused substantially longer waiting times; these problems were particularly acute in 2022 and 2023. Real-time waiting times for JES are posted on JES's website as well as on a large billboard on the highway proximate to the facility.

JES employs CCGH's state-of-the-art information technology (IT) system, which is used by the hospital, all of its subsidiary organizations, and most physicians affiliated with admitting privileges at the hospital. Conversion to the system was accomplished smoothly.

JES holds professional and general liability insurance protection in the amount of $1,000,000 per occurrence and $3,000,000 in aggregate, as well as umbrella liability in the aggregate of $10,000,000. It also maintains property damage insurance with a maximum coverage of $30,000,000. JES is insured for workers' compensation claims up to $1,000,000 per claim and per employee with a policy limit of $1,000,000. Finally, JES assumes the cost of professional malpractice liability coverage for all its employees.

JES conducts an ongoing assessment of quality of care. It also compares its performance with that of the CCGH emergency department. As noted, waiting and service times in the facility are shorter than in hospital-based ERs, and the level of patient satisfaction is high. Analysis has shown lower use of radiology services and similar use for ultrasonography and CT scans versus at the hospital emergency department. Use of laboratory testing was similar in both settings.

A special study was conducted on JES patients with a cardiac-related diagnosis. The study results indicated that only 75.5 percent of patients receiving a diagnosis of ST-segment elevation myocardial infarction met the American Heart Association's recommended "door-to-balloon" time of 90 minutes. This is an area of current investigation.

Another special study evaluated the hospital length of stay for patients admitted from JES versus from the hospital emergency department. An average length of stay of 5.3 days was found for JES admissions, versus 7.2 days for patients admitted from the hospital-based emergency department. This is another area of ongoing study.

With help from CCGH, and using advice garnered from the Advisory Committee, JES has developed a marketing program for the facility. Ms. Fowler has on-site responsibility for the program and reports that it is one of her most enjoyable activities.

The program focuses on two primary messages:

1. "JES provides outstanding emergency care close to your home (Jasper)," and

2. "You won't have to wait for care at JES."

Prior to JES's opening, members of the community were invited to tour the facility and meet members of the staff; health and safety information and devices were distributed at the tours. Since the opening, the marketing program has consistently informed the community about the range of services available at JES, as well as differentiated the facility from urgent care centers and physician's offices. A variety of approaches are used to communicate with potential clients of the facility, including Internet, texting, radio, outdoor advertising, and direct mail. JES has an informative website and an active Twitter account.

Health education is a large part of the program, and JES has assembled helpful resource banks of information about the types of healthcare needs that call for emergency services, such as stroke, chest pain, difficulty breathing, and accidents. This information is available on JES's website and through periodic direct mailings to the community. In addition, several collaterals are employed in the marketing program, including such items as thermometers; sunscreen, sunglasses, and hats; water bottles; and poison information cards, all featuring the JES name and logo. The marketing campaign focuses on the Jasper community and its needs, and JES representatives meet periodically with local political and business leaders to enhance their local profile.

Measures of the effectiveness of the initial marketing initiatives have been favorable. JES's name recognition in Jasper is extremely high, and more than 85 percent of respondents to an anonymous survey conducted by phone and online rated JES as providing excellent or very good care. Respondents described JES with phrases such as "high quality," "excellent and efficient care," "clean and quick," "close to where I live," and "great place if you have an emergency with your child." When asked who owns or operates JES, surprisingly only 30 percent of respondents answered CCGH. The majority did not know or thought the owner or operator is "probably MIDCARE."

Utilization

Utilization of JES in visits is shown in table 10.3. The facility opened in April 2020, and volume steadily increased during the first several months of operation. The impact of the pandemic is seen in the table data throughout 2021–2023, as people were reluctant to use healthcare services of any type during that period. In 2024, volume has picked up, and it is hoped that the increase experienced this year will continue into the future. JES has ample capacity to increase utilization substantially.

Approximately 45 percent of JES's patients come from within three miles of the facility and 75 percent from within 5 miles, the majority of them from the greater Jasper area. Patient case mix severity, based on billing data, is shown in table 10.4. Only 40 percent of patients were reported to be severely or critically ill, and one-quarter of patients had illnesses of low or minor severity. Anecdotally, JES providers note that patients seem to be presenting with more severe illnesses than in the past, although this pattern is not reflected in the actual billing-based data.

Table 10.5 displays the most common diagnoses of patients to the freestanding ER in 2024. The diagnoses shown are not substantively different from data in preceding years, although the percentage of visits attributed to upper respiratory infection and bronchitis/pneumonia showed an increase from earlier years. Infectious disease specialists at CCGH suspect this may be due to the pandemic, which was still relatively prevalent until mid-2024. Table 10.6 displays the patient–payer mix.

JES has exhibited an interesting pattern of utilization seasonality. During the winter months and throughout the pandemic, utilization related to respiratory ailments (bronchitis, pneumonia, influenza) increased versus the overall annual experience. In addition, as consumer participation in high-deductible health plans has become more prevalent locally, consumers have been reluctant to use health services, including emergency services, and delay receiving care. Many at JES believe this has led to a somewhat sicker patient population using the facility, although diagnosis data do not necessarily bear this theory out. Finally, as the consumer has become responsible for a greater portion of healthcare expenses, the level of bad debt at JES has increased over the last two to three years.

Table 10.7 displays JES's operating statement for years 2020–2024. The statement reflects the impact of a small annual increase in charges, as well as a shift from commercial payers to Medicare and Medicaid. As a wholly owned subsidiary of CCGH, JES does not issue a separate balance sheet. It is hoped that the end of the pandemic will enable JES to redirect its payer mix to a higher percentage of commercial business and that its marketing strategies will be designed to accomplish this shift.

CCGH imposes a management fee on JES of 6 percent of net income. This fee covers the costs of integration with the hospital's data management system and ongoing consultative services. In discussing the fee, Ms. Fowler stated, "The fee certainly has an impact on our bottom line, but at the same time, working with the hospital's IT system has been incredibly valuable and helps connect us with any ACO or other value-based system that might come along. We absolutely could not succeed without this link. Also, the consultative help we get from the hospital staff has been great. They were particularly helpful when we set up our telehealth program. They really understand who we are and what we are trying to accomplish as a provider organization, and they are there when we need them."

Table 10.1
JES Advisory
Committee

Name	Title	Occupation	Residence	Term Expires
Seymour Shilcraft	Chairperson	Attorney	Jasper	2025
Valerie Campos	Vice Chair	Social Worker	Capital City	2026
Jacqueline Dulik		Accountant	Capital City	2027
Barbara Beck*		Nurse	Capital City	2025
Denzel Owusu*		Emergency Physician	Capital City	2026
Della Autry		JIDA Staff	Jasper	2027
Malika Bhatt		Banker	Jasper	2027
Gregory Williamson		Business Owner	Jasper	2025
Gloria Fletcher		Insurance Broker	Jasper	2026

Notes: *Employee of Capital City General Hospital; JIDA: Jasper Industrial Development Authority.

Table 10.2
JES Staffing

Employee Type	Full-Time	Part-Time
Physicians	4	5
Registered Nurses	4	5
Radiology Technicians	4	5
Pharmacy (including techs)	0	4
Administration	2	2
Transport/Aide	4	5
Housekeeping	2	5
Total	**20**	**31**

Table 10.3
JES Total Visits
per Year

Year	2024	2023	2022	2022	2021
Visits	3,806	3,313	3,260	3,281	1,985

Severity	Percentage
Critical	17%
Severe	23%
Moderate	35%
Low/Moderate	17%
Minor	8%
Total	**100%**

Table 10.4
JES Case-Mix Severity of Patients, 2024

Diagnosis	Percentage of Visits
Acute Upper Respiratory Infection	3.8
Chest Pain	3.4
Bronchitis/Pneumonia	2.7
Abdominal Pain	2.2
Urinary Tract Infection	2.1
Asthma	1.6
Otitis Media	1.4
Headache	1.4
Syncope/Altered Consciousness	0.9
Back Pain	0.9
Substance Abuse	0.9
Total	**21.3**

Table 10.5
JES Most Common Patient Discharge Diagnoses, 2024

Table 10.6
JES Patient–
Payer Mix:
Percentage of
Patients

Payer	2024	2023	2022	2021	2020 (April)
Private Insurance	57	60	62	63	64
Medicare	23	17	17	18	20
Medicaid	18	19	18	16	14
Other	2	4	3	3	2
Total	**100**	**100**	**100**	**100**	**100**

Table 10.7
JES Operating
Statement,
USD $

	2024	2023	2022	2021	2020
Revenue					
Total Net Operating	6,862,939	5,815,947	5,522,450	5,420,250	3,175,200
Expenses					
Personnel					
Physician Compensation	2,198,011	2,133,991	2,112,862	2,071,433	1,508,325
Nurse Compensation	559,859	543,552	538,170	527,618	384,188
Radiology Compensation	351,652	341,410	338,030	331,402	241,312
Pharmacy Compensation	181,865	176,568	174,820	171,392	124,800
Administration	142,082	137,944	136,578	133,900	97,500
Transport/Aide	166,236	161,394	159,796	156,663	114,075
Housekeeping	172,630	167,602	165,943	162,689	118,463
Subtotal	3,772,335	3,662,461	3,626,199	3,555,097	2,588,663
Other Costs					
Occupancy Costs	667,340	647,902	635,199	622,744	455,667
Drugs/Supplies Costs	243,387	236,298	231,665	227,123	165,437
General/Administration	330,958	321,318	315,019	308,841	225,982
Management Fee	483,124	372,672	355,411	345,845	188,712
Subtotal	1,724,809	1,578,190	1,537,294	1,504,553	1,035,798
Total Expenses	5,497,144	5,240,651	5,163,493	5,059,650	3,624,461
Net Earnings Before Taxes	1,365,795	575,296	358,957	360,600	–449,261

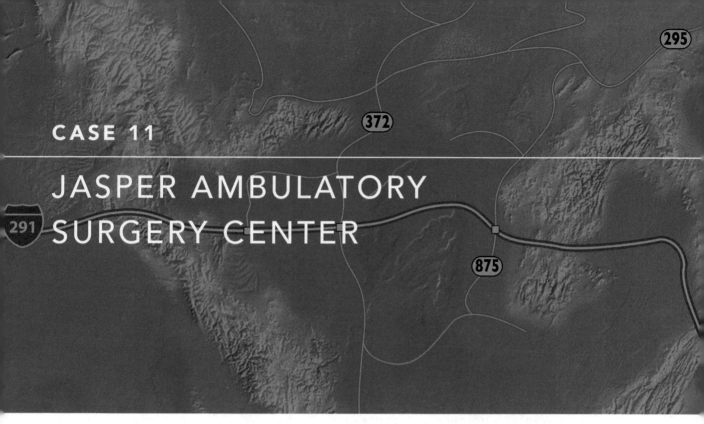

CASE 11

JASPER AMBULATORY SURGERY CENTER

Jasper Ambulatory Surgery Center (JASC) is jointly owned by Capital City General Hospital (CCGH) and Capital City Physicians Group (CCPG), one of several distinct physician/hospital organizations within the medical staff. JASC is the newest of three ambulatory surgical centers owned by such physician/hospital collaborations, the only one involving CCPG, and the first outside of Capital City. It is operated as a for-profit entity. The 6,500-square-foot facility is owned by CCGH with space rented to JASC. It is located 8 miles east of the center of Jasper on property adjacent to the soon to be completed interstate highway, about 24 miles from the heart of Capital City. JASC opened in March of 2023 with the intent of providing non-inpatient surgical services to the growing community in southern Hillsboro County. JASC operates Monday through Friday from 7:00 a.m. to 4:00 p.m. and Saturday from 8:00 a.m. to 1:00 p.m. Development of such centers is a major component of CCGH's strategy to expand its market beyond Capital City. The organization is accredited by the Accreditation Association for Ambulatory Health Care (AAAHC), receiving its initial accreditation 12 months after opening. The center is also Medicare certified and has Medicare deemed status.

Beginning in 2020, CCGH conducted exploratory discussions with MIDCARE about a joint ambulatory surgery project located in Jasper. CCGH had already opened one joint venture physician/hospital ambulatory surgical center in Capital City. Resistance to the proposal from MIDCARE surgeons, however, made it apparent that such a project was not viable, at least in the short term, and CCGH decided to proceed with the project without the proposed affiliation. MIDCARE is currently finalizing its certificate of need plan to develop a freestanding ambulatory surgical center/emergency room in Jasper.

CCPG was established by the physicians involved to serve as a vehicle to develop joint ventures with the hospital, including but not limited to ambulatory surgery. The group is composed of eight physicians specializing in orthopedic surgery, ophthalmology, gastroenterology, and anesthesiology. The two anesthesiologists practice exclusively at JASC, while the other physicians maintain active practices at JASC and have admitting privileges at CCGH. There are no formalized arrangements between CCGH and MIDCARE or Medical Associates physicians.

OWNERSHIP AND GOVERNANCE

JASC is structured as a joint venture. The hospital has 51 percent of ownership with CCPG holding the minority share. The number of surgeon shares outstanding is established by the board, and owners are required to buy in to the organization at a level fixed by the JASC board. The original offering authorized 20 shares of stock to be issued, 18 of which are authorized and issued. Each current shareholder owns a full share in the organization, and the hospital holds ten shares. Offering of partial shares and the sale of existing shares are both permissible, subject to board approval. The original owner investment was $50,000 for a full share.

Each physician owner earns a percentage of net profits; the percentage is agreed upon by the board members. According to the bylaws, owners are required to begin to reduce their practice/ownership share upon reaching age 65, and shares can no longer be held by physicians over the age of 72; in effect, owners' shares are bought back by the organization.

Table 11.1 is a list of physician owners of JASC, by specialty, age, and number of cases.

The governing board of the center retains responsibility for the overall operation and performance of JASC. As such, its purview is expansive, including but not limited to fundamental items such as the following:

- ◆ Defining the mission, goals, and objectives of JASC

- ◆ Adopting appropriate bylaws for administration of the organization

- ◆ Adopting bylaws to govern delivery of clinical care within the organization

- ◆ Ensuring the quality of care delivered

◆ Ensuring the organization operates in compliance with relevant industry legal and ethical standards

◆ Maintaining the financial viability of the organization

◆ Recruiting and retaining appropriate management personnel

◆ Recruiting, credentialing, and retaining high-quality clinical staff

◆ Ensuring patient rights and confidentiality are respected

The governing board of the center is composed of seven individuals:

◆ Lukas Fremont, president, is associate vice president for Clinical Outreach at CCGH, a position he has held for approximately eight years. He lives in Capital City, and his term expires in 2027.

◆ Greta Maeweather, RN, vice president, is a surgical nurse who has worked at CCGH for approximately seven years; she currently works at JASC. She has prior clinical experience in an ambulatory surgical center in a midwestern state. She lives in Capital City, and her term expires in 2026.

◆ D'Wayne Taylor, secretary, is the manager of Data Informatics at CCGH, a position he has held for three years, following a number of years as a data analyst in the financial services industry. He too lives in Capital City. His board term will expire in 2026.

◆ Penelope Purita, MD, at-large, is a practicing gastroenterologist whose main office is on the west side of Capital City. She performs surgery at both JASC and CCGH. She lives in Capital City and her term expires in 2027.

◆ Liliana Frances, MD, at-large, is a practicing ophthalmologist whose main office is in Capital City, adjacent to CCGH. She also resides in Capital City. She performs surgery at both JASC and CCGH, and her board term will expire in 2027.

◆ Franklin Cody, DO, at-large, is a practicing orthopedic surgeon whose principal office is in Capital City, adjacent to CCGH. He performs surgery at both JASC and CCGH. He lives in Capital City, and his term will expire in 2026.

◆ Reginald Stuyvesant, at-large, is an insurance broker in Jasper. His board term will expire in 2026.

Board terms are three years long, and members can serve no more than two consecutive terms. Initial board members were awarded terms of either two or three years. Board committees and membership are indicated below. The full board meets quarterly, and each subcommittee is required to convene no later than one month preceding this meeting.

Executive: Fremont, Maeweather, Taylor

Quality Management, Improvement, and Safety: Cody, Frances, Maeweather

Infection Control: Purita, Cody, Taylor

Tissue: Purita, Cody, Frances

Data Analytics: Taylor, Stuyvesant, Fremont

MANAGEMENT

JASC is a jointly owned subsidiary of CCGH, and Charlotte Nieswander, RN, AANP, MBA, is the administrator. Ms. Nieswander received her baccalaureate nursing training in University Town and later earned her master's degree. After practicing as an adult nurse practitioner at CCGH for eight years, she completed an MBA program at On-Line University and served in various administrative capacities at CCGH for another four years before being appointed as JASC's inaugural administrator in 2023. Her colleagues feel she is extremely competent, although her management style has been described as relatively "direct" and occasionally abrasive. In particular, her relationship with surgeons at JASC has at times has been rocky.

Ms. Nieswander is responsible for developing contractual relationships with area insurance companies and employers, and she estimates that this activity accounts for at least a quarter of her time. The organization has service relationships with all local insurance carriers and Medicare and Medicaid and is also working to develop bundled pricing contracts with area employers as well as carriers for specific orthopedic cases such as total knee replacement surgery. In all negotiations, JASC seeks to be identified as an in-network provider; to date it has been successful with this approach, although Ms. Nieswander reports that negotiations have become increasingly price-sensitive since the pandemic.

JASC's medical director is an elected position chosen by the center's medical staff. The director serves a three-year term (no term limits apply). The current medical director is Ling Yuan, MD, a practicing ophthalmologist. Dr. Yuan has practiced and served as the medical director of JASC since its opening. As medical director, Dr. Yuan receives a stipend to support her administrative responsibilities. She is respected by her fellow physicians and gets along well with Ms. Nieswander. It is likely, however, that at the end of her current term, Dr. Yuan will elect to return to a full-time surgical practice. Dr. Yuan does all her surgical work at JASC and maintains no other office.

Warnette Sims, RN, is the director of Nursing and Operations. She has been a surgical nurse for 15 years, having worked in both hospitals and freestanding ambulatory surgery centers. She is responsible for scheduling surgery, staff training and development, overall clinical care, infection prevention, and general human resources for all JASC employees.

Data Manager Bonnie Warlock, CHDA, has worked at JASC since the organization's inception. Ms. Warlock worked at CCGH for 12 years in a data analyst position, and at JASC she is responsible for all aspects of information storage, retrieval, and analysis. She has an excellent relationship with the "data team" at CCGH, and they often collaborate on cutting-edge analytical projects. Assisted by CCGH, Ms. Warlock has also taken the lead in developing a new telehealth program implemented by JASC. Ms. Nieswander considers data management to be one of JASC's significant strengths.

The JASC management team has excellent relationships with managers at CCGH and frequently consults informally with them regarding organizational issues and challenges.

MISSION AND VALUES

The stated mission of JASC is as follows:

We provide excellent ambulatory surgical care in selected specialties in a safe, efficient, and cost-effective manner.

In achieving this mission, JASC will adhere to this set of core values:

1. We will treat all patients and employees with kindness, openness and compassion.

2. We will maintain ongoing quality improvement programs to monitor standards of care and strive to ensure high standards of safety.

3. We will foster an environment of patient education.

4. We will employ a team approach to care including patients, families, physicians, nurses, and other staff.

5. We will maintain an environment supportive of professional growth and opportunity.

6. We will adhere to a professional code of ethics and honesty.

7. We will run our business in a manner consistent with sound business practices.

8. We will seek to improve the efficiency of our organizational policies and practices.

9. We will maintain status as an accredited ambulatory surgery center.

10. We will strive to maintain an atmosphere of respect and innovation.

QUALITY OF CARE

JASC takes great pride in the quality of its surgical services. Working with managers at CCGH as well as with outside consultants, the organization developed and implemented a surgical improvement plan that includes online incident and complications tracking. These reports are further analyzed to identify indicators potentially in need of additional study. The organization monitors and evaluates the effectiveness and safety through postoperative contacts with patients as well as frequent and periodic peer-review audits. Feedback from these audits is used to continually improve delivery and outcomes of care. The organization is proud of the fact that feedback surveys indicate extremely high satisfaction from patients and referring physicians. Over 85 percent of patients indicate that they would highly recommend JASC to others for their care.

Several focused studies of quality were completed in 2024, including complication rates by surgeon, patient transfer rates to the hospital following a procedure, percentage of on-time case starts, and turnover time between cases. Generally, results of these studies for physician owners met expectations of the Quality Management subcommittee of the board, although complication rates for one of the orthopedic surgeons exceeded expected levels. These results are currently being discussed by the board. Analysis of on-time case starts among non-owners revealed a substantial number of late starts among orthopedic surgeons, who claimed the operating suite was not available for use at the scheduled time; this problem did not arise among physician owners.

During and following the pandemic, JASC implemented an extended system of telehealth for pre- and some postsurgical visits. These visits have generally been well received by surgeons and patients.

In March 2024, the JASC board conducted a survey of non-owner physicians who had utilized the facility. Respondents were generally quite positive regarding their experiences, noting:

> "JASC gives me the opportunity to work around my surgical schedule, rather than theirs. They are much more accommodating than the hospital."

> "They know what they're doing for the routine stuff. I know I can get my work done in less than one hour, have the patient in recovery, and be on my way."

"They do a great job of turning over the rooms—there is very little downtime for me."

"The quality outcomes here seem to be at, or at least close to, what I can do at the hospital."

At the same time, negative comments were received, including:

"Not all of the technical staff are up to par."

"The anesthesiologists are OK I guess, but I feel we are governed by their schedules."

"I cannot always get the equipment I need for procedures that I don't do frequently. I have more flexibility at the hospital."

"They need to revisit the procedures for sterilization. For now they are OK, but if the place keeps growing, they're not going to be able to handle the load—too many trays all over the place. It's a challenge."

"Sometimes I get a late start for my knee cases—the rooms aren't ready or the ortho staff is finishing up somewhere else."

"They should open a new procedure room for the endoscopy workload—it's crowding out other work that could be done there."

"Most of the nursing staff and administrators are great. Charlotte (Nieswander), though, can be a bit difficult to work with. With her, it's 'my way or the highway'."

In 2023, there was an incident of employee theft of fentanyl at another ambulatory surgery center jointly owned by CCGH and a different physician group in Capital City. The incident received significant media coverage, and JASC still receives a number of questions regarding the theft from prospective clients.

SERVICES OFFERED

JASC staff offer an array of services in the facility's three operating rooms and two procedure rooms. The most frequently performed procedures are listed in table 11.2. This list has not changed substantially since the facility opened. Monthly utilization at JASC is shown in table 11.3.

Payers, notably Medicare and Medicaid, have been substantially increasing the list of outpatient surgical procedures that are reimbursable. The board is pleased with the direction the facility is going in terms of volume of cases, particularly in gastroenterology, where procedure volume has increased markedly from 2023 to 2024. Surgeons from other specialties—including otolaryngology, pain management, general surgery, urology, gynecology, plastic surgery, and podiatry—frequently utilize the facility. Cardiologists have also expressed an interest in using the facility; however, to this point the board has felt an expansion into cardiology would require substantial investments in new staff and equipment. While generally quite pleased with utilization trends, a small number of physician owners have expressed concerns that the volume of cases by non-owners could potentially make scheduling a substantial challenge.

STAFFING

JASC nonphysician staff includes 35 full- and part-time individuals. All nurses are RNs. Table 11.4 displays the staff by position and employment status.

A total of 25 physicians (MD/DO) and two podiatrists performed surgery at JASC in 2024.

FINANCIAL INFORMATION

The payer mix of JASC for 2024 is displayed in table 11.5. Ms. Nieswander's goal is to increase commercial insurance by at least 10 percent over the next two years and to reduce Medicaid and self-pay case volume. Financial information regarding staffing is provided in tables 11.6 and 11.7.

JASC has begun to generate a significant profit, as shown in table 11.8, and both CCGH and CCPG have indicated their satisfaction with the manner in which development has proceeded, particularly considering that the facility opened in the midst of the pandemic. It is hoped that with the pandemic's easing, further development will be accelerated. Table 11.9 displays the JASC balance sheet.

Name	Specialty	Age	Number of Cases, 2024
Ling Yuan, MD	Ophthalmology	49	208
Liliana Frances, MD	Ophthalmology	45	248
Franklin Cody, DO	Orthopedic Surgery	53	203
Anika Kathbamna, MD	Orthopedic Surgery	52	197
Penelope Purita, MD	Gastroenterology	48	352
Alejandra Munez, MD	Gastroenterology	53	289
Steve Craigworthy, MD	Anesthesiology	58	1063
Jimmy Crawford, MD	Anesthesiology	47	950

Table 11.1
JASC Physician Owners by Specialty, Age, and Number of Cases

Rank	Procedure	CPT Code	Percentage of Total Procedures
1	Cataract surgery, with intraocular lens insert	66983	27%
2	Colonoscopy and biopsy	45380	11%
3	Upper gastrointestinal endoscopy, biopsy	43198	11%
4	Anterior cruciate ligament (ACL) reconstruction	29888	8%
5	Carpal tunnel release	64721	8%
6	Spinal injection	62310	5%

Table 11.2
JASC Most Frequently Offered Services, 2024

Table 11.3
JASC Utilization by Specialty and Month

	Number of Cases				
	OPH	ORTHO	GI	Other	Total
2024					
January	41	34	41	17	133
February	44	37	46	19	146
March	49	41	56	34	180
April	41	49	52	37	179
May	38	48	63	46	195
June	38	43	67	55	203
July	29	48	63	51	191
August	41	52	75	63	231
September	43	59	77	82	261
October	46	55	79	74	254
November	50	59	73	81	263
December	42	55	68	68	233
Total	**502**	**580**	**760**	**627**	**2,469**
2023					
January	0	0	0	0	0
February	0	0	0	0	0
March	21	17	19	2	59
April	32	21	15	12	80
May	31	29	17	15	92
June	37	35	37	13	122
July	31	33	58	17	139
August	42	42	44	27	155
September	41	42	52	44	179
October	39	47	55	52	193
November	38	45	49	51	183
December	32	38	25	18	113
Total	**344**	**349**	**371**	**251**	**1,315**

Note: OPH: ophthalmology; ORTHO: orthopedic surgery; GI: gastroenterology.

	FT	PT
Administrative	3	2
RN	8	2
OR Tech	3	3
Transport	1	1
Other Healthcare	2	0
Non-Healthcare	3	2
Total	**20**	**10**

Table 11.4
JASC Staffing as of December 2024

Notes: (1) FT: full-time; PT: part-time.
(2) Facility is open 250 days per year.

Payer	Percentage of Cases
Medicare	37%
Medicaid	4%
Commercial	49%
Workers' Compensation	3%
Self-Pay	5%
Other	2%

Table 11.5
JASC Payer Mix for 2024

Table 11.6
JASC Key
Personnel and
Salaries

Name	Title	Salary ($)
Nieswander	Administrator	104,000
Yuan	Medical Director	40,000
Sims	Director of Nursing and Operations	85,000
Warlock	Data Manager	55,000

Note: As of December 31, 2024.

Table 11.7
JASC Average
Salaries by Staff
Type, 2024

Title	Salary ($)
RN	70,000
OR Tech	65,000
Transport	35,000
Other healthcare	45,000
Administration	30,000
Other: Non-healthcare	35,000

Note: These figures do not include benefits.

	2024	3/1/23–12/31/23
Revenues		
Gross Patient Revenue	5,029,029	2,817,298
Allowances	1,202,891	635,243
Net Patient Revenue	**3,826,138**	**2,182,055**
Expenses		
Employee Salary/Wage	1,721,000	1,075,101
Employee Benefits	567,930	354,783
Supplies/Drugs	702,172	209,432
Office Supplies/Exp	40,217	20,450
Equipment Repair		
Maintenance	53,097	48,372
Rent	195,000	195,000
Utilities	50,147	35,008
Interest	67,500	67,500
Insurance	40,300	36,050
Purchased Services	65,214	59,897
Depreciation	80,058	38,928
Total Expenses	**3,582,635**	**2,140,521**
Earnings Before Taxes	**243,503**	**41,534**
Federal Tax 38.9%	94,723	16,157
State Tax 8.9%	21,672	3,697
Earnings After Taxes	**127,109**	**21,681**

Table 11.8
JASC Statement of Operations: March 1, 2023, and CY 2024 ($)

Table 11.9
JASC Balance
Sheet for Fiscal
Years Ending
December 20XX
($)

	2024	2023
Assets		
Current Assets		
Cash	449,207	212,523
Accounts Receivables: Net	71,324	54,736
Inventory	89,364	85,334
Prepaid Expenses	9,423	3,546
Subtotal	**619,318**	**356,139**
Property, Plant, and Equipment		
Equipment and Leasehold Improvements (Gross)	1,576,271	1,427,382
Accumulated Depreciation	118,986	38,928
Equipment and Leasehold Improvements (Net)	1,457,285	1,388,454
Total Assets	**2,076,603**	**1,744,593**
Liabilities and Net Assets		
Liabilities		
Current Liabilities		
Accounts Payable	121,374	74,356
Accrued Expenses	16,530	8,436
Subtotal	**137,904**	**82,792**
Long-Term Liabilities		
Notes Payable (2.25%)	300,000	150,000
Total Liabilities	**437,904**	**232,792**
Net Assets		
Common Stock	20 shares authorized, 18 issued (1 each per 8 physician owners and 10 for hospital @ 50,000 par value)	
Authorized and Issued	900,000	900,000
Development Fund	89,907	100,000
Retained Earnings	648,792	511,801
Total Net Assets	**1,638,699**	**1,511,801**
Total Liabilities and Net Assets	2,076,603	1,744,593

CASE 12

THE OAKS: A CONTINUING CARE RETIREMENT COMMUNITY

The Oaks was founded in 2018 as a tax-exempt corporation and is situated on a campus five miles east of Jasper near the new highway. It is nationally accredited by CARF International and, based on formal inspection, licensed by the state. In 2019, The Oaks purchased 138 acres of land from Jefferson Partners, a private equity firm that also owns and operates nursing homes, assisted living facilities, and adult day care centers. In 2020, it secured its initial construction funds from the sale of tax-exempt bonds by the state Health and Educational Facilities Authority. Currently, The Oaks is the only Type A continuing care retirement community (CCRC) between University Town and Capital City. The closest competition is in the western suburbs of Capital City.

MISSION, GOVERNANCE, AND MANAGEMENT

The mission statement states, "We strive to assist senior citizens maintain their freedom and independence as they age by providing a safe, secure, and nurturing living environment." The Oaks is governed by a seven-member board of trustees (see table 12.1). Trustees serve five-year renewable terms. The current trustees founded The Oaks and have indicated their willingness to remain as trustees at least until all construction has been completed.

The construction and development of The Oaks is being conducted in four phases. When completed, it will have 200 residential apartments. Phase one, begun in 2020, included the main one-story central building with offices, common spaces, dining facilities, health/wellness center services, assisted living services, recreational services, and other amenities. Attached to the central building is a residential wing with 50 apartments. Phase one was opened in January 2022 and included the site preparation for phase two. Phase two, completed in February 2023, added two residential wings with 50 apartments, a Memory Care Unit, and site development for phases three and four. Phases three and four are scheduled for completion in February and August 2026, respectively. Transportation services are provided, as is on-site parking. Services include the following:

◆ *Assisted living services* that help residents maintain independent-style living with access to daily assistance for chores and other tasks.

◆ *Short-term rehabilitation* provided by physicians, therapists, and nurses. This service is available 24/7.

◆ *Memory care* for residents with cognitive impairment, Alzheimer's disease, or other dementia-related conditions.

◆ *Skilled nursing care* involving short-term and long-term skilled nursing care.

Based on a multiyear contract with Jefferson Partners, skilled nursing care for the residents of The Oaks needing these services is provided by Jasper Gardens. Jasper Gardens is located in close proximity to The Oaks. Any skilled care service needed by a resident not covered by Medicare is paid directly by The Oaks. Efforts are underway to assess The Oaks' need for in-house skilled nursing care that could be added at the completion of phase four development.

The Oaks has a multiyear contract with Medical Associates (Jasper) to provide on-site medical care using the facilities of the Wellness/Health Center. Medical Associates physicians are available to residents either by appointment or as needed. Any fee not covered by health insurance is paid for by The Oaks. Medical Associates also provides telehealth consultation with residents.

The 138-acre campus provides many opportunities for residents to exercise on walking and bicycle trails. A community garden is also maintained for the residents. There is a coffee shop and a library adjacent to the main office. Many tennis and pickleball courts are also available for residents. An outside amphitheater is the site of concerts and community events. Future plans involve expanding the dining options and providing studios for art, dance, woodworking, sewing and quilting, and pottery.

The monthly fee covers all residential expenses. The fee includes membership in a local health club with an indoor pool, and laundry and cleaning services. Each residential unit at The Oaks has a 24/7 emergency call system. All residents are also provided long-term care insurance. Primarily for residents who travel, the monthly fee can be reduced by 30 percent for up to two months in any 12-month period. Current Internal Revenue Service regulations indicate that a percentage of the entrance fee and monthly payments can be deducted as a prepaid medical expense.

ACCOMMODATIONS AND FEES

Each existing residential wing has 50 apartments. Apartments range from 500 to 1,500 square feet and have either one or two bedrooms with or without a separate den. Some first-floor units also have direct external access. The selected apartment determines the fees associated with living at The Oaks (see table 12.2). Residents are responsible for furnishing their apartment and purchasing renter's insurance. The facility's utilization report is shown in table 12.3.

MANAGEMENT TEAM

Appointed in 2019, Jane McDonald Douglas, CPA, is the executive director and chief financial officer of The Oaks. She is a graduate of State University and was previously the vice president of operations for another CCRC located in the state. Prior to that, she was the chief financial officer for an assisted living community and a financial analyst with a national consulting firm. She is an ex officio member of the board of trustees. She directly supervises the business office.

Kathleen Kirk, APRN, is vice president of Professional Services. She supervises the operation of the health and wellness center, 24-hour nursing care when needed, the memory care unit, the 24/7 help line, and all assisted living, health, medical, and social services. She is also responsible for the contractual arrangements with Medical Associates, Jasper Gardens, and contracted and employed therapists and counselors.

William Epstein, Jr., is the vice president of Administration and supervises all non-professional services. He is a licensed nursing home administrator and former CEO of two long-term care facilities. He is responsible for all nonprofessional services, including housekeeping; maintenance; food services, including restaurant operations; building and grounds; and transportation services.

Margaret Bethany is the director of Marketing. Prior to joining the staff at The Oaks, she was the associate director of sales at a CCRC located in Capital City. She has a degree in marketing from State University. She is responsible for marketing and sales, all publications and advertising, and relations with the Resident's Council. Her staff includes recreational therapists and others who plan and provide programs and events for the residents.

CONSTRUCTION TEAM

The Oaks has contracted for comprehensive architectural and construction services with Moses Development, Inc., of Capital City. General project oversight is provided by a special committee composed of trustees Morrison and Hirsch, Executive Director Morrison, and Vice President Epstein. Legal services are provided by Giles and Giles of Jasper. A clerk-of-the-works reports directly to Vice President Epstein.

CONSTRUCTION FINANCING

Project financing has been furnished by the state Health and Educational Facilities Authority. Moody's currently rates these bonds as Baa. Financing rules also require that The Oaks must meet specific financial ratios after the completion of all construction and three quarters of operations. Specific ratios include net operating margin, days cash on hand, cash to debt ratio, and debt service coverage. Current funding does not include the construction of an on-site skilled nursing facility connected to The Oaks. Current financing will only construct the needed general unfinished space. How this new space is used will be determined and financed in the future.

RESIDENT DEMOGRAPHICS

Eighty-five residential units are currently occupied, with a total of 161 residents. Seventy-six of the units are occupied by two persons, and nine are occupied by one individual. The age of residents ranges from 58 to 85. The average age for men is 75.3 and for women is 78.7 years of age. Based on current deposits by future residents, this general demographic is expected to continue. During 2024, residents accounted for a total of 62 inpatient days in skilled care nursing services at Jasper Gardens and 45 patient days in area hospitals. During 2024, there were two resident deaths. Prior to moving into The Oaks, current residents resided in Jasper (74), Capital City (58), University Town (8), and Statesville (3). Eighteen of the current residents came to The Oaks from an out-of-state residency. During the pandemic, both residents and employees were tested for the virus. Seven positive tests were recorded among employees and two among residents. In response, the organization implemented aggressive isolation/positive protocols, and the virus appears to have not spread further. The Oaks was also very conscientious about social distancing and other approaches proven to be successful, although the isolation protocols proved daunting to enforce.

The residents of The Oaks elect a five-person Resident's Council to represent their interests. Its president attends all meetings of the board of trustees. Allocated funds by the board, the Resident's Council directs specific recreational activities based on the desires of the membership. Annually, a formal survey is conducted of all residents with a report sent to the board of trustees with action recommendations. Members of this council also make themselves available to chat with prospective residents.

FUTURE PLANS

A recent interview with Executive Director Jane Douglas indicated some of the future plans for The Oaks. She noted that The Oaks has obtained a multiyear land option adjacent to the interstate between University Town and Jasper. When asked to comment on recent efforts to hold nonprofit corporations liable for "the appropriate payment in lieu of taxes," she declined to comment. She did announce that development/construction phases five and six would begin in six to nine months and that approval of the local planning and zoning boards has been secured. Douglas indicated these new development/construction phases would involve "single-family cottages" specifically designed for "our clientele." She also indicated that The Oaks will be partnering with a national "elder housing corporation" to design and build the homes.

The statement of operations and balance sheet for The Oaks are displayed in tables 12.4 and 12.5, respectively.

Table 12.1
The Oaks Board
of Trustees

Name	Position	Residence	Term Ends
Reese Morrison	President	Jasper	2025
Wanda Charles, RN	Vice President	Capital City	2026
Paul Shuey	Secretary	Jasper	2026
Gayle Wyman, CPA	Treasurer	Capital City	2027
Jayne Winters	Member at Large	Jasper	2028
Melvin Seed	Member at Large	Jasper	2025
Elroy Hirsh	Member at Large	University Town	2027

Table 12.2
The Oaks
Schedule
of Fees and
Occupancy

Fee Schedule as of December 31, 2024		
Apartment Size	**One Bedroom**	**Two Bedrooms**
Entrance Fee	$ 300,000–610,000	$ 725,000–915,000
Refundable Percent	90%	80%
Monthly Fee:		
One Person	$ 3,650–6,000	$ 6,800–7,400
Two Persons	$ 3,800–7,500	$ 8,300–8,900

Residential Occupancy as of December 31, 20XX		
	Resident Units	
	Occupied	**Available**
2022	42	8
2023	60	40
2024	84	16

Residential Units	Construction Phase		
	One	Two	Three/Four
To Be Available			100
Available	50	50	0
Occupied	48	36	0
Deposits	1	13	12

Table 12.3 The Oaks Utilization Report as of December 31, 2024

Revenue	
Residential Service Fees	6,267,900
Earned Entrance Fees	2,807,053
Investment Income, Net of Fees	5,112,847
Health Insurance Payments	38,252
Other Operating Income	24,339
Net Assets Released from Restriction	42,551
Total Revenue	14,292,942
Expenses	
General and Administration	4,834,983
Resident Services	680,083
Dining Services	2,132,375
Nursing Services	1,112,866
Environmental Services	1,519,625
Facility Costs and Utilities	1,124,892
Depreciation and Amortization	3,647,784
Interest	240,840
Total Expenses	15,293,448
Gain (Loss) from Operations	−1,000,506

Table 12.4 The Oaks Statement of Operations: January 1–December 31, 2024, USD $

Table 12.5
The Oaks
Balance Sheet
as of December
31, 2024, USD $

Current Assets	
Cash and Cash Equivalents	69,224
Entrance Fees and Accounts Receivables, Net	11,625,383
Prepaid Expenses and Other Current Assets	142,494
Total Current Assets	**11,837,100**
Restricted Assets	
Land and Improvement	8,273,716
Building and Improvements	23,661,692
Furniture and Equipment	3,787,292
Work in Progress	14,223,572
Subtotal	**49,946,272**
Less Accumulated Depreciation	6,242,339
Total Restricted Assets	**43,703,933**
Other Assets	
Investments	52,867,556
Total Other Assets	**52,867,556**
Total Assets	**108,408,589**
Current Liabilities	
Current Portion of Long Term	2,630,447
Accrued Payables and Expenses	345,292
Accrued Salaries and Wages	256,440
Accrued Interest Payable	86,395
Total Current Liabilities	**3,318,574**
Long-Term Debt, Net of Current Portion	
Future Resident Deposits	132,502
Refundable Entrance Fee Liability	48,010,629
State Authority Construction Bonds	62,353,448
Total Long-Term Debt	**110,496,579**
Total Liabilities	**113,815,153**
Net Assets	−5,406,564
Liabilities + Net Assets	108,408,589

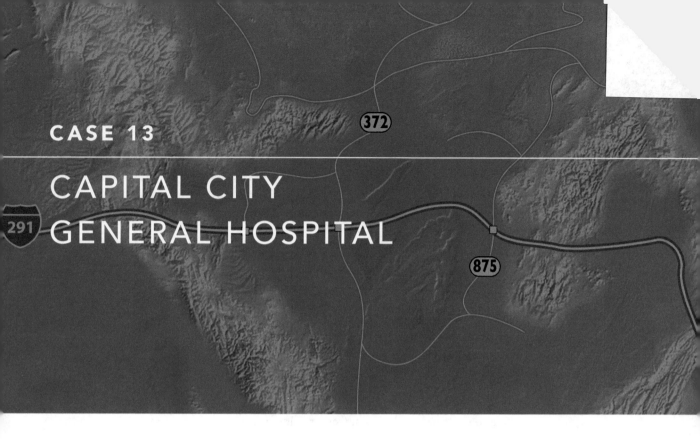

CAPITAL CITY GENERAL HOSPITAL

Capital City General Hospital (CCGH) was founded in 1894 and was originally owned and operated as a municipal department of Capital City. In 1963, it was incorporated as a private tax-exempt corporation. In 1990, it joined Capital City Health, which comprised a group of healthcare organizations in Capital City and the surrounding area. Today, Capital City Health has grown to include CCGH and a number of community hospitals, urgent care and freestanding emergency rooms, ambulatory surgical centers, outpatient services, and long-term care facilities. It is located in Ward I of Capital City.

Over the last 40 years, CCGH has expanded its mission to include specialized services, teaching, and research, serving many areas of Capital City and its adjacent communities.

MISSION AND GOVERNANCE

The mission of CCGH is "to strive to meet the health needs of all who live in the communities we serve." Currently, the hospital operates 220 inpatient beds and, in conjunction with Capital City Health, provides services at 16 sites in the greater Capital City area. It is the only Level I trauma center in Capital City and maintains Air Evac services for all regional hospitals. It is a designated teaching hospital and has formal affiliation agreements with two medical schools located in the state.

Governance of the hospital is provided by a seven-member self-perpetuating board of trustees; each member serves a four-year term and may be reappointed. The current members are as follows:

Name	Profession	Residence	Board Role
Ronald Jenkins, JD*	Attorney	Capital City	Chair
Marie Hyde*	Banker	Capital City	Vice Chair
Eloise Thierry, CPA*	Accountant	Capital City	Treasurer
Prescott Harrington*	Business Executive	Capital City	Secretary
Nancy Moore, Ed.D.	Educator	Capital City	At-Large
Walker Augustus	Business Executive	Capital City	At-Large
Judith MacArthur, RN	Retired	Capital City	At-Large

(* = also serves on the board of Capital City Health)

Carla Warren, MD, is the current CEO and serves as an ex-officio member of the board. She is also the president and chief operating officer of Capital City Health.

OPERATIONAL STATISTICS

Except during the recent pandemic, CCGH has continued to grow and develop. Over the last 15 years, it has expanded its teaching and research mission and become the primary referral hospital for areas outside of Capital City, especially those areas west and south of Capital City. Operational statistics for CCGH are displayed in table 13.1.

MEDICAL STAFF

Currently, the medical staff includes 377 members in a variety of specialties. All are board certified. Annually, the hospital also offers internships and residencies to approximately 30–40 physicians. Except for the hospital-based physicians, all maintain practice relationships with group practices located in Capital City. Some also have consulting medical staff privileges at hospitals located outside of Capital City, such as Jasper. CCGH Medical Staff Specialties are listed in table 13.2.

Based on numerous sources, CCGH has an excellent regional reputation for its research and quality in cardiovascular surgery and orthopedic surgery. It also operates a regional cancer center to serve the surrounding areas, including Hillsboro County.

Financial Reports

The financial reports in tables 13.3 and 13.4 reflect the continued growth and development of CCGH. It has maintained a high investment grade bond rating (AA) for over 15 years. CMS Core Measures for CCGH are displayed in table A.5 in the appendixes.

	2024	2023	2022	2021
Patient Days	78,930	74,262	68,345	70,223
Total Discharges	15,005	14,155	13,256	14,002
Inpatient Beds Licensed	314	314	314	314
Inpatient Beds Staffed	292	292	292	292
Outpatient Visits	135,632	128,395	106,330	114,239
Emergency Room Visits	23,360	21,445	20,795	19,667
Births	1,198	1,193	1,320	1,212
Employees (FTEs on 12/31)	621.4	604.2	587.2	601.8

Note: FTEs: full-time equivalents.

Addiction Medicine	Neurology	**Table 13.2** CCGH Medical Staff Specialties
Allergy	Obstetrics and Gynecology	
Anesthesia	Oncology/Hematology	
Audiology	Ophthalmology	
Cardiology	Oral and Maxillofacial Surgery	
Cardiothoracic Surgery	Orthopedic Surgery	
Child and Adolescent Psychiatry	Otolaryngology	
Colon and Rectal Surgery	Palliative Medicine	
Dentistry	Pathology	
Dermatology	Pediatric Dentistry	
Electrophysiology	Pediatrics	
Emergency Medicine	Physical Medicine/Rehabilitation	
Endocrinology	Plastic Surgery	
Family Medicine	Podiatry	
Gastroenterology	Psychiatry	
General Surgery	Pulmonary Medicine	
Geriatric Medicine	Radiation Oncology	
Hospital Medicine	Radiology	
Infectious Disease	Rheumatology	
Internal Medicine	Sleep Medicine	
Interventional Cardiology	Thoracic Medicine	
Interventional Radiology	Urology	
Nephrology	Vascular Surgery	
	Wound Care and Hyperbaric Medicine	

Table 13.3
CCGH
Statement of
Revenues and
Expenses for
the Year Ending
December
31, 2024 (in
thousands $)

Revenue	
Net Patient Revenue	614,941
Other Revenue	92,876
Total Operating Revenue	**707,817**
Expenses	
Salaries and Benefits	423,914
Services and Supplies	205,859
Depreciation and Interest	36,331
Other	30,472
Total Operating Expenses	**696,576**
Gain from Operations	11,241
Non-operating Revenue	5,845
Net Profit or Loss	17,.086

Assets	
Cash and Other Current Assets	242,066
Long-Term Investments	478,371
Plant, Property, and Equipment—Net	275,464
Other Assets	19,098
Total Assets	**1,014,999**
Liabilities	
Current Liabilities	160,232
Long-Term Liabilities	356,329
Total Liabilities	**516,561**
Net Assets	
Without Donor Restrictions	446,931
With Donor Restrictions	52,507
Total Net Assets	**498,438**
Liabilities + Net Assets	**1,014,999**

Table 13.4
CCGH Balance Sheet for the Fiscal Year Ending December 31, 2024 (in thousands $)

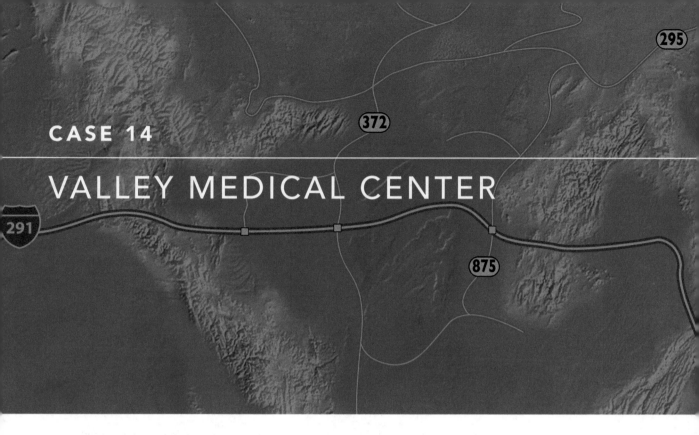

CASE 14

VALLEY MEDICAL CENTER

Valley Medical Center (VMC) was founded in 2022 and is owned and operated by Muroc Health, Inc., a publicly traded corporation that owns and operates hospitals, clinical laboratories, and urgent care centers in many states. During the Chapter 7 bankruptcy involving Osteopathic Medical Center, Muroc acquired the assets of the former Osteopathic Medical Center (OMC). This acquisition also included the license for the hospital. Prior to the acquisition of the assets, Muroc also obtained commitments from select members of the OMC medical staff and professional staff to base their practices at the new Valley Regional Hospital.

VMC officially opened 15 months ago. It includes a Level II trauma center and is located in Ward III in Capital City adjacent to well-developed bedroom communities serving Capital City. VMC has established a number of signature programs mirroring Muroc Health's commitment to telehealth and providing gratis consultation to physicians in private practice. Since the acquisition, Muroc has invested in both the physical facility and the staff.

MISSION, VISION, AND VALUES

According to the medical center, "The mission of VMC is to improve the health of the community. This mission is accomplished by the provision of health services and information to the community in collaboration with The Muroc Health System and other resources."

VMC's vision statement is: "VMC will be recognized as a leader in its service offerings. That leadership recognition will be derived from the relationships formed with patients, colleagues, and the community, and from the commitment and capabilities of each staff member endeavoring to accomplish this mission."

VMC's values include the following:

◆ "Respect for the individual and a recognition of the collective power of individuals working together.

◆ Creativity and optimism as essential ingredients of a better future.

◆ Integrity and compassion as a basis of positive human relationships.

◆ Initiative and flexibility as abilities necessary to thrive in changing times.

◆ Commitment to superior customer satisfaction.

◆ Providing services that are efficient and high quality."

COMMUNITY ADVISORY BOARD

This board reviews hospital programs and issues. It is also responsible for maintaining effective relations with community leaders and interest groups. Based on recommendations of the medical staff, the board also reviews medial staff appointments. Terms on this board are five years and can be renewed. See table 14.1 for a full list of board members.

Mr. Darrell Blueberry is the president and CEO of Valley Medical Center.

OPERATIONAL STATISTICS

Although impacted by the recent pandemic, VMC continues to demonstrate positive growth and development (see table 14.2). It continues to expand its teaching and research activities and has multiyear contracts with a number of academic programs in nursing, allied health, and medicine.

In 2025, based on the challenges confronted during pandemic, VMC significantly increased the size of its intensive care unit and was able to secure extra per diem professionals through the Muroc Health System.

MEDICAL STAFF

VMC currently has a medical staff of 253, and all are board certified. Except for the hospital-based physicians, all maintain practice relationships with group practices located in Capital City. Some also have consulting medical staff privileges at hospitals located outside Capital City. The hospital also supports members of its medical staff maintaining consulting privileges at one or more community hospitals. Based on the leadership of Muroc Health, Inc., VMC has established in-house training programs and designated specific staff to help physicians use the regional and systemwide telehealth consultation system. VMC medical staff specialties are listed in table 14.3.

VMC typically has 12–15 interns and residents in emergency medicine, family medicine, and urology. Muroc Health, Inc., also owns and/or manages the following organizations in Capital City: Valley Orthopedic Center, Valley Ambulatory Surgery Center, Valley Endoscopy Center, Valley Hospital Medical Group, Valley Imaging Centers, and Valley Urgent Care Centers.

FINANCIAL REPORTS

VMC's Statement of Operations is displayed in table 14.4. Muroc Health, Inc., does not release balance sheet Information on specific holdings. CMS Core Measures for VMC are in table A.5 in the appendixes.

Table 14.1
VMC Community
Advisory Board

Name	Profession	Committee Role
David Wirth, DO	Physician, Retired	Chair
Amos English	Newspaper Editor	Vice Chair
Sylvia Fish, CPA	Accountant	Treasurer
Michael Washington, PhD	University President	Secretary
Amy Close, DO	Physician	At-Large
General Marie Forrester, RN	US Air Force, Retired	At-Large
Nancy Gunter, RN	Capital City Home Care, Inc.	At-Large
Robert Mayo, JD	Attorney	At-Large
Melvin Idegwe	Member, City Council	At Large

Table 14.2
VMC
Operational
Statistics for CY
20XX

Statistics	2024	2023	2022	2021
Patient Days	53,005	60,034	63,828	59,334
Total Discharges	12,865	12,856	9,804	12,003
Inpatient Beds Licensed	240	240	240	240
Inpatient Beds Staffed	212	212	225	210
Outpatient Visits	126,954	121,345	103,294	122,776
Emergency Room Visits	21,832	21,056	24,560	20,691
Births	1,047	1,004	856	1,201
Employees (FTEs)	821.4	816.3	745.2	801.8

Note: FTEs: full-time equivalents.

Allergy	Obstetrics and Gynecology
Anesthesia	Ophthalmology
Cardiology	Oral and Maxillofacial Surgery
Cardiothoracic Surgery	Orthopedic Surgery
Child and Adolescent Psychiatry	Otolaryngology
Colon and Rectal Surgery	Palliative Medicine
Dentistry	Pathology
Dermatology	Pediatric Dentistry
Emergency Medicine	Pediatrics
Endocrinology	Physical Medicine/Rehabilitation
Family Medicine	Plastic Surgery
Gastroenterology	Podiatry
General Surgery	Psychiatry
Geriatric Medicine	Pulmonary Medicine
Hospital Medicine	Radiation Oncology
Infectious Disease	Radiology
Internal Medicine	Rheumatology
Interventional Cardiology	Thoracic Medicine
Interventional Radiology	Urology
Nephrology	Vascular Surgery
Oncology/Hematology	Wound Care

Table 14.3
VMC Medical
Staff Specialties

	2024 ($ in thousands)
Revenue	
Patient Revenue—Net	602,996
Other Operating Revenue	103,634
Total Revenue	706,630
Expenses	
Salaries and Benefits	403,242
Services and Supplies	199,635
Depreciation and Interest	44,121
Other	16,243
Total Expenses	663,241
Gain (Loss) from Operations	43,389
Taxes	10,342
Profit (Loss)	33,047

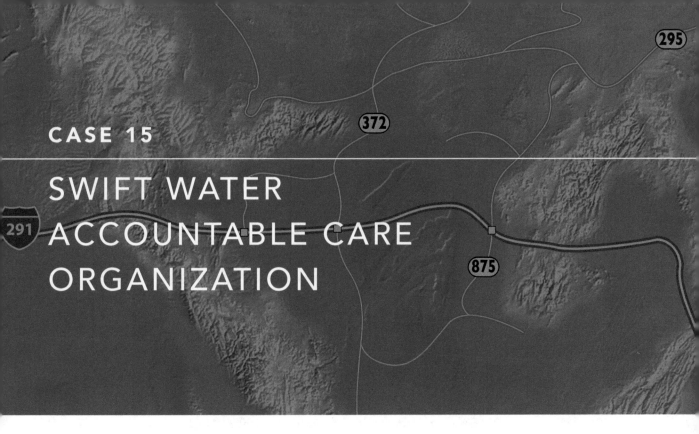

CASE 15

SWIFT WATER ACCOUNTABLE CARE ORGANIZATION

I n June 2022, Swift Water Accountable Care Organization (SWACO) was incorporated, spearheaded by a collaboration between Capital City General Hospital (CCGH), a 295-bed acute hospital, and Capital City Primary Care Association (CCPCA), a group including 32 physicians, approximately 30 percent of the primary care physicians on the hospital's medical staff. SWACO is a track 1, level A risk-sharing ACO enrolling Medicare covered lives. As of December 31, 2024, SWACO has 5,759 covered lives, with a goal of reaching 9,000 by the end of 2026.

SWACO became the first local ACO and one of only three in the state. The organization grew out of a core group of approximately 15 primary care physicians on the medical staff of CCGH who have taken on value-based contracted care for about ten years. The ACO has a preliminary agreement with Columbian Manor, a 154-bed skilled nursing facility in Capital City, to participate in the organization in the first quarter of 2025 as a full-risk-bearing member. To date, no other cooperative agreements have been established.

After working initially to strengthen linkages within Capital City, in recent months the organization has expressed interest in expanding to other nearby communities, potentially including Jasper and/or Middleboro. SWACO has also targeted other healthcare providers for inclusion in the initiative. Of particular interest are linkages with behavioral health organizations.

Mission and Vision

The stated mission of SWACO is to:

Coordinate an integrated network to provide high-quality healthcare services in and around Capital City through the delivery of value-based patient care.

In particular, SWACO was created to coordinate the effective management of chronic health care conditions such as coronary artery disease, neoplasms, stroke, and diabetes. The organizational vision is to achieve the Quadruple Aim of healthcare through an appropriate and effective implementation of value-based care. This vision entails the following:

◆ Achieving better health outcomes

◆ Achieving demonstrable cost containment

◆ Creating a more positive clinician experience

◆ Improving the patient experience

A key component of accomplishing this vision is to successfully build upon the telehealth platform, whose foundation was built during the recent pandemic. Future plans for the ACO call for investment in clinical programs, services, and delivery systems to reach new populations, including those in need of behavioral health care. One issue that continues to challenge the successful growth and development of the ACO is the variability in medical record systems among the various provider groups. While the majority of ACO physician practices utilize the same information system as CCGH, not all do, and as new groups are added to the network, coordination of systems will become more difficult. This problem will be exacerbated when Columbian Manor is fully integrated into the ACO.

According to Centers for Medicare & Medicaid Services (CMS) requirements, the ACO must provide certain public information annually. The key components of this report are summarized in the following sections.

Organizational Information

The ACO participants are CCGH and CCPCA, and the members of the governing board are listed in table 15.1. The types of ACO participants that formed the ACO include:

◆ Hospitals employing ACO professionals

◆ ACO professionals in a group practice arrangement

◆ Networks of individual practices of ACO professionals

SHARED SAVINGS AND LOSSES AND QUALITY PERFORMANCE MEASURES

Data regarding SWACO's savings and losses are presented in table 15.2, and quality-related data can be found in table 15.3.

Table 15.1
SWACO
Governing
Board

Name	Title/ Position	Member's Voting Power Expressed as Percentage	Membership Type	Member's Legal Business	Board Committees
Allepo, Simon		100%	Medicare Ben.	Independent	3,4
Bullard, Francine		100%	ACO Partic.	CCPCA	3
DeGregorio, Nicholos		100%	ACO Partic.	CCGH	3,5
Ecotopaulos, Vincent	CFO	100%	ACO Partic.	CCGH	2,6
Granger, Phoebe	Clinical Officer	100%	ACO Partic.	CCPCA	1,5
Gupta, Anjoli		100%	ACO Partic.	CCPCA	3,4
Hernandez, Valentina		100%	ACO Partic.	CCPCA	1,6
Lukanfoss, Harris	CEO/Chair	100%	ACO Partic.	CCGH	1,5,6
Nelson, Rodney		100%	ACO Partic.	CCPCA	2,4

Notes: Committees: 1 = Executive and Nominations; 2 = Finance; 3 = Contracting; 4 = Value Oversight; 5 = Patient Experience; 6 = Compliance. Ben. = Beneficiary; Partic. = Participant.

Table 15.2
SWACO
Share Saving
Distribution

	2023	2022	2021
Proportion Invested in Infrastructure	10%	100%	0
Proportion Invested in Redesigned Care Processes/Resources	50%	0%	0
Proportion of Distribution to ACO Participants	40%	0%	0
Financial Distribution ($)	938,353	136,309	0

Note: ACO: accountable care organization.

ACO Quality Measure Number	Measure Name	SWACO	ACO Mean
ACO-1	CAHPS: Getting Timely Care, Appointments, and Information	85.92	85.86
ACO-2	CAHPS: How Well Your Providers Communicate	91.42	94.11
ACO-3	CAHPS: Patients' Rating of Provider	95.32	92.69
ACO-4	CAHPS: Access to Specialists	73.53	81.54
ACO-5	CAHPS: Health Promotion and Education	59.28	60.44
ACO-6	CAHPS: Shared Decision Making	62.49	62.78
ACO-7	CAHPS: Health Status/Functional Status	74.29	73.79
ACO-34	CAHPS: Stewardship of Patient Resources	25.48	26.17
ACO-45	CAHPS: Courteous and Helpful Office Staff	95.32	92.84
ACO-46	CAHPS: Care Coordination	84.38	86.89
ACO-8	Risk Standardization, All Condition Readmission	14.93	14.86
ACO-38	All-Cause Unplanned Admissions for Patients with Multiple Chronic Conditions	53.89	58.15
ACO-43	Ambulatory Sensitive Conditions Acute Composite (AHRQ) Prevention Quality Indicator (PQI #91))	1.39	1.87
ACO-13	Falls: Screening for Future Fall Risk	86.38	84.04
ACO-14	Preventive Care and Screening: Influenza Immunization	75.29	74.77
ACO-17	Preventive Care and Screening: Tobacco Use: Screening and Cessation Intervention	69.3	78.04
ACO-18	Preventive Care and Screening: Screening for Depression and Follow-Up Plan	68.39	70.4
ACO-19	Colorectal Cancer Screening	73.6	73.84
ACO-20	Breast Cancer Screening	77.39	73.84
ACO-42	Statin Therapy for the Prevention and Treatment of Cardiovascular Disease	83.2	82.17
ACO-27	Diabetes: Hemoglobin A1c Poor Control (>9%)	14.29	13.88
ACO-28	Controlling High Blood Pressure	78.39	75.04

Table 15.3
SWACO Quality Performance Results

Note: ACO mean data from 2019.

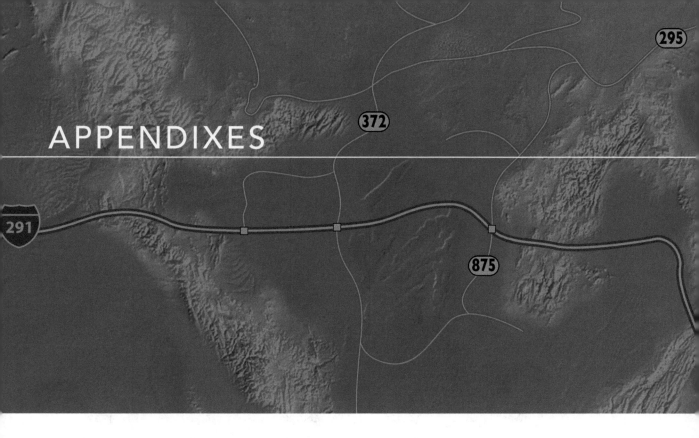

APPENDIXES

A ppendixes include supplemental information on Capital City. Although not located in Hillsboro County, Capital City is near Jasper. As stated in case 8, Jasper is slowly becoming a commuter town for Capital City, as an increasing number of Jasper residents work in Capital City. The opening of the new interstate highway will significantly reduce the travel time between Jasper and Capital City. Capital City also remains the medical referral center for Hillsboro County.

	2024	2019	2014	2009
All Races				
Ward I	42,578	40,293	41,250	40,320
Ward II	51,031	50,392	52,395	50,395
Ward III	35,950	35,202	31,595	31,370
Ward IV	52,262	51,673	38,200	38,145
Total	**181,821**	**177,560**	**163,440**	**160,230**
White				
Ward I	16,646	19,241	25,949	26,646
Ward II	39,041	38,668	44,057	42,599
Ward III	27,990	27,212	25,350	25,971
Ward IV	49,726	48,936	35,387	37,123
Total	**133,403**	**134,057**	**130,743**	**132,339**
Black				
Ward I	24,087	19,202	13,612	12,096
Ward II	10,560	10,294	7,218	6,826
Ward III	7,004	7,067	5,365	4,516
Ward IV	1,322	1,612	1,590	597
Total	**42,973**	**38,175**	**27,785**	**24,035**
Other				
Ward I	1,845	1,850	1,689	1,578
Ward II	1,430	1,430	1,120	970
Ward III	956	923	880	883
Ward IV	1,214	1,125	1,223	425
Total	**5,445**	**5,328**	**4,912**	**3,856**

Table A.1
Capital City
Population by
Race

2024	Under 5	5–14	15–24	25–44	45–64	65–74	75+
Total	**181,121**	**12,316**	**25,538**	**24,560**	**54,155**	**38,219**	**15,646**	**10,687**
Male	85,992	6,096	13,127	12,157	23,287	19,244	7,698	4,383
Female	95,129	6,220	12,411	12,403	29,888	19,975	7,948	6,284

Table A.2
Capital City Age Profile by Sex

	2024	2019	2014	2009
Live Births	2,745	2,257	2,163	2,051
Death (Except Fetal)	1,456	1,379	1,362	1,398
Infant Deaths*	18	19	21	22
Neonatal Deaths+*	11	12	14	14
Postneonatal Deaths**	7	7	7	8
Maternal Deaths	3	1	4	2
Out-of-Wedlock Births	890	689	565	315
Marriages	1,367	1,358	1,433	1,325

Table A.3
Capital City Vital Statistics

Notes: *Under 1 year; +*Under 28 days; **28 days–11 months.

Table A.4
Capital City
Resident Deaths
by Cause of
Death

Cause of Death	2024	2019	2014	2009
Diseases of the Heart	404	407	376	361
Malignant Neoplasms	301	321	300	298
Cerebrovascular Diseases	96	94	85	80
All Accidents	75	66	60	50
Pandemic	73	135		
Chronic Lower Respiratory Disease	60	71	69	60
Influenza and Pneumonia	54	40	30	41
Diabetes Mellitus	50	49	34	31
Alzheimer's Disease	48	39	30	18
Intentional Self-Harm	20	19	17	15
Nephritis, et al.	18	25	20	20
Septicemia	13	20	20	12
Total Leading Causes	**1,212**	**1,286**	**1,041**	**986**
All Deaths	**1,456**	**1,379**	**1,362**	**1,398**

Category	CMS Core Measure	NA	MID	WH	CCGH	VMC
Sepsis Care	Percentage of patients who received appropriate care for severe sepsis and septic shock (%)	60%	62	60	63	63
Cataract Surgery Outcome	Percentage of patients who had cataract surgery and had improvement in visual function within 90 days following surgery (%)	11%	16	12	13	18
Colonoscopy Follow-up	Percentage of patients receiving appropriate recommendation for follow-up screening colonoscopy (%)	91%	92	88	89	90
Heart Attack Care	Average median number of minutes before outpatients with chest pain or possible heart attack who needed specialized care were transferred to another hospital (minutes)	58	45	63	30	45
Heart Attack Care	Percentage of outpatients with chest pain or possible heart attack who got drugs to break up blood clots within 30 minutes of arrival (%)	57%	56	49	56	63
Emergency Department Care	Parentage of patients who left the emergency department before being seen (%)	2%	1	2	2	1
Emergency Department Care	Percentage of patients who came to the emergency department with stroke symptoms who received brain scan results within 45 minutes of arrival (%)	72%	74	72	80	78
Emergency Department Care	Average (median) time (minutes) patients spent in the emergency department before leaving from the visit (minutes)	146	133	122	187	115
Preventive Care	Percentage of healthcare workers given influenza vaccination (%)	91%	92	91	93	92
Cancer Care	Percentage of patients receiving appropriate radiation therapy for cancer that has spread to the bone (%)	91%	90	84	92	92
Pregnancy & Delivery Care	Percentage of mothers whose deliveries were scheduled too early (1–2 weeks) when a scheduled delivery wasn't medical (%)	2%	1	2	2	2

Table A.5
Performance Against CMS Core Measures for MIDCARE Hospital, Webster Hospital, Capital City General Hospital, and Valley Medical Center in Capital City— Most Recent Data

continued

Table A.5
Performance
Against CMS
Core Measures
for MIDCARE
Hospital,
Webster
Hospital,
Capital City
General
Hospital, and
Valley Medical
Center in
Capital City—
Most Recent
Data
(continued)

Category	CMS Core Measure	NA	MID	WH	CCGH	VMC
Use of Medical Imaging	Percentage of outpatients with low-back pain who had an MRI without trying recommended treatments first (%)	39%	32	41	34	33
Use of Medical Imaging	Percentage of outpatient CT scans of the abdomen that were combination double scans (%)	6.40%	6.5	6.8	6.1	6.3
Use of Medical Imaging	Percentage of outpatients who got cardiac imaging stress tests before low-risk outpatient surgery (%)	4.20%	4.4	4.6	4.2	4.9
Complications	Rate of complications for hip/knee replacement patients (%)	2.4%	2.1	2.7	1.8	1.8
Complications	Deaths (rate) among patients with serious treatable complications after surgery (%)	16.4	16.1	15.3	15.7	12.5
Complications	Central line-associated bloodstream infections (CLABS) in ICU and select wards (SIR); see Note	1.0	1.0	1.1	1.0	0.9
Complications	Catheter associated urinary tract infections (CAUTI) in ICU and select wards (SIR); see Note	1.0	1.0	1.0	0.8	1.0
Complications	Surgical site infections (SSI) from colon surgery (SIR); see Note	1.0	0.9	1.0	0.8	0.9
Complications	Surgical site infections (SSI) from abdominal hysterectomy (SIR); surgical site infections (SSI) from colon surgery (SIR); see Note	1.0	1.0	1.1	1.0	0.9
Complications	Methicillin Resistant Staphylococcus Aureus (MRSA) blood infections (SIR); Surgical site infections (SSI) from colon surgery (SIR); see Note	1.0	0.9	1.0	1.0	1.0
Complications	Clostridium difficile (C.Diff) intestinal infections; Surgical site infections (SSI) from colon surgery (SIR); see Note	1.0	1.0	1.0	0.9	1.0
Death Rates	Death rate for COPD patients (%)	3.8	8.2	8.3	8.1	6.5
Death Rates	Death rate for heart attack patients (%)	12.0	10.3	10.8	12.8	11.2
Death Rates	Death rate for heart failure patients (%)	13.0	3.3	10.9	9.9	9.2
Death Rates	Death rate for pneumonia patients (%)	16.9	16.2	16.6	15.7	15.9
Death Rates	Death rate for stroke patients (%)	16.4	13.3	16.2	14	13.6
Death Rates	Death rate for CABB surgery patients (%)	3.00	3.00	3.00	3.00	3.00

continued

Category	CMS Core Measure	NA	MID	WH	CCGH	VMC
Unplanned Hospital Visits	Rate of readmission after discharge from hospital (hospital-wide) (%)	15.5	13.7	14.8	14.2	14.7
Unplanned Hospital Visits	Rate of readmission for COPD patients (%)	19.6	20.1	21.3	18.3	19.5
Unplanned Hospital Visits	Rate of readmission for heart attack patients (%)	16.1	15.4	16.3	16.1	15.7
Unplanned Hospital Visits	Rate of readmission for heart failure patients (%)	21.9	20.4	22.1	22.4	20.9
Unplanned Hospital Visits	Rate of readmission for pneumonia patients (%)	0.2	14.3	16.6	15.7	13.2
Unplanned Hospital Visits	Rate of readmission for coronary artery bypass graft (CABC) surgery patients (%)	0.1	13.2	11.4	9.6	12.2
Unplanned Hospital Visits	Rate of readmission after hip/knee replacement (%)	16.6	3.0	4.0	4.0	3.0
Unplanned Hospital Visits	Rate of unplanned hospital visits after an outpatient colonoscopy (per thousand)	16.4	16.2	16.6	15.3	15.9
Unplanned Hospital Visits	Rate of inpatient admissions for patients receiving outpatient chemotherapy per 100 chemotherapy patients (%)	12.7	13.4	13.2	12.4	11.7
Unplanned Hospital Visits	Rate of emergency department (ED) visits for patients receiving outpatient chemotherapy per 100 chemotherapy patients (%)	5.9	4.2	4.8	4.9	4.7
Psychiatric Unit Services	Patients discharged on antipsychotic medications who had body mass index, blood pressure, blood sugar, and cholesterol level screening in the past year (%)	77.0	73.0	78.0	82.0	80.0
Psychiatric Unit Services	Patients assessed and given influenza vaccinations (%)	81.0	83.0	85.0	84.0	85.0
Psychiatric Unit Services	Patients with alcohol abuse who received or refused a brief intervention during their inpatient stay (%)	84.0	74.0	72.0	80.0	71.0
Psychiatric Unit Services	Patients with alcohol abuse who received a brief intervention during their inpatient stay (%)	77.0	78.0	77.0	80.0	72.0
Psychiatric Unit Services	Patients who screen positive for alcohol or drug use disorder who, at discharge, either received or refused (1) a prescription for medication to treat their disorder OR (2) a referral for addiction treatment (%)	73.0	74.0	73.0	80.0	79.0

Table A.5
Performance Against CMS Core Measures for MIDCARE Hospital, Webster Hospital, Capital City General Hospital, and Valley Medical Center in Capital City— Most Recent Data
(continued)

continued

Table A.5
Performance
Against CMS
Core Measures
for MIDCARE
Hospital,
Webster
Hospital,
Capital City
General
Hospital, and
Valley Medical
Center in
Capital City—
Most Recent
Data
(continued)

Category	CMS Core Measure	NA	MID	WH	CCGH	VMC
Psychiatric Unit Services	Patients screened positive for an alcohol or drug disorder who received a prescription for appropriate medications OR a referral for treatment (%)	62.0	68.0	62.0	69.0	64.0
Psychiatric Unit Services	Patients who use tobacco and who received or refused counseling to quit AND help to quit tobacco or had a reason for not receiving medication during their hospital stay (%)	82.0	82.0	80.0	80.0	81.0
Psychiatric Unit Services	Patients who use tobacco who received counseling to quit and medications to help them or had a reason for not receiving medication (%)	47.0	49.0	51.0	50.0	59.0
Psychiatric Unit Services	Patients who use tobacco at discharge received or refused a referral for outpatient counseling and a prescription for treatment (%)	60.0	56.0	57.0	62.0	60.0
Psychiatric Unit Services	Hours that patients spent in physical restraints for every 1,000 hours of patient care (hrs)	34.0	30.0	21.0	24.0	27.0
Psychiatric Unit Services	Hours that patients spent in seclusion for every 1,000 hours of patient care (hrs)	27.0	31.0	22.0	35.0	27.0
Psychiatric Unit Services	Patients discharged from an inpatient psychiatric facility who received (or whose caregiver received) a complete record of inpatient psychiatric care and plans for follow-up (%)	68.0	69.0	63.0	71.0	69.0
Psychiatric Unit Services	Patients whose follow-up care provider received a complete record of their inpatient psychiatric care and plan for follow-up within 24 hours of discharge (%)	59.0	59.0	60.0	62.0	60.0
Psychiatric Unit Services	Patients discharged from an inpatient psychiatric facility on two or more antipsychotic medications and multiple prescription were clinically appropriate	65.0	67.0	64.0	69.0	66.0
Psychiatric Unit Services	Patients hospitalized for mental illness who received follow-up care from an outpatient mental health center within 30 days of discharge (%)	49.0	50.1	50.3	48.9	50.1

continued

Category	CMS Core Measure	NA	MID	WH	CCGH	VMC
Psychiatric Unit Services	Patients hospitalized for mental illness who received follow-up care from an outpatient mental healthcare center within 7 days of discharge (%)	28.0	31.0	43.0	29.0	45.0
Psychiatric Unit Services	Patients readmitted to any hospital within 30 days of discharge from an inpatient psychiatric facility (%)	21.0	21.1	13.2	21.4	16.3
Payment & Value of Care	Medicare payment per case for heart attack patients ($)	25,526	25,845	27,340	31,670	24,378
Payment and Value of Care	Medicare payment per case for heart failure patients ($)	17,670	17,005	17,354	19,450	18,430
Payment and Value of Care	Medicare payment per case for hip/knee replacement patients ($)	20,959	20,341	23,540	24,359	21,575
Payment and Value of Care	Medicare payment per case for pneumonia patients ($)	18,322	18,993	16,893	18,932	18,403
Payment and Value of Care	Death rate for heart attack patients (%)	12.7	11.3	10.4	12.9	12.4
Payment and Value of Care	Payment for heart attack patients ($)	25,526	22,453	23,585	27,459	24,992
Payment and Value of Care	Death rate for heart failure patients (%)	11.3	10.6	10.9	10.9	10.3
Payment and Value of Care	Payment for heart failure patients ($)	17,670	16,982	15,340	21,540	17,602
Payment and Value of Care	Rate of complications for hip/knee replacement patients (%)	2.4	2.3	2.1	1.7	1.9
Payment and Value of Care	Payment for hip/knee replacement patients ($)	20,959	20,045	19,542	22,549	20,056
Payment and Value of Care	Death rate for pneumonia patients (%)	15.4	13.4	14.4	16.3	15.2
Payment and Value of Care	Payment for pneumonia patients ($)	18,322	18,023	16,440	19,354	18,893

Table A.5 Performance Against CMS Core Measures for MIDCARE Hospital, Webster Hospital, Capital City General Hospital, and Valley Medical Center in Capital City— Most Recent Data *(continued)*

Notes: CCGH: Capital City General Hospital; MID: MIDCARE Hospital; NA: national average (median); VMC: Valley Medical Center; WH: Webster Hospital. SIR is a ratio of observed/expected; any number greater than 1 indicates higher than expected.

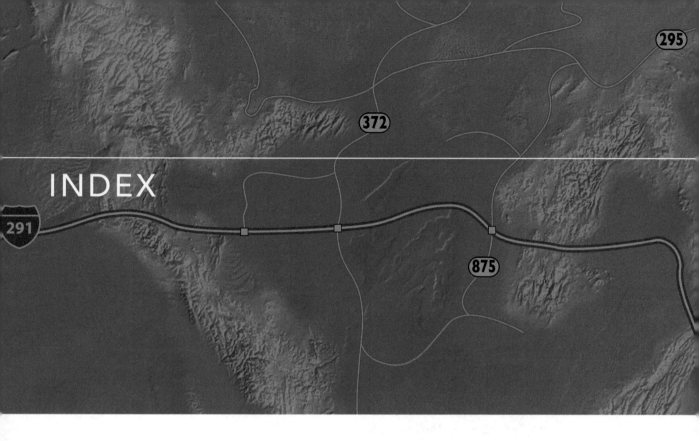

INDEX

Note: Page numbers with t indicate tables.

Lee F. Seidel, PhD, is professor emeritus of health management and policy at the University of New Hampshire (UNH) and a former visiting professor in the executive MBA in health administration program at the University of Colorado, Denver, where he also chaired the program's Curriculum Committee. He taught capstone courses in both settings and courses in financial management and healthcare systems at UNH. He is the founding director of the UNH Center for Excellence in Teaching & Learning, and he managed the center for 15 years. UNH awarded Dr. Seidel the Jean Brierley Award, its highest honor for effective teaching. He is a former chairman of the board of directors of the Association of University Programs in Health Administration (AUPHA).

Prior to his academic career, he worked with Arthur Andersen and Company and for the Office of the Mayor, City of New York. Dr. Seidel holds an MPA and PhD in health administration from the Pennsylvania State University. He is a graduate of Hobart College.

James B. Lewis, ScD, is associate professor emeritus of health management and policy at the University of New Hampshire (UNH). At UNH, he taught baccalaureate- and graduate-level courses in health finance, health marketing, social marketing, strategic planning, strategic management, health reimbursement, managed care, and introduction to the healthcare system. He has also directed the university's undergraduate and graduate programs in health management and public health and served as department chair for several years. He currently co-teaches the capstone course in the Executive MBA in Health Administration at the University of Colorado, Denver.

Dr. Lewis is a graduate of the University of Pittsburgh and holds an MBA from Northwestern University and an ScD from the Johns Hopkins School of Hygiene and Public Health. Prior to his academic appointment, he was a healthcare management consultant specializing in strategy and strategic planning, having been a principal with the firm of William M. Mercer and the national manager of healthcare strategic planning for Coopers & Lybrand. In these positions, he provided advice to dozens of healthcare organizations, insurance companies, and purchasers of healthcare services.